praises for

OPEN MIKE

"Mike has boldly expressed the sentiments of many men who often cry in the dark or remain silent about the internal traumas that manifest externally. He shows that honesty is truly the best medicine."

– Michael Strahan,
American Television Host

"I could tell you how long I've known Mike Hill, but that would do a disservice to our friendship, because it's not measured by time, but by moments. And as much as I've enjoyed those moments growing from friends to brothers, I've enjoyed more watching him overcome personal and professional traumas to become who he is today. His journey is amazing, and I have the utmost respect for it, and for him."

Jay Harris,
ESPN Anchor

A Memoir

OPEN MKE

MIKE HILL

13TH
&
JOAN

13TH
&
JOAN

For permission requests, write to the publisher, addressed "Attention: Permissions Coordinator," 205 N. Michigan Avenue, Suite #810, Chicago, IL 60601. 13th & Joan books may be purchased for educational, business or sales promotional use. For information, please email the Sales Department at sales@13thandjoan.com.

Printed in the U. S. A.
First Printing, August 2020

Library of Congress Cataloging-in-Publication Data has been applied for.

Hardcover ISBN: 978-1-7342346-9-5
Paperback ISBN 978-1-73426346-7-1
E-Book ISBN 978-1-7342346-8-8

This is dedicated to my Grandma Lillian.

Thank you for teaching me to always
believe in myself more than anyone else
will and to always seek happiness.

May words of truth set us free.

-Mike Hill-

FOREWORD

THERE'S A STORY behind every person. There's a reason why they're the way they are. Had Mike not written *OPEN MIKE*, I can say with absolute certainty that I would not be his fiancée today. Number one, I don't believe that he would have ever proposed to me in the first place, and number two, I never would have accepted if he had. I truly believe in timing, destiny, and God. Not necessarily in that order. Although Mike and I knew people in common, it was only by the grace of God (and Steve Harvey) that our worlds would eventually collide. I have to be honest, the beginning of our relationship was a slow burn, a flicker at best. We definitely developed a friendship first, and both probably would have been fine with just being friends if that was God's will. God had other plans. I never imagined in my life the inferno of love that would become famously #CHill. Ironically, chilling with Mike was so much easier said than done. Little did I know that Mike has been carrying untold stories of pain and sadness inside since he was a child. The traumas we experience growing up do not magically disappear when we become adults, although I do believe that we are ultimately the magicians of our life. Reading *OPEN MIKE* gave me incredible insight, history, and clarity of not only who this man is today, but his tumultuous journey to how he got here. Once you have admitted and accepted your flaws, no one can hold them against you. Imperfections and flaws in a person give them no choice but to thrive in any situation, no matter how dark it is. Mike is a giver, and although it is commendable, it is my least favorite thing about him. Why? Because he gives to everyone except himself. As his fiancée and future wife (God willing), I take issue with that. I believe Mike is deserving, and he is also worthy. It saddens me that because he is still fighting his demons, he has not fully realized it yet.

It is difficult to walk toward your future if you are still fighting the demons of your past. Refusal to settle for less than you deserve is necessary, even though it's what you expect (and are sadly familiar and comfortable with).

The decision to thrive is always the only option when there is nowhere else to go but up. Some people were born to settle, and some people would die if they had to. I know in my heart that Mike is the latter.

OPEN MIKE opened (no pun intended) the door for Mike physically, emotionally, spiritually, and mentally to regurgitate his past, heal, and indulge in his future. It is a chance to inspire others in pain, take ownership of his life (past and present), and make sense of his truth. His WHOLE truth. It's his time to let go for once, and not play it safe. To risk it all in the name of love, not for his family, but mostly for himself. To allow him to confront his past, mistakes, and the demons that haunted him for years. You only get one life, but you get as many chances as you want to make it the life you have always dreamed of. Learn from your mistakes and have more lessons than regrets. Take off the mask of trying to convince the world who you want us to believe you are and be the man who loves and believes in himself without approval or validation from others. Where you go from here is between you and God. He is our only judge. The reset button has been pushed. Mike, I pray you flourish and create the life you were born to have. You can't call yourself a king if you don't feel worthy of the crown. Trade the mask for the crown. It's a better fit. Find your peace, my love. It should never be negotiable.

I love you.
Cynthia

Preface

THE BACKSTORY

I'VE BEEN TELLING people about the backstory of my life for many years. Stories about how I came to be who I am on television, how I resolved to be a better father and a better man, and how that evolution allowed me to discover love. Everybody kept saying, "You need to write a book. You need to write a book." My initial thought was *Who am I to write a book?*

I'm not a big celebrity. I'm not an A-list or B-list person, so I also wondered *who is going to want to read it?* As time passed and more lessons were garnered, writing the book became a necessity for my personal healing.

The first time that I sat down to put pen to paper was in 2014, and I managed to write five or six pages. At the time, I wasn't sure if I could go the distance. I put the pen down and didn't think about much more. God continued to send people and signs that would serve to reinforce that I needed to write this book.

In 2017, I found myself seeking clarity surrounding the series of events that had taken place in my life. I needed to understand myself more. On the outside, I was seemingly happy and content, but it was not authentic. My life was wonderful, in many ways both personally and professionally, but there was also something that was eating at me. That something was literally killing me. I would not come to realize that holding everything that had happened to me over the years could be likened to internal bleeding. I was hemorrhaging from the pain of unresolved trauma and emotions. The only way that I could save my life was to put pen to paper.

By 2018, I realized that I needed to make amends with some of the people whom I had hurt and those who hurt me. One source of my unresolved pain was the first young lady whom I had ever told I loved. After mustering up the strength to utter the words to tell her, she looked at me like I was crazy. Her lack of reciprocity hurt. I buried that hurt, so the pain went unresolved for many years. Little did I know, that decision would affect many of my relationships. In a hasty decision, I wrote to her on Instagram and admitted that she hurt me. It might seem crazy to the average person, but that action started me on a mission to heal. She wrote back with a response that changed my perspective. She said, "You know what, I'm so sorry. I was in a different stage of my life. I was going through something at that time with my mom. I was a miserable person. I'm sorry. I hope you can forgive me. I'm so glad things worked out for you. But please forgive me, and I hope you can let it go."

Her words opened my eyes and allowed me to release. That release took place on the paper. Writing became my therapy. The more I wrote, the more clarity I attained. My mind and my heart were regurgitating all of the incidents that plagued my memory for so many years. Tears streaming down my face upon remembrance cured me. I realized that I was in a funk, and every time I wrote, it was like poison coming out of my body. What was really inside of me was a cocktail of the trauma, stress, hurt, depression, and anger that I had suppressed for so many years. All of these factors combined were literally killing me.

By 2019, I knew that writing this book was a direct request from God. I had lived and learned long enough to know that a request of this magnitude also meant that getting to the finish line would not be easy. With my first draft of the manuscript written, I began my quest to find a publisher to help me finish what I had started. After showing the rough manuscript to Cynthia, she immediately sent it to a dear friend, Dr. Ian Smith, and he loved it. He was amazed and as a favor, shuffled it around to a few of his cohorts in the literary industry. There were people who told me, "Don't write this out. It's going to destroy your career. With the #MeToo movement and the things you're saying, you can't say that. You can't put these names in there."

After having come so far in my journey and quest to tell my story, fear set in. I tabled the effort once more. And as much as I wanted to let it go, there was something inside of me that would not allow me to table it for too long. I knew that I had to share my journey. I knew that God would not have placed it in my heart if He had not wanted me to help others.

After connecting with my publicist Kita Williams, I began to discuss the manuscript and my desire to get the book out to the world. She immediately began vetting publishers. We talked to three different publishers, but Ardre Orie at 13th & Joan Publishing House had the energy and excitement that made me feel comfortable. I knew that in her company, my story had found a home. The opportunity to work with this team was a godsend. Everybody else I felt was wasting my time.

We got busy strategizing and reconstructing the new developments that had manifested in my life since picking the manuscript back up now with absolute intent to publish. I began to write about my trials and tribulations on a quest to be the best father possible and to discover self-love. Everyone around me now recognized that I didn't want to write the book; I needed to write it.

As you begin to turn these pages and access my truths, I ask that you have an open mind and understand the circumstances and the why of who I once was and who I strive to be today. If you have an open mind, you can see my hard-earned evolution. This truth that I speak of has released me. It is because of this book that I will never be in bondage again. The words placed atop these pages signify my truth—but more importantly, my freedom.

ACKNOWLEDGMENTS

I'M STILL A work in progress, but I couldn't have gotten this far without admitting that I needed help. There have been plenty of people who have been there for me in different ways. A heartfelt thanks to my mother, Linda, and brother, Preston, who have always supported and prayed for me. As much as you have supported me, you have also been the first to get me to see my faults. For this, I am eternally grateful.

To my kids, Ashlee and Kayla, who have grown with me and been patient with me while I figured it all out.

J.R. and Natara, thank you for making me strive for more and never wavering when times were tough.

To the fans who have watched and given me fuel throughout my broadcasting career, I sincerely appreciate you. For all of the mental therapists, who help men and women who fight with being transparent and their demons, you are God's angels.

Much love to those same patients who have decided to seek help and the people in their lives who encourage and support it.

Obviously, I want to acknowledge Cynthia Bailey for your support, and for accepting me for who I am. Thank you for walking with me as I get better. And, of course, I wish to acknowledge God for everything I've gone through. The good and bad in my life has made me better. I know that He is the source of my strength.

IS THIS THING ON?

WHO IS MIKE Hill? For 49 years now, I've tried to answer that question for others. As I get older, I'm realizing my life has become too complex to even answer it for myself. The person many of you reading this book see is a sportscaster. "That guy" who used to be on *that* network and did a few shows. Maybe some of you see me as "that dude who is about to marry the reality show star." Recognizable, but hardly famous.

Some of my friends know me as the person who likes to make others laugh. Good ol' Mike. Always accommodating. Nice most of the time. Has a profound thought or able to hold an intelligent conversation from time to time but bound to say something inappropriate if you're around him long enough. *Yeah, I admit I have about as much of a filter as a Camel's cigarette at times.* I accept it. I know it's a part of me that makes up who I am.

Then there are my kids. They are my heart and joy, the main reason why I hustle hard every day. I think they just view me as that old man who likes to act silly. It hasn't always been easy because of the issues I've had with their moms, but I'm sure they love me. I'm sure they're proud. They tell me that. And I see it because I feel it.

I could be wrong, but most of those who *really* know Mike Hill like the man he's *become*. God knows I've been through a lot to get here. I witnessed domestic violence as a child. My biological father was not around. I discovered my stepfather was a hit man who spent the last nine years of his life in prison for murder-for-hire. I felt alone, depressed, and contemplated whether the world would be better off without me. Senseless violence took the life of my best friend. I watched friends deal and/or get hooked on drugs. I had marriages which, at times, became tumultuous because I was a terrible husband. I dealt with racism and politics in this business I call a career—and yes, that includes ESPN.

Yes, I've dealt with plenty of ups and so many downs. However, I've survived thanks to the grace of God, good friends, family, and angels along the way.

I'm sharing all of this hoping to inspire someone who's trying to overcome obstacles. Even the obstacles they've placed in their own way. I think it's time to share what I experienced and how I overcame it. I may not have all the exact details, but it's how I remember it, and it's my truth.

One of the most important rules in broadcasting is to be careful what you say around a hot microphone. It's gotten a lot of people in deep shit and even ruined careers. However, it's time to go against that for the purpose of this book. I'm telling it all, and I'm speaking through an open mic.

A few of the names have been changed to protect the guilty!

Introduction

I NEED TO BE SEEN.
I NEED TO BE HEARD.
I NEED TO BE LOVED.

IF I DARE to utter the words, "I need to be seen," I simply mean that God has a purpose for me. In no way am I putting myself on a pedestal. I am simply stating that what God has done and is doing in me deserves to be seen by the world. The need to be seen is not my claim to fame, or me searching for random reinforcement through glory—that's not the goal here. My purpose is to make sure that I put all of me out in the open for the world to see so that I can make the difference that God wants me to make.

God has placed something inside of me that I knew about even when I was a kid. I knew that I was going to be something someday. I didn't know what that something was, but I knew it was going to make a major impact in this world. There were times that I tried to suppress it and to be overly humble. I didn't want to come across as cocky or overzealous. All I knew was that my purpose needed to be seen, and that God was responsible for the light that had been placed inside of me.

I'd be lying if I said that I believe I've reached my full potential. There is still so much more inside of me that God is developing. I recognized that the work being done in me resonated with others after I began a series of Mike Check posts on my social media platforms. These posts were instances of me baring my soul and remaining transparent about moments of profound evolution in my life that happened as a result of the work that I was doing to be better and to heal from many of the elements that far too often plagued my existence.

To have people commenting things like, "I needed to hear this. Thank you. I was lost. I felt like I didn't know where to go, but this was right on time" resonated with my soul. Their words were confirmation that I needed to be seen.

There were other profound moments of life that further proved that God was not finished with me. Coming out of the military to pursue broadcasting was an unlikely path. I was rejected more times and in more ways than I could count, but I never lost faith. God did not allow me to give up or to throw in the towel. Landing the gig at ESPN was simply the hand of God moving while molding a platform for me to eventually give him the glory through the work being done in me. Landing the gig at Hyperdrive on Netflix was more proof.

Crossing over from sports to the entertainment sector was huge. So much happened in between. Some days felt like sunshine and many like the raging storms of life. Each of the moments prepared me for one of the greatest gifts that life would offer: meeting Cynthia, the love of my life who saw and accepted me. Today, now fully accepting of myself, I am a living witness to the wondrous work that God has done in me.

There have been many people in my life who resolved to tell me who I was and what they saw in me, but no one saw me the way that God did. And today, I see with the vision that He has given me. I see who He has called me to be, and I see His purpose for creating me. In him, there are no limitations or records of fault or wrongdoing, only potential for growth.

And because I know who I am and from where I came, I am liberated. When you are seen and you see yourself, you let go of fear. In this space, you take chances on yourself. For the first time in my life, I have been able to just breathe.

The most liberating element of knowing who and whose you are is feeling confident in laying it all on the line. When you resolve to tell your story, there is no man or woman who can speak on your behalf. Writing this book has given me the liberty to take back my narrative. And though I have no way of knowing how the world may react, I have peace that surpasses all understanding in knowing that this is all a part of God's will for my life. My journey, my story—albeit some of the ugliest moments of my life and some of the most beautiful moments fused together—is me baring my soul to the world. I'm willing to accept that some may laugh or make jokes about my truths, but the need to be seen, the assignment that God has tasked me with, still remains.

Today, more than ever, I recognize that my experiences have the potential to help someone along their journey. I recognize that each of our stories are purposed to ensure that someone else has the information that they need to not make the same mistakes or to learn from the trials and tribulations that we will inevitably experience.

The truth is we're all human, and we are all going to make mistakes. Our ability to come out better on the other side of those mistakes is what really counts. Not only are we obligated to learn from our transgressions, but we are also responsible for righting our wrongs. The stories inside this book are a series of the highs and lows that resulted from the wrong turns I made in life. And although it has been an extremely difficult journey, I own each moment because I am the better for it. At the time while life was playing out, I didn't always realize how my actions affected the lives of those around me. It is my belief that God puts us through things to give us perspective and to teach us about the capacity in which He has created us. One of my favorite quotes from Cynthia states, "I don't have any regrets; I have life lessons."

The most tumultuous moments of our lives only become regrets if you don't learn the lessons that life gives you. From cheating to lying and being fake, I was guilty of it all. These moments were the by-product of me operating in a capacity less than what God had planned for me. In those moments, I caused great pain to people that I was responsible to and for. I can see the pain that my daughters still feel to this day because of my past. They recognize that I hurt their moms, and they are old enough now as young women to understand. Although not easy, I owed it to them to allow God to do the necessary work in me.

Who wants to be wrong? Who wants to get things wrong? In life, it's about success. Failure is an option, but nobody wants to fail. To admit that you've done something wrong is huge, but it's imperative that you do. Admitting that you're wrong is imperative. To get to that point is a process, and you have to work on yourself. No one's perfect at all, but at the same time, when you make the same mistakes on a continual basis, you have to begin doing the work to turn it around. It takes a lot of strength because you never want to admit that you're wrong and a failure. With the grace of God and counseling, I got there.

In the pages of this book is the truest, most raw depiction of my journey. Nothing about this has been pretty, but every moment has been worth it because it has allowed me to be who I am today. It is not possible to have this magnitude of transformation and not give God the glory. I Need to Be Seen. His work in me is miraculous, and there must be witnesses to what He can do. I Need to Be Heard. No matter how ugly the truth is, God has painted my soul in a beautiful way. I Need to Be Loved.

And whether or not we admit it, we all have the same desire to be seen, heard and loved. This is how we have been divinely wired, but first we must believe that we are worthy and deserving of each of these gifts of life, for in them, true joy is bred. My story is proof of what God can do. It would have killed me if I had not written it. The weight of the transformation of my life became so heavy that I was forced to write it. Today, I know that it was my calling to be a living testimony and to share God's hand in my life. He saved me and placed these words in my heart. My only wish is that these words touch your heart the way God has touched mine.

Chapter 1

PRESHOW

> *It's a sound and image that will never leave me, and unfortunately, it's the first image I can remember of my life. It's like a nightmare that plays on a loop. Something you'd love to erase, but it's obviously stamped in the mind with a permanent solution. Screams of terror, so loud and bloodcurdling that it rips through the essence of your soul. It's a damn shame that your first memory is your mom getting her ass beaten by the man that's supposed to love and protect her.*

I WAS BORN August 19, 1970 in the Bronx, New York to Linda Edwards and James Maxwell. My birth certificate says my name at birth was James Michael Maxwell, but I'm hardly a junior. I can't remember much about my biological father early on in my life because he was rarely *in* my life. More on him later.

How would I describe my early childhood? I guess rough at times, but I never knew I was poor. I mean, I *was* poor, but sometimes you don't know how bad you have it until you're shown something better later. This didn't happen for me until much later in life.

I'd have to give the credit to my mom for shielding me from this. Like a lot of women, she did the best with what she was given, which many times wasn't very much. I can still remember nights when she'd say, "How 'bout some pancakes or cereal for dinner?" At the time, I thought it was because I had done something special. Some kind of treat. At least, she made it feel like a treat, shielding me from the reality. That reality was that there was nothing else to eat in the house. She made do.

I know for sure I got my strength from her because she's been through it. Remember that famous quote from Oprah's character Ms. Celie in *The Color Purple*? *"Alls my life I had to FIGHT!"* Ms. Celie must have gotten her inspiration from my mom. Unfortunately, for a great deal of her life, that line could be taken in the figurative *and* the literal sense.

My mom's first marriage happened when she was still a teenager—not even out of high school. There was a reason for that. She was pregnant with my older brother, Preston. Of course, it's rare to see kids be forced to wed because they're having a kid these days, but back in the day, they called that a good old-fashioned shotgun wedding. *Crazy, because I don't know which one of my family members would've forced them to wed.* Anyway, something or someone did, but like so many others, it didn't work out. I'll just leave that at that.

I honestly don't know much about my mom's time with my biological father, James or Jimmy, as everyone called him. I know some of the things she's told me, and it ain't pretty. I know she met him through my aunt, her sister, Francine. Francine worked in a grocery store and Jimmy was a butcher. From what I've heard, he was a damn good butcher, but as a man, he was far from prime cut. *Look, I'm not out to disparage him. He's my father and I'll always respect that, but this is "Open Mike" and we're keeping it real throughout.*

So how would I describe him? Tall, handsome dude who talked the talk but definitely didn't walk it, and to put it kindly, was not the most educated man in the world. Jimmy did have a charisma about him. His voice was commanding. The rare times I did talk to him on the phone, after my mom left him, he'd always start with "Hello, son." But I could barely call him "Dad." He just didn't feel like one to me.

The only time I can remember me, him, and my mom being in the same household together was that vivid first memory I described earlier. Of course, I may have been about two or three, so forgive me if the details aren't exactly accurate, but here's what I remember.

We were in an apartment, and I remember a lot of screaming. However, it didn't sound like the scream of pleasure. Maybe it was my young ears not knowing any better. Like I said, this could easily have been a dream, but even if it is, it more than likely still happened in my mom's reality. I remember hearing my mom scream, "Help! Help!" at the top of her lungs. Unfortunately, this would be a plea I'd hear from her on too many occasions in my childhood. What was craziest about this memory is that my parents were pretty much naked while they fought in front of me. I was on the bed, jumping up and down, as if what they were doing was just a game for my entertainment. After a few minutes, two people came through the front door like firemen about to put out this hot blaze. It was my grandmother, Lillian, and her boyfriend, Eddie. Then, the fighting stopped. Once again, it's the only memory I have of my biological parents ever being together, but I wish I could erase it forever. *We'll get back to Jimmy later.*

I'll tell you what. My mom really knew how to pick her men...*terribly.* Not long after Jimmy, she met Richard Hill, and they got married. Richard was from Alabama, and he had some sort of job lined up down there (or so he said). Not long after the wedding, my mom packed me and my brother up, and we moved south.

We moved to Bessemer (or as they call it down there, BEH-MA), Alabama. I can still remember the first time I laid eyes on this new "dream home" we were going to move into. When I tell you this shit looked like it was built in the middle of a corn field, I'm being nice. There were weeds and shrubs taller than me (and I was over 4 1/2 feet at the time). We did have two addresses: 2109 and 2111 Berkley Ave. That's because the house was a duplex that they built a door between to make it one big house.

Bessemer gave me my first experience with racism, although I didn't even know it at the time. *That's just how innocent childhood is or "should" be.* A few doors down from our house lived this older white lady named Betty and her long-time boyfriend, Jack. Once again, this is decades ago *in Alabama.* The deep South. However, Betty was one of the nicest ladies I've ever met in my life. She had genuine love for two things: Bear Bryant, head coach of the University of Alabama football team, and her beer. She was also very sweet to me and my family. In fact, she would actually take care of me from time to time when my parents had to work.

While Betty (and Jack) were sweet, some of her relatives who would come around weren't so cordial. I mean they weren't mean, but they just didn't say much. At least, to *this* little preteen black boy at the time. Well, one day, I remember playing in Betty's front yard with Betty's grandniece (or it could've been her granddaughter, I really don't remember the relation). Anyway, the two of us were digging for something and I cut my hand. I started to bleed and when the little girl saw this, she said, "Ew, that's BLACK blood!"

I was in pain, but now a little confused. I looked down at my hand, and it looked pretty damn red to me, so I showed it to her and replied, "No, it's red." She ran in the house and told Betty, and apparently she said something to Betty that embarrassed her because Betty came out as red as my blood. Betty began to help me and clean me up, but she was apologizing for her niece/granddaughter while she was. I was even more confused because I didn't know why. It wasn't until *years* later, thinking back on that story, that I realized she wasn't talking about the color of my blood but the color of my skin that blood was leaking through. I don't think I ever saw her again, but that little girl was too young to make a racist remark like that on her own. It was taught in her home. I wish she and many others had been raised in Betty's home. We probably wouldn't have a lot of the problems we have today.

Believe it or not, we were one of the more "well off" families in the neighborhood. Oh, it was a shit-poor neighborhood, but our household was one of the best. *We actually eventually got a side deck, with a glass sliding door. It came off the track all the time because it was built by a dude my stepfather got a hook-up from, but it was a glass, sliding door.* I even had my own room that I didn't have to share with anybody. Sure, the roof leaked, and water would come crashing down on me in the middle of the night during a storm, but for the most part, I was dry. The lights were on most of the time, and I never went hungry. We had a mouse (not a rat) problem, and the roaches were big enough to skate on at times, but like I said, some of the families in that hood had it so much worse. So while it was bad, it wasn't terrible.

Even though I have a brother and two sisters, we didn't grow up together. My brother Preston (who's my mother's only other child) left to go live with his father when I was young, and I've never shared the same household with either of my sisters, Belinda or Maria. In fact, all four of us spent our childhoods in different cities.

I love them all, and we're all pretty close now, but growing up, I was closest to my brother. I've actually known him my entire life. As for my sisters, I didn't "meet" Belinda until I was fourteen and she was sixteen, and I didn't get to meet Maria until she was five and I was around fifteen. So even though I have siblings, I sort of grew up an only child, and I think that had an effect on my social skills in life. In fact, I know it did.

I didn't really fit in in Alabama. Even though I spent my formative years there, it never has and still to this day doesn't "feel" like my home. Now some of the people I grew up with there will read this and go, "Oh, he thinks he's too good to claim us...well, fuck him then!" And that's exactly how harsh it might go. You have to understand, I don't mean it as disrespect. It's just how I've always felt. It's part of my make-up.

I've never really felt like I've fit into just one particular category either. I'm complex like that. Sort of in the middle.

The good thing about being "in the middle" is that everyone kind of knows a little something about you. I can relate in one way or another with just about everyone, but I never fully feel bonded. Honestly, I kind of like it that way. Yep, I can have a conversation with Flavor Flav or Barack Obama and feel comfortable talking to either. It suits me. The only problem is, some of the people you're actually talking to or you're around don't get you. I'm that brother that can come across too "street" for certain people or too "corny" for others. Imagine having that problem in the hood. Is there such a thing as a thuggish nerd? Well, I guess I was it.

Once again, growing up, I never truly fit in. At least not with the people I grew up around. I always felt different. Especially in Bessemer. Like I didn't belong, but I faked it long enough to try and not stand out. At times, that and, of course, dumbass peer pressure would get me in trouble. One time, it almost got me killed.

It started off pretty innocent. I was playing football down the street from my house at this church with some fellas in the neighborhood. All of a sudden, a car pulled up. The driver was this older dude that I had seen but hardly knew. I was about thirteen or fourteen, but he was around nineteen. A few of the guys I was playing with knew him better, and he said, "Y'all lil niggas want to go for a ride?"

A few of them said, "Yeah." I was kind of stuck. I kind of knew it was a bad idea, but since some of the other guys got in, my dumb ass went right behind them.

The drive started off cool. Just kind of cruising. And then something hit me. Like a spidey sense or something. At that moment, I realized, "Oh shit, this car is stolen." I promise

you, as soon as I realized that, it felt like I was on an amusement park ride, and he started driving like we were on one.

We were hitting top speeds on residential streets. Then, all
of a sudden, we were on 19th Street. The reason I remember
that particular street is because, on the south side of Bessemer, there's this *huge* hill known as the 19th Street hill.
Looks like it goes up for miles or something. Now there's
a smaller hill you have to go up and back down before you
get to the big one, and we were going up this smaller hill.
I mean, we were flying up this hill.

I was in the back with some other guys, and I was scared
as shit. All of a sudden, we were getting close to an intersection, and I could see the light turning yellow. Even as
fast as we were going, there was no way we were going to
make it before it turned red. We got closer and someone
yelled out, "Take that shit" (meaning run the light), and
the driver did just that.

Remember I just said we were flying up this hill? Well,
when he got to that intersection at the top of that hill,
because we were going so fast, we literally took flight. I
ain't even going to lie, I started screaming like a seven-year-
old girl. It was like something out of the movies. When we
finally landed, the driver had lost control of the car. He tried
to spin it back, but before he could, we fishtailed and hit
this truck parked right outside of a church, and I mean we
hit that truck *hard*. Luckily, no one was in it and luckily
for us, we didn't hit it hard enough to stall.

He regained control of the car and took off. As we drove
up that mountain of a hill, we looked back and saw people
rushing out of the church. The impact was that loud. We

somehow got away and later ditched the car in these woods, but I don't think I stopped shaking until a few days later.

I learned a very important lesson that day. If your gut is telling you something is wrong, believe it. Don't allow any amount of peer pressure or what your friends "think" is cool to influence your decisions. **Now I ain't gonna lie, I didn't always remember my own lessons,** but that incident certainly made me think about my future options more intelligently. So believe me, you have the God-given ability to be more of a leader than a follower. At least don't follow dumbass friends who get into cars with guys dumb enough to steal them.

I learned a lot about life from my mistakes, but mainly from the mistakes of others. I owe being the man I am today to the women in my life. That being my mom and grandma. My father figures weren't the best in the world. Well, since we're keeping it real, there was little that was good about them. The lessons I did learn from them were from the mistakes that they made. I wanted to make it a point to make sure I didn't repeat their errors. *That didn't always go as planned.* Also, some of the lessons I did get from them would actually harm me or others in a strange way.

I didn't have much of a relationship with Jimmy, my biological father, but I remember two things he tried to teach me. The first was actually pretty good. I don't know how the conversation started, but when I was around nine, I was visiting him, and he told me to never put my hands on a woman in anger. He said, "Son, the best thing you can do if a woman makes you angry is to just take a walk." Spectacular advice. Hooray and gold star for Jimmy. I actually remember being proud that he told me this. So proud I told my mom, and her reply was, "Well, too bad his ass never took a walk when it came to me."

The second lesson he taught me came at the end of that same summer when I was visiting him and Ruthie. Ruthie was Jimmy's wife. Ruthie was this super sweet Puerto Rican lady, and I absolutely loved her. *Hell, I still adore that lady and her son Michael to this day.* Her cooking, especially her rice and peas, were delicious. She made the rare occasions I stayed with Jimmy special. I felt so much love. So much that when that summer visit was wrapping up, I began to cry because I didn't want to leave. (Not like snot crying, but tearing up some.)

Now, you'd expect a dad to be like, "It's going to be okay, son. We're going to miss you too." Nope. Not this one. He was like, "Hey, stop crying, Michael. You're a man!" (*No, Pops, I'm fucking nine years old*). He continued, "In fact, from here on out, no more tears."

Now imagine me, a nine-year-old who desperately wants to have a relationship with a man who was never around, getting that advice. And as emotional as I was at that point, I was just happy to get any advice from him. So I took it to heart and held on to it. For a long time. I may have actually been a crybaby before then, but that shit hardened me. The problem is, it hardened me and affected several relationships, because I never wanted to show any sort of tender emotion if I was hurt. I mean, I could cry in a movie or fake cry to make a woman do something (more on this later), but if I was ever hurt by *anyone*, you'd never know you got to me. Some of you may think that's a good skill to have, but it's unhealthy if you keep it bottled up. I did a lot.

Now, I'll cut Jimmy a little slack or give him the benefit of the doubt because I know what it's like to have kids and no longer be with the mother. However, I honestly don't think he cared too much. Just keeping it real... (You'll hear me use that phrase a lot in this book.) The only significant thing my biological father ever gave me was that name I had at birth. And obviously, I even changed that later.

Let me stop. Let me give him credit for the yellow polo shirt he got me when I visited him when I was nine. The Pierre Cardin suit he got me that same summer and the luggage he bought me because my mother shamed him by sending me to see him with a suitcase that had a rope wrapped around it to keep it together. Hard times, man.

The one lesson I got from Richard also had an adverse effect on my life.

> *Now before I go any further, I've learned not to blame others for my issues, but this is only after having a revelation from someone special that my issues are of my making—or at least, I choose to continue to have them.*

Anyway, back to Richard's lesson. One night, I was with him in a shot house around the corner from where we lived. *For those who don't know, a shot house is someone's house where they sell you alcohol. Of course, this is very illegal, but common down South.* He was drinking, and there were a few other people in this particular room. One of them was this guy named Lil Son. The other was a woman named Cassandra, but they called her "Muck Muck." Don't ask.

I was sitting there while my dad was drinking, and it was summertime because I had on shorts. Lil Son started making comments about my legs. "Mike, boy, you sure got some pretty legs. Your legs are like lady legs." *Weird as shit, right?* Of course, I was around ten or so, so I didn't understand it. All of a sudden, Lil Son came over and started rubbing my legs.

I didn't know what was going on at that point, but luckily Richard sternly (but in sort of a joking manner) said, "Michael, don't let that man touch your legs."

Now I'll tell you something about my relationship with Richard. I don't know if I fully respected him, but I sort of feared him. It was odd, because I wanted to be accepted by him, but I knew he had many flaws that I wanted nothing to do with. But when I was younger, and he told me to do something, I felt a sense of urgency to get it done. So when he told me to make Lil Son stop touching my legs, I reacted. I pushed Lil Son's hands away and told him to stop, and he did.

Now Muck-Muck, having seen everything that had just happened, all of a sudden wanted some of those "beautiful legs." So she came over and started rubbing my legs. Once again, I was nine, maybe ten. I really didn't know shit about sexuality. I knew I liked girls and not boys, but damn, I was still young, and this shit was confusing me. I was thinking if Richard didn't want Lil Son touching my legs, well, that logic must apply to Muck-Muck. So I forcefully pushed her hands away and said, "Get off me." Now Richard gave me another lesson. He said, "No, Michael, if a woman wants to do that, let her do what she wants."

I included this story because I think it affected my behavior for many years of my life. For so long, if I was ever in a situation where a woman wanted me to do something, I almost felt obligated to please her. I know it sounds freaking ridiculous, and it is, but that was my mindset. There have been many times where I flirted, touched, and even had sexual relations with a woman just because that's what *she* wanted, and not necessarily what I wanted. I'm glad things have changed. They needed to.

I've always loved women. I mean, I was a ladies' man before I was a man. It's always been a blessing and my biggest vice. Charming, but at the same time, I "wasn't shit." Ask just about any woman that's had to deal with me.

My first girlfriend was a girl who would later become my stepsister. (My mom married her dad much later in life... we'll get to that.) Her name was "Karrie." We were babies, so it was innocent, but Karrie taught me how to kiss. Her parents (yeah, her mom too) and my family were actually pretty tight. They'd come over with her younger brother "Kevin" on occasions, and the kids would all hang in a room together.

One night, while the adults drank, us kids were in the room playing as usual. Now, in the past, Karrie and I would kiss every now and then, but it was just a little innocent peck. Well this night, I went in for the kiss with my lips tight and she took it to the next level. That girl nearly drowned me with her tongue. I remember thinking that it was very wet, but I liked it, and from there, well, I was hooked.

Karrie and I rarely saw each other because we lived in different states. However, we stayed in touch with letters *(yeah, people actually wrote and MAILED them with a STAMP back then)*, and when we saw each other, we'd always have fun. That is until one day, when we were around ten or eleven. We were at her parents' place, I believe in Virginia, and we got caught making out in the basement. We were behind this door, and all of a sudden her dad (my future stepdad) came downstairs. I still don't know how we didn't hear him, but he got down there without us knowing. All I remember was him swinging open that door and catching the two of us hugged up. We jumped up, and as soon as we did, he grabbed Karrie, and I believe she must have said something smart, because he slapped the living shit out of her. He didn't do anything to me. He didn't even look at me. He didn't have to. I'm pretty sure he realized I was already nervous as hell. I may have even peed on myself a little.

Despite being scared out of my freaking mind, I liked the feeling of being physical with a girl. Even though I wasn't having sex, it was super satisfying, and all I knew was I wanted more.

The problem with a child discovering sexuality is if he/she doesn't have proper guidance, it can be seriously detrimental to his future. Besides Richard's "advice" I told you about earlier, I never received the "talk." Not from Richard. Damn sure not from Jimmy. And my mom's approach was more about how I treated a girl/lady rather than what to do if I got or how to get the "treats."

Yes, every parent should choose when it's the right time to have that "talk" with their kids, but it's so important to have. It's also important to ask your kids those questions they may find embarrassing. Sure, it may be awkward, but I'm sure it would be even more awkward if they didn't have proper preparation and had to come and tell you about a pregnancy or worse.

I was about twelve (yup, that young) the first time I attempted to have actual intercourse. Emphasis on attempted because it was pretty much a total failure. I had no idea what I was doing. I was with this older girl from the neighborhood who tried to give me some on the side of my house. What's even more crazy about this is we had an audience. At least two other kids were there just watching. Watching me fail miserably. Sure, our pants were down, but she kept saying, "That's my thigh. That's my pelvis," and then pulled her pants up and left, so I knew I hadn't done "it" right. At least, not yet.

> *Looking back, luckily I failed because you'll notice I didn't say anything about protection. Man, I could've been a great grandpappy right now. Whew!! Talk to your kids, please!*

While it wasn't pretty on the side of the house, it was worse inside it. To say there was no love between my mom and Richard was an understatement. Sure, I'd come home in the middle of the day every now and then and that bedroom door would be closed, but if they were making love, that love sure didn't follow them out of their room.

The two of them were a brutal mix that any scientist would tell you was combustible. Richard was a violent, jealous alcoholic that was a ticking time bomb, and my mom, with her sharp and lethal tongue, would always find a way to cut his already-short wick shorter.

Arguments were almost daily. Physical fights were too often, especially when I was younger, but what's even crazier is I don't remember one time that the police showed up to our house because of a "domestic" situation. I guess it was just routine for the area I grew up in. Even when my mom got stabbed by this man—*Oh, did I forget to mention Richard actually stabbed my mother?*

I remember being brought home by Richard's cousin Freida, who was also someone my mom would talk and socialize with. When we got there, Richard was sitting on the porch, and Freida said, "Where's Linda?" Without any emotions, he responded by saying, "She in there," gesturing inside the house. Immediately, I could feel something was wrong, but I was young, so what did I know? Upon walking in the house, Freida began to call out to my mom, and when she didn't answer, my feelings intensified. Of course, we didn't live in a huge house, so it didn't take long to realize my nightmarish feeling was all too real. Lying in the bathroom in a pool of blood was my unconscious mother. How she got there I found out much later in life.

She told me that Richard had been gone all weekend. Just hadn't come home. On Sunday, she needed to get groceries for the house, but he had the car and she had no way to get to the store. Of course, this was before cell phones or even pagers, so she had no way to even reach out to see when he was coming back. Having no other options, she went around the corner to where Freida lived and asked her if she'd watch me and if she could borrow her car to go to the store.

According to my mom, after buying groceries, she got home and didn't even turn the car off because she just planned to run in, drop the bags down on the counter, and return Freida's car because Freida had to go to work.

This is when I believe my mother faced the devil himself, just in the form of man. When she got into the house, the man who had been a ghost all weekend suddenly wanted to be home. He didn't have roses, apologize for leaving his family without protection, or bring food because he was gone all weekend. He didn't even ask, "Can I grab those bags for you, dear?" Nope! This "man" asked her, "Where you been?" Now, I know he wasn't always the smartest man in every room, but damn, Captain Obvious, remember my mother had *groceries* in her hands. Her reply was a smart one but very appropriate in this situation.

"Where does it look like I've been, Richard?" My mom told me she doesn't remember anything after that except waking up in a hospital.

It may have been a good thing she doesn't remember, because I wouldn't want anyone to have to recall or relive what she endured. Beaten black and blue. Eyes closed. Stabbed in the back, and my mom also believes he shot her in the leg with "something." She had to spend thirty days in the hospital.

Police tried to interview her, but when they tried, she was so drugged up, and according to my mom, Richard's mom and sister tried to discourage them by saying, "She's on all this medicine. She doesn't know what she's saying."

Sounds horrible and nearly unbelievable. However, you have to remember this was down South and in the '70s. Domestic violence victims down there didn't get much justice back then unless they ended up dead. Luckily for my mom, she didn't end up that way. Unfortunately for Richard's next wife, she didn't end up so lucky. More on this later.

Chapter 2

FADE IN

BEFORE I BECAME a person talking about sports for a living, I thought I'd be the one playing them for a living. Problem was, I wasn't that good. Sure, I played (and actually did quite well for myself playing football or basketball on the Air Force bases where I was stationed), but I knew early on that athletic scholarship offers weren't going to be flooding my mailbox.

The reality about my athletic prowess, or lack thereof, was exposed one day when I was going to play some basketball with my cousins, Reggie and William, who everyone called "Main." It's really supposed to be "Man," but down South, with everyone's country accent, they pronounced it "Main." Reggie and Main were much older. Around this time, I was about fourteen, so they had to already be in their twenties.

Anyway, we were riding to the gym, and they had a cooler of beer in the back seat with me. They were drinking the brew, and—doing what older cousins usually do to younger cousins—they offered me one. I replied, "Nawwww, I'm an athlete." Not "What are you talking about? I'm too young," but "I'm an athlete." They kind of snickered, and we continued our ride to the gym.

Now, once again, I'm not the greatest ball player in the world, but I thought I had potential. We were playing, and on this day, I was absolutely *terrible*. I was playing with older guys, but I would've gotten run off the floor by some five-year-olds on that day. After about two hours of this humiliation, we got back into the car, and they went back to drinking their cold ones. After a few moments, Reggie said, "You sure you don't want one? I don't think that athlete thing is gonna work for you." He and Main busted out laughing, and realizing he was telling the truth, I reached into that cooler. I popped the top and had my first of what would become many more alcoholic drinks.

I also smoked my first joint with them, and I got so high with Reggie before the 1985 NCAA Championship game between Georgetown and Villanova that when we got to my house, I literally fell out of the car when we parked. I was laughing so loud and hard that Reggie had to pick me up, stuff me back into my seat, and drive around until I was able to stop laughing, because my mom would've absolutely known I was high and killed us both.

Now, I'm not blaming my older cousins for introducing me to marijuana and alcohol; it just happened. I would've likely tried them anyway, and more than likely with someone less responsible who wouldn't have taken care of me the way they did. In fact, those two were and still are, to this day, guys I admire and have always looked up to. They teased and picked on me like a little brother, but they also looked out for me like one. Honestly, they were the only real male role models I had growing up. I owe them a lot because I don't even want to imagine what my childhood could've turned into without them.

Ironically, they were Richard's nephews, but they were nothing like him. I still don't know how my stepdad turned out the way he did. Looking at his side of the family, many of them were scholars, some with good jobs and even pastors. His sister even married the pastor who baptized me at an early age.

Even though I wasn't blood, I felt loved by them. However, I just wish they would've or could've done more to stop Richard from beating my mom. Eventually, I did.

Like I mentioned earlier, arguments were a common occurrence, and the physical fights were way too often. Not like every day or every week, but they happened enough. Usually, I'd hear it happening, and I remember my body just going into shock. You ever have one of those dreams where you know you're dreaming, but you can't wake up or move? Feeling paralyzed? That's what it was like for me. Once again, I was a kid, so I just felt helpless. Until this one time, when I'd had enough.

It happened on a Saturday or maybe during the summer. All I know is I was home and it was in the daytime, so I know there was no school. The fighting began like it usually did with an argument and screaming back and forth. The threat from him like, "and I'll beat yo ass" and my mom saying something else before he followed up on his promise. Like I said, usually fear would paralyze me, but this time, the anger of hearing my mom scream just pissed me off.

Our house was full of guns—none of them legal—and I wouldn't be surprised if one or two had a body on them. Usually, they were hidden in spaces only Richard and maybe my mom knew about, but there was one gun I knew of because it was mine. It was a rifle, and Richard had given it to me because I always wanted to go hunting with him. I only actually used it once for hunting, but this time, I was going to use it again...on Richard.

I jumped up and ran behind the closet door where the rifle was kept. I grabbed it and ran into the room where my mother was being attacked. Gun in hand and in the ready-to-shoot position, I turned the rifle on Richard and told him...

Honestly, I don't know what I said, because I felt like I was having an out-of-body experience.

I'd like to think I said some cool, hard shit like, "Go ahead, make my day" like that famous Clint Eastwood line, but it was probably something more like, "Leave my mommy alone." Whatever it was, I made my point. He looked at me, half angry and half afraid, and went, "Boy, what you gonna do with that gun?" But he didn't move. Now I don't know why I thought my mom was going to be proud of her baby running in to protect her, but that wasn't the reaction I got. She started screaming hysterically, "Michael! Put that gun down!" I would ask my mom later in life what would make her react that way, and she said, "He just wasn't worth it."

As terrible as Richard was to my mom, he was actually pretty good to me. He loved me as if his blood ran through my veins, and I actually felt that love. I hated the way he treated my mom, and that he'd blow his money on alcohol and maybe even drugs, but like I said, there was a hard-to-explain respect for him. It could've been fear, but I know one thing: as long as people knew he was my dad, *I* didn't have to fear shit.

In the neighborhood, he went by several names. Richard, of course. "Black Richard" or "Crazy Richard" too. There was a reason why he had that latter name. He earned it! He was a guy who was not to be "f-ed with." Even though I didn't grow up in a great neighborhood in Bessemer, we could leave our doors wide open when no one was home and no one would dare go in. That's because of Crazy Richard.

I almost saw him in action firsthand, and looking back on it, had things turned out differently, I might have been a witness to a murder. It started because I got robbed around the corner from our house. *Yep, someone must not have known I was Crazy Richard's kid. I mean, it was dark and it's not like I wore a sign around my neck indicating I was.*

A friend of mine named Rick and I were coming home from basketball practice. Not long after we split to go to our separate homes, I heard Rick screaming my name. "Mike! Mike!" I was about a half block from my house, but I ran back to see what was going on with my homie. When I ran back around the block, I saw him standing there with this man, and Rick seemed shook. Of course, the spidey senses were going off again. I knew some shit was not quite right, but I was not going to be a punk and leave my boy by himself. So I ran up, and as soon as I did, this man showed me this gun and stuck it right in my chest. I thought I was dead on the spot. You don't know fear until someone pulls a gun on you, which actually has happened a few times in my life.

Anyway, with the gun in my chest, the man said, "Y'all look like the 'lil motherfuckers that stole my money."

I was stuttering at this point. "N-n-n-n-n-nawl, man, you, you, you got the wrong ones."

He said, "Run your pockets," which means take everything out of your pockets. "I know you got some money." We had stopped at this neighborhood bakery after practice to get some donuts, and he could've seen us spending money in there and followed us. Regardless, he knew. I had about nine dollars in my pocket, which, to a fourteen-year-old down South in the '80s, was a lot of damn money. He saw this money, snatched it, and ran off.

Now I'd gone from just scared to scared and pissed. To this day, I *hate* a thief. I'll give you anything I have, if I can afford to and you really need it, but don't take shit from me without me knowing or doing it forcefully. That was the first time I'd ever been violated, and I was upset. It was time to find Richard. I threw down the bag of donuts I had in my hand and ran home. Well, Richard wasn't there, and my mom was at work. However, Richard's car was outside, so he couldn't have been far. If he wasn't home, he must have been at this lady's house named Ms. Chick, who ran a shot house. I ran there, and bingo!

I walked inside and tears were streaming down my face. Richard saw me and he jumped up. "Michael, what's wrong? What's wrong, man?" I told him what had just happened, that I just had been robbed at gunpoint, and I witnessed a transformation. I saw an inferno in this man's eyes, and he went completely silent with the exception of "Who is he?" I didn't know, and he asked, "What does he look like?" I said I could point him out if I saw him.

We walked out of that shot house and went to our house right around the corner. He went in his room, into his closet, and grabbed something. *I don't think it takes a rocket scientist to figure out what "that" might have been.* We were walking out of the house, and there was a golf club in a corner. Now I don't know why there was a golf club in the house; no one there *ever* played golf, but I guess I was about to learn because he picked it up and gave it to me. We walked around that neighborhood for a good thirty minutes. Luckily for this dude, we couldn't find him, or I KNOW I would've been a witness to a brutal felony, and with that golf club in my hand, maybe even a co-defendant. God always looks out, and He certainly looked out for that guy, and for US, that night.

I also believe things happen for a reason, and that night, thanks to me being a victim, I learned a valuable lesson.

After not being able to find the guy, some people wisely convinced my dad to call the cops, and he did. When they showed up, they acted suspicious and treated *me* like I'd done something wrong or like I was lying. *Why the hell would I do something like that?* I was thinking. They even put *me* in the back of the police car. I remember being in that back seat and realizing for the first time that there's no handle to get the hell out, and I was staring at a cage in front of me. My lesson was, *I'm never going to feel like this again. I can't* ever *get locked up.*

While I was back there, my mom just happened to come home from work. Once again, this was before cell phones, and I don't think anyone called her job, so imagine her shock when she saw a squad car in front of her house and her little boy in the back seat. She lost her damn mind, and went off on those cops. "Take my son out of that car!" She came to the window and was screaming, "Un-un, I don't care what happened. Get him out of there right now." They did, and I just remember being super relieved afterwards.

Being in that situation also gave me my first indication of how some law enforcement view us. Of course, that's very apparent today. Remember, I was a child and I was the victim, but my skin criminalized me in their eyes. When I was in that police car, I didn't feel served or protected. I felt judged and neglected. Being treated like this by cops wasn't rare in my community, and my situation (at least this first one) was mild compared to many others. It's part of the reason why a lot of black and brown folks don't trust cops. I know they're not all bad, but there are enough bad ones to give the good ones a bad name. It's why I'm so passionate about changing the system.

While Richard might have been the "crazy" one, my mom was and sort of still is to this day not someone to be messed with. Oh, she's super sweet, loving, kind, and God-fearing, but she can lay the fear of God into someone too. Especially with her mouth.

I told you about my first encounter with racism with the little girl in Betty's yard earlier. Another one came not long afterward. And this time a white woman got turned black after the ass-whooping my mom gave her.

There was this convenience store around the corner from our house. Not even two blocks away. My mom would send me there to grab small things for her. Cigarettes, toilet paper, a Pepsi, etc. *My mom has kept Pepsi in business by herself for decades.*

Anyway, one day I was there, and there was a white lady behind the counter. She was new, or at least I had never seen her before. I don't know what led up to her saying it, but she said something to me and ended her sentence with, "you lil nigger." Now look, I was still very young at this point, but I knew it wasn't right for *her* to call me that.

Let me tell you something. It hurt. It wasn't like the little girl saying "black blood" when I cut myself. This was something that cut into my soul, and ironically made my blood boil. Yes, I could've cursed her out, yelled, and made a scene—and believe me, a lot of kids would have—but my mom always told me to respect adults. I mean, she wouldn't want me to be a fool and let them hit me, but I felt if I cursed this woman out and my mom found out about it, my mom would have "that ass." So I did the next best thing. I went home and I told "Mommy." I'm sure that white lady wished I would've just cursed her out, yelled, and made a scene.

I didn't go to the store with my mom after I told her, but the witnesses who were there said my mom *whooped her motherfucking ass*! Once again, I'm not trying to make my mom out to be a bad person, because she's not at all. In fact, my mom would later tell me that she had a friend's baby in her hand and merely threatened the lady because she was talking slick to her. I'm also sure she went up there and asked her what I had said first. My mom is about justice, but also making sure her sons are accountable for their actions. Obviously the answer wasn't a sufficient one, and this lady paid the consequences.

What I did witness was hearing police cars show up and a commotion that spread throughout the neighborhood. I started walking around the corner toward that store and I saw at least three cops trying to arrest my mom. They were *not* having much success because they could not contain her. Of course, I would never advise anyone to do this now. Thinking back on this brings chills because of the epidemic that's plagued this nation today of unarmed black people being gunned down in the streets. Yes, my mom was resisting, but she was only armed with her 5'6" frame, sharp tongue, and anger of still knowing this racist woman had called her son out of his name and SHE was being arrested. I do remember thinking, "Damn, I didn't know she was that strong," but eventually, the police controlled her and put her in the squad car without beating, choking, or killing her. *Over 30 years later, I'm wondering why that's still so hard for some cops to do today.*

I went to Jess Lanier High School in Bessemer. My first year, it was pretty mixed: half black, half white. Then they decided to shut down Abrams, the all-black high school across town, and merge its students with Lanier's. Shit changed. Most of the white folks rolled the hell out and transferred to McAdory High, and Lanier became black as shit in every way. Shit just got run down. Not that blacks were losing their damn minds (some were, but so did the white kids when they went there), but it was as if no one gave a damn anymore. The contrast was my first experience of seeing how much some people care when it affects blacks as opposed to whites.

I wasn't the popular kid in high school, nor was I the shy kid no one knew. I was really just a dude. Smart, but never fully applying myself. Cute, but not "fine," as the girls used to say back in the day. Charismatic, but a little too talkative for some teachers. I was the class clown, and I loved that role. It's the first time I knew I wanted to entertain for a living.

I was in class one day and the teacher, I think his name was Mr. Cook, was giving us instructions. Now, Mr. Cook was a *huge* man. At least, he looked like that to me as a child. Still, he was a guy that, teacher or not, you probably didn't want to piss off. He rarely smiled—all business. Anyway, he was giving his lecture or whatever it's called, and someone did something in the class that did not please him. He went in. I'm talking about full tilt.

The class got super quiet and I saw my opportunity. I said, in a really proper manner, "Mr. Cook, have you ever thought about anger management...I just don't want to see you die from stress, brother." He gave me this look of amazement like *What the F did you just say?* I continued, "You see, here's an opportunity for you to take a softer, gentler approach. You're really just a big teddy bear inside," and I ended it with, "Coochie coochie cooooo."

The class lost its mind. They were rolling on the floor. This even got a grin from Mr. Cook. I know deep down he wanted to laugh, but he held it in. He kicked me out of his class, and I got detention, but I was hooked on entertaining people.

The only thing I liked more than entertaining or making people laugh in high school was girls. You thought I was going to say sports, huh? I believe the only reason I played sports some years is because I thought it would get me more access to girls.

Now, for the rest of this book, there will be a lot of name changes. Partly because I ain't trying to be sued, but honestly, I just can't remember a lot of the names.

When I was a freshman in high school, I played basketball, and one of my best friends (in fact, I actually considered him my best friend at the time) was this guy named James Mason (not his real name). James and I were super tight; we did a lot together, and both played basketball. James was slightly better. Honestly, he was much better because he made the varsity team as a freshman, while I played JV.

Our team had a student manager named Tania Hall. She was pretty, a year older than me, and also my girlfriend. We'd talk on the phone a lot. I'd get a kiss after school but nothing deeply sexual. We'd sit together on the bus during away games, etc. Everything was cool with us. That is, until one night my silliness revealed my first moment of betrayal.

I called Tania one night and decided I was going to play on the phone. The phone rang. Her sister answered and I changed my voice, pretending to be a salesman looking for Tania. Her sister was not in the mood. Now you have to understand, this was before the days of caller ID, so she had no idea who it was, but she knew it was someone joking around on the phone.

After a few seconds, she finally got frustrated and said, "Who the hell is this? Is this that James boy calling here again?"

I was still in play mode and said, "James who, ma'am?"

She replied, "I know this you, James Mason."

Game over. My regular voice was all of a sudden back. I said, "This is Mike!" Of course, her sister knew me and who I was to Tania, and I could feel her emotions through the phone even though I couldn't see her. She quickly went, "Oh shit," and just hung up.

I was pissed, because I was wondering *why* James had been calling for Tania in the first place—and how did he even get the number? Long story short, they had been messing with each other behind my back. My best friend and my girl. Betrayal hurt like a bitch. I was upset with Tania, but way more incensed with James. I wanted to kick his ass, and once it got out what he did, my teammates thought he was foul. Especially since *they* began sitting next to each other on the team bus.

There was a rap group in the '80s named Whodini who had a hit song called "Friends," and I knew the lyrics. Look up the lyrics. It talks about two-faced, low down, dirty, back-stabbing people that we call friends. *(Damn, am I still bitter about that one?)* Anyway, one night after a game, someone was playing it on the bus, and I went in with the verses, right in James' and Tania's faces. The whole bus was cracking up. Tania got upset and looked like she wanted to cry. James made a few threats, but he knew better. I would've and probably should have f'ed James up.

Maybe I should've whooped his ass. Maybe it would've made me feel better because before that, I was probably overly trusting of people. Probably a little naïve. However, because of that, it's still hard for me to trust people to this day. I'm getting better, but I've got to get to know you very well before I do.

By the time I was fifteen, I had already grown to be about six feet tall, and I thought I was cute. Girls at least thought I was, even though back then, I was skinny as hell. That's why I never got the "fine" moniker. Just, "Oh yeah, he cute!" It was a quiet confidence though. I never went around saying

I was the shit because (a) I really wasn't and (b) my mom always kept me grounded.

She and my Grandma Lillian are the main reason why I am doing what I do today. They were the first people to really believe in me and tell me that there's something more than what I'm surrounded by in my environment.

My mom was about that work and action too, though. I used to tell her that I wanted to be an actor. I mean, I'd tell her over and over and over again. Then one day I started to tell her about my dreams, and she cut me off like an edit. "Stop," she said. "I don't want to hear this anymore. What are you *doing* to make that happen?" I didn't have an answer. She continued, "Until you have a plan about how you're going to do this and *show* me that you're serious about doing it, I don't want to hear it anymore."

I was a bit shocked and at first confused, but it's some of the best advice anyone could have given me. Too many people say they want something, but many of those people don't take the action necessary to get it. Sure, a few things may fall in their laps every now and then, but usually that real success has to be obtained by the person seeking it. Sometimes you even have to take chances. You will never develop your wings until you have enough courage to leave the nest. So go for yours, like I did mine. Even though my first step into the acting world was just to get on TV, period.

However, before my TV dreams, I had that desire, like a lot of other kids, to be a professional athlete. Not as an NFL or NBA player though. Hell no! I was going to play baseball. I was going to be a New York Yankee. My grandmother and many other family members lived in a building directly across the street from Yankee Stadium in the Bronx.

I've always loved sports, but I absolutely *loved* the Yankees. Reggie Jackson (funny story about him later), Dave Winfield, Don Mattingly, Willie Randolph—those were my guys. If I went on top of the roof of the building, I could actually see inside the stadium. At least, the infield. My goal in life was to get inside and star in that stadium. So much so that one afternoon, I looked out my Grandma Lillian's window and over at the stadium and told her, "One day, I'm going to play right over there."

At the moment, I was talking about being over there as a player. Of course, it didn't work out that way, but it still *worked out*!

When I was younger, I loved doing two impressions; they were two sports icons. The first was my favorite athlete of all time, Muhammad Ali. First time I remember seeing Ali, he was nearing the end, but he still had that charisma. I had a half fro like him at the time, and we were the same complexion, so I felt like I was a part of him. He was magical—larger than life, and I was glued to the set anytime he was on it. And, of course, I had to listen to every word he said, which made it easier to emulate him.

I remember seeing a few of his fights of course, but the most memorable one is one I kind of wish I could forget. However, it taught me something I've held on to for years. It was when he fought Larry Holmes, and I remember crying because my hero was getting beaten so badly. He was losing, but you'd never know it. Ali was still smiling. Still confident. Even in defeat, you'd never know he'd been defeated.

I've tried to take that approach in my life. Even when you're down and people have counted you out, never give up or lose confidence in yourself. Smile and believe that a better day is coming. However, and this is very important, if that smile from *within* isn't genuine, and you don't actually believe it will be better, it won't benefit you. *Listen closely.* Talk to someone about it. Preferably a good therapist who you can trust and you feel comfortable releasing your fears and insecurities to, but talk to someone. You HAVE to let that shit go or it will consume you. Don't let it win.

The other sports figure gained a lot of his popularity because of Ali, and that's Howard Cossell. Before there was a Stephen A. Smith, Colin Cowherd, Michael Wilbon, or Tony Kornheiser, Cossell was the mouth of sports. He was smart but very opinionated and didn't give a damn if you disagreed or not. This was long before this was vogue. Like Ali, if he was on my set, I was watching, and more importantly, listening.

These two icons and my impressions were the start of my broadcasting career, believe it or not. One Christmas, I got a cassette player. *Yeah, look it up if you're under 35.* Of course, I recorded and played music on it, but more than anything, I recorded myself. One of the things I would do was an interview between Ali and Howard Cossell, in their voices. "This is Howard Cossell speaking sports. I'm here with the loquacious [yeah, I even had his vocabulary back then] man formerly known as Cassius Clay, *now* known as Mo-ha-med Ah-Li! Champ, how are you?" Then, in my Ali voice, "Better than that hairpiece, Cossell." I'd just make up stuff on the flip and actually got pretty good at it.

One day, Richard, for whatever reason, was listening to my tapes and he came across one of my recordings. He actually went and played it for his drinking buddies, and they all started laughing. They thought I sounded just like both

Ali and Cossell. That moment, like the classroom moment with Mr. Cook, was like a light going off blinking toward my destiny.

While I knew what I wanted to do, or at least which sort of direction I wanted to go in (in a professional sense), my personal life has always been, and in some ways still is tattered. Once again, I have always loved me some women. My problem is jumping in a relationship too soon before figuring out who I'm actually with. You sometimes get infatuated by the catch or what you believe is the perfect woman for you, but many times, you find out that ain't nearly the case.

Another problem I had, until recently actually, is not being able to fully let go and dive in. I've always held a little bit back because I never wanted to get hurt. Sure, it's selfish, and I've missed out, and my dumb ass has hurt many women in my past, but for me, it was about self-preservation. I felt that searing pain in my heart when I was fifteen, and it's something that stuck with me for a long time and had an effect on many relationships.

I was in the tenth grade and feeling myself. Once again, I was known as that cute, funny guy, but never fine. However, it was enough to get the attention of one of the finest girls in my high school. Her name was "Jackie." She was tall, with a pretty complexion and long hair. A transfer student, she was two years older. Even though she was a senior and I was just a sophomore, it didn't matter. To me, that's what I should expect at that time. A little cocky, I know, but that's just who I was at the time.

Even though I had lost my virginity a year earlier *(to a girl named Love—can you believe that shit?)*, Jackie and I were never fully intimate. We kissed, hugged, and talked on the phone, but never did anything more. Mainly because I didn't have a car at the time (even though I had lied to her and told her I was sixteen, not fifteen), she lived in Birmingham, which was fifteen miles away, and her mom was strict as hell. She couldn't go anywhere. In fact, the only time we truly hung out outside of school was the night I wish I could've kicked Cupid's ass for making me fall for this girl.

It was a Friday night and we were at Jess Lanier's football game. Our school just happened to be playing Jackie's old school that night in Birmingham. Honestly, because of how strict Jackie's mom was, it's the only reason why she was at the game. That, plus her older brother brought her.

Of course, all her old friends were also there, and I remember just walking around that stadium the entire night holding hands. Of course, I didn't mind. *Did I tell you Jackie was fine as hell and she was MY girl?* I was proud. But I was also tired and asked her if we could just sit down for a second. She said okay, but she also wanted to walk on the other side of the field again, where people from her old school were.

I said cool, and we walked over. Once we got there this time, I noticed this guy looking in our direction and his friends giving that *awwww shit* expression. I knew something was up, but need I remind you I was fifteen and I was not fully up on game at this point.

Before the game was over, we decided to go to the parking lot where Jackie's brother's car was parked. She and her brother had been drinking wine coolers before, and she wanted to go back out for a few more sips. Of course, I wanted to go for a "taste" myself, if you know what I'm saying. We got to the car and had a few drinks, and then began to wet each other's whistle. It was only kissing and touching, but I was really into it. Not as much in a sexual sense, but I was emotionally engulfed in this girl. I mean, my heart, mind, and body were all saying at once, "I love this...I love her." This was the first time my little tender heart had ever felt like this. Man, I've just got to share this.

So the radio was playing *(in my memory it was a slow song by Luther Vandross. More than likely it was some Big Daddy Kane or Eric B & Rakim. But this is MY special moment. So allow me to embellish some)*. We were embraced. My love was building. I pulled away slowly. I looked into Jackie's eyes, while holding her hand and softly told this gorgeous seventeen-year-old girl, "I love you." Three little words, but they left my mouth so smoothly. So magical. It was the first time I had ever told a girl I loved her, and it felt simply liberating and amazing...for just a split second. The reaction on Jackie's face was as if I had farted in her mouth and told her it was breath spray. It's almost as if she was looking at a stranger, and if I had a mirror, I probably would've seen that same fool. I swear I heard the DJ scratch the record on the radio. There was no "I love you back." No "Me too." No "Awww, that's sweet, lil boy."

She just let go of my hand, took another sip of her wine cooler, and said, "Let's go."

I was stunned. A little hurt that what I'd said wasn't reciprocated, but still happy because that entire weekend, I stayed at my cousins' house and it was Jackie this, Jackie that. My cousins probably saw little hearts floating over my head every time I said her name. So I didn't talk to her that entire weekend because her line was busy every time I called. Man, this was my *lady* and I *loved* her. I loved her until we got back to school that Monday.

I was walking down the hallway, and a friend of mine named Karen came up to me. She asked curiously, "Are you and Jackie still together?" You ever have someone ask you and tell you something at the same time? Like a rhetorical question THEY know the answer to but YOU don't? That's the tone she had.

My response was an innocent, unassuming, "Yeah."

Her look was like, "I know something that he should know but I don't really have the heart to tell him." She just said, "All right" and walked off.

I was young. Still a bit naïve, but I wasn't dumb. I knew something in the water was foul, but I didn't quite know what it was yet—until the next period, when we were walking between classes. I hadn't seen Jackie since that Friday night, but as I was walking between classes, I spotted her. However, she wasn't alone. She was walking down the hall coming toward me, and she was holding hands with this dude named "Gary."

They walked right past me. People in the hallway knew we had been dating and they were wondering what I was going to do. The answer? I tore that motherfucking school up! At least, that's what played out in my mind at that moment. In reality, all I did was absolutely nothing. I just stood there with a look of embarrassment on my face and severe pain in my chest. I was humiliated, but the heartbreak superseded that. There was never any explanation from Jackie. I even found out later that the dude who was eyeing us at the football game was her ex-boyfriend, and the reason she was parading me around the stadium was just to make him jealous. I can't even remember talking to her the rest of that school year. All I knew was that that was a pain I never wanted to feel again.

It's sad, and yes, I get it, it happened when I was fifteen, but I held that for many years, and it's the excuse I used for never truly giving a woman everything I had or revealing the inner me. I've said things but could never let go. I always had to have a back-up plan.

If I'm being totally honest with myself, it was also my crutch. It was really my excuse for my abhorrent relationship behavior (more on this later). I honestly didn't fully get past this until Jackie and I communicated over social media just recently and she explained what she was going through in her life at that time and apologized. Of course, looking back, she didn't need to. Just like me, she was a kid, and just like me, she needed to work out her issues through therapy. With the grace of God, I still am.

If it wasn't for girls and me clowning around, I could have been an excellent student. I really didn't have any excuses not to be. My mom made sure I had everything I needed when it came to my education, but I just didn't fully apply myself. I passed classes, but with Cs. I know I could've done better, but I just got bored too easily. Plus, I loved the girls and talking in class too much.

Chapter 3

CUE

IN A CRAZY way, my unruly behavior in class actually started my journalism career. I had an English teacher in the ninth grade named Mrs. Sanders. Now, this was a lady who didn't take any shit and was quick to put you out of her class if you acted too much of a fool.

One time during a PTA meeting, this woman snitched on me so hard. As soon as my mom walked in her class, with me right behind her, she belted out, "Lady, I've been waiting to tell you just how terrible Michael is in my class."

She went on to tell my mom about my talking, and how much I disrupted her class, and my mom told her, "If he does it anymore, you have my permission to beat his ass." Now, this was after this type of punishment was outlawed in my school, and I knew she couldn't follow through on it, but she reminded me every time she could. And if she didn't, a classmate named "Vonnie," who witnessed my mom giving her permission, would blurt it out herself. Thanks, Vonnie!

Well, Mrs. Sanders was also the journalism teacher at Jess Lanier. At the end of my tenth grade year, I had to pick a few electives for my junior year. Classes such as home economics, shop, etc. Well, I just so happened to run into Mrs. Sanders, and she asked me if I had picked my electives yet.

I replied, "No ma'am. Not yet."

She said, "Well, why don't you sign up for journalism?"

Now this came as a shock. Remember, this was the woman I had come to believe didn't like me very much. So why was she asking me to sign up for a course that she taught so that *I* could be back in her class? Odd but heck, why not? Next school year, I got my courses and I saw journalism was on my schedule. I was kind of intrigued with the course, even if I did have to be back in tough-ass Mrs. Sander's class. However, there was one problem. Mrs. Sanders wasn't teaching the class anymore. A lady named Mrs. Bedford had taken over journalism.

My theory is Mrs. Sanders knew she wasn't going to be the teacher when she asked me to sign up for that class, and I don't think she was that fond of Mrs. Bedford. So I guess I was supposed to be the problem child for the teacher she had a problem with. Whatever the reason, I'm thankful to Mrs. Sanders. Sometimes God will use the most unbelievable methods or unlikely people to put you on the path He wants you on. Obviously, that path led to the journey I've been on since.

Being on the student newspaper actually gave me more confidence. I found a class that was fun, and I was actually really good at it. So much so that I went from being a sportswriter on the newspaper to sports editor to chief editor within a year. I even won the journalism Student of the Year award at graduation. That confidence leaked into other classes, and I became an overall better student. Still not great, but better.

I felt like I had an out from Bessemer. I always knew there was something much better out there. *Let me make something clear here, I'm not trying to dump on Bessemer. Sure, it has its problems, but it also has some great people in the city that I love and respect very much.* Like I said, I had the privilege of being born and having family in New York, and I saw that way of life every summer, so I knew there was more, but I needed to find a path to escape. I knew by my junior year in high school that college wasn't going to be my bag. I just wasn't disciplined enough to stay the course academically, and money would be an issue for my family. Therefore, I was thinking about joining the military. My cousins Main and Reggie were both in the Air Force by this time, and they seemed to be doing quite well for themselves, so I was strongly considering it.

I had to leave because at times, I absolutely dreaded going home. Yes, the physical abuse had come to a stop since I had pulled the gun on my dad and had what amounted to a man-to-man talk in which he said he'd never hit her again, but the arguments and the mental abuse were excruciating. They argued all the time, and so I tried to spend as much time away from home as possible.

I'd go to my cousins Martin and Niecy's house on the weekends, but during school days, I'd just hang out with my boys Vincent and Durand. Vincent lived with his grandma in the projects, but Durand lived in a nice, new neighborhood. Last house on a cul-de-sac. It was just him, his mom, and his granny, but me and Vincent would be there all the time. His family treated us like family because we acted like brothers. Still, to this day, if we see each others' moms, we refer to her as "ma."

We did everything there. Ate, watched movies, brought girls by for "fun," drank alcohol, and smoked...weed! Now, the girls, alcohol, and smoking happened when his mom wasn't home, most of the time, but I'm pretty sure she knew some of the things that were happening.

Before I go any further, let me preface this by saying we weren't addicts. We didn't smoke all the time or even often. But one night, when Durand's mom wasn't there, we got lifted. When I say we smoked a lot that night, Snoop Dogg would've said, "Damn, cuz, y'all smoking a lot." Here's the problem with me smoking a lot or even at all. I've got asthma and it was really bad when I was younger.

After I left Durand's, I got home and got to my room without running into my parents, but I was already coughing a lot. Later that night, I had the most severe asthma attack I've ever had. I don't know if you've ever seen someone have an asthma attack, but if not, imagine a heavy dude sitting on your chest while you're being choked at the same time. It's horrifying. My inhaler wasn't helping, and I knew I needed to go to the hospital for a treatment, but I was not about to ask my mom to take me out of fear she'd find out I had been smoking. Hell nawl!! I was coughing like crazy, and finally my mom heard me and asked if I was all right. I could barely breathe, but still I said, "Yeah, I'm okay."

Well, after about another hour, I couldn't take it anymore and finally stumbled into my parents' room. I mean, I was sipping air, taking very shallow breaths at this point. She took me to the hospital. I got that treatment, and she never found out I had been smoking. *Well, after she reads this she will. And she might still try to whoop my ass because that whole night was dumb.* I could've really died. Unfortunately, it wouldn't be my only close call with death during my early years.

Around this time, I began seeing this girl named Ariana. She was gorgeous, but remember that guy Gary that was walking the school hallway with my girlfriend, Jackie? Well, it was his half-sister, and honestly one of the reasons I started messing with her is to sort of get back at him. *I know it's messed up, but again, I had a messed-up way of thinking back then.* No male role models taught me any better.

Messing around with Ariana was fun, but also gave me one of the most embarrassing moments of my childhood. We were at a high school football game one Friday night, but decided we were going to ditch the game a bit early to huddle up ourselves. Down the street from the stadium was this post office. We walked down the block and realized our best chance at privacy was on the side of that post office. It was night and no one could see us, so we started making out. Our clothes were on but let me tell you, no one could dry hump better than me back in my day. Problem on this night was I didn't stay dry. I was into it. She was *really* into it. She was making these sounds like I was actually penetrating her and after a while, it began to feel that way. A few minutes later, or maybe it was a few seconds later, I got this sensation. Fellas, you know what that sensation is. I knew I should just stop and let this subside, but it was feeling *way* too good, and the next thing I knew, I was like a postman on the side of that post office, because I had just delivered.

As soon as it happened, my mind quickly went from "Oh, that felt good" to "Oh fuck, this ain't good." I pulled back and said to Ariana, "Hold on a second." At this time,

I don't think she knew what had just taken place, because I couldn't believe what had just happened. I left her and walked near the front of the building to where some light was. I looked down at the blue pants I had on and it looked like someone had thrown a cup of baby oil on my crotch. "Shit!" *What am I going to do? I still have to take her back to the stadium, where hundreds of people are under bright ass lights.*

I played it cool. I went back and got her, and we started walking back to the stadium. She said with a bit of a smile, "Everything okay?" Of course, I played it off and said, "Yeah, I think I got a cramp cause my thigh was hurting." Obviously I was lying, but I wasn't about to admit to this girl what happened. I had a sweater on and I was trying to pull that damn thing down low like it was a dress or something, but it was not going far enough. Everything was cool, or so I thought, until we got back to the stadium.

As soon as we walked up, I saw this dude I knew, and the first thing he said to me right in front of Ariana was, "What's up, Mike? Damn, cuz, what happened to you? Did you nut on yourself?"

Yes, I had. However, I still had to deny it, right? "Naw, man. I don't know what the hell that is." Ariana, to her credit, played it off and didn't even trip or say a word. At least not then.

A few weeks later in the school gym, I was cracking jokes with one of her female friends and she said, "I heard you failed P.E." Now, we were in gym, but I wasn't failing the class, and besides, that shit ain't funny. So while I've still got this confused look on my face, she quickly followed up with, "This P.E. stands for premature ejaculation." Cut the hell out of me. I looked right at Ariana, and from her look and the laughter of everyone in that circle, I knew she had told everyone what had happened.

Why would I expect her to keep that to herself? It's just human nature to spread gossip, and when it's factual gossip, it's even harder to contain.

The reason I included this embarrassing story is it gave me my first taste of karma. Remember, my main reason for pursuing her was to get back at "Gary." I mean, she was a gorgeous young lady but I was bitter and out for revenge. Well, that backfired. I couldn't control my emotions and obviously I couldn't control "other things," and I ended up looking stupid.

However, I didn't have anyone to talk to about these issues, so instead of learning a valuable lesson on why I shouldn't be spiteful, my twisted little ill-informed mind looked at it as another reason why I couldn't trust a woman. The irony is, because of my intentions, she shouldn't have trusted me from the start. *Young men, please find someone you can talk through all your issues with before it does severe damage later in your life.*

Even with counseling, I admit, I still have trouble letting people in. By nature, I *want* to trust people, but it's gotten harder and harder over my years to do so. I just know eventually they will let me down because they have so many times. Even if they're some of your closest friends, you will likely eventually feel betrayed by the majority of the people you meet. There are few exceptions in my life to my own rule. Darryl Bice was one of them.

I met Bice through some mutual friends going into my senior year of high school, twins named Ronald and Donald

Aldridge. I was hanging with Ronald pretty tight around this time. He lived in Birmingham (which is, again, fifteen miles north of Bessemer and one of the few metropolitan areas of Alabama, if you want to call it that).

Ronald and I were at this skating rink one Friday night, and he introduced me and Bice. I just remember thinking to myself, "This dude is wild and crazy as hell." Bice was one of those guys that just didn't care. Not necessarily in a reckless way, but in a nice, over the top, no fear type of way. Even though I was a little more serene when it came to him, he brought out that extra energy in me.

The night I met him, I gave him a ride home from the skating rink. He had been drinking a soda in a cup and when he got out of my car, he threw the cup up in the air, ice and all, with it landing on the roof of my Honda Civic as I drove away. It sounded like a barrage of hail had just come down on my roof. I was pissed. "I know this motherfucker didn't just throw something on my car after I just gave his ass a ride home."

I was about to stop the car, get out, and confront him, but fortunately, Ronald was in the car and said, "Man, that's just what Bice does. Let it go." I did and drove home.

The next day, Bice called me. We started kicking it, and it wasn't long before I considered this crazy-ass, sometimes-reckless dude my best friend in the world. He became part of the family. If you saw me, you saw him. We did almost everything together.

Around this time, I had gotten a job at this spot called Jefferson Home Furniture and met a dude named Stanley Hall, who worked there too. Stanley's dad was one of the biggest weed dealers in Birmingham, and Stanley had to work for him from time to time. Yes, I said "had" to work for him. Even though Stanley was out of high school and lived rent-free with his grandmother, he said he was still basically forced to work for his dad from time to time, if he expected some of the necessities of his life. *Who am I to judge?*

Bice, Stanley, this guy named John Jones, and I were hanging pretty tough back then. Bice and I more regularly, but that was my little crew back then. I'd still hang with Vincent and Durand from time to time, but I was spending more time in Birmingham than Bessemer at this time. We weren't in any fraternity, but we called each other "frat," short for fraternity, because we felt like brothers.

However, once again, of all the people I was hanging with back then, I felt like Bice would be the guy I could always trust and rely on the most. He didn't have much, but he'd give you his last, and he'd ALWAYS have your back.

This was on full display back in December of 1987. I remember it because it was a Christmas party at the Jefferson Civic Center thrown by this popular Birmingham DJ they called "Showboat." It was packed. Everyone from all over seemed to be there, including me and my crew.

I had been dealing with this girl named "Denise," but we had broken up months ago, so I was a free agent, having fun. I was talking to several girls at this time, including this girl named "Tonya Thompson." She was smoking, pretty, and had money. Her dad owned a popular night club in the city. Tonya and I had met months before, and it wasn't anything serious but talking on the phone every now and then.

Well, I knew she'd be coming to the party that night, but she hadn't arrived yet. I was dancing with this other girl, when all of a sudden, I saw her walking by. She looked at me dancing with this girl, gave me a smirk, and kept walking. I played it cool. Finished up my dance and started looking for her. When I found her, she was talking to this guy (who I later found out was her ex) and his homeboys. Now, you have to understand, I had been drinking heavily and maybe even had some weed before going into that party, so my courage was on ten. I walked right up to them and just extended my hand toward Tonya, as if to say, "It's time to go." *I mean, that's some real young mack shit, if I do say so myself.* With her ex looking like *Who the fuck is this dude?* she grabbed my hand and started walking away with me. Well, it almost cost me my life.

As I was walking through the crowd, I heard a girl scream, "Look out!" and a second later, felt my head get pushed from behind. Down South, they call that being "yoked," and it's a huge form of disrespect. I dropped Tonya's hand, and I turned around, pissed and ready to fight the world. I almost had to. By the time I turned around, the guy who'd "yoked" me had darted through the crowd, but I was more than determined to find him. I found Bice and the others and told them, "I got beef," and we were on the hunt.

I was looking for this dude and finally I spotted him. We locked eyes and the people between us saw us looking at each other and they knew it was about to go down. When I tell you that the crowd parted between us, it was like Moses was there with his staff, because soon it was just me, him, and opportunity. I ran toward him and we started throwing blows, and before long, three of his friends had joined in. I was fighting these four dudes by myself, and I must say, I wasn't doing that bad. But of course, I could have used some help. Where were John and Stanley? I don't know. Where was Bice? He had been on the other side looking for the same dude, but it didn't take long for him to find the melee because in a matter of seconds, he had joined in. I knew this because I saw him out of the corner of my eye just run into the fray and stab this dude square in the ass. Soon as this happened, I heard a *pop, pop, pop*. It wasn't firecrackers. The good and bad thing about most people with guns: they aren't that accurate. That's why they need semi-automatic weapons. Luckily, back on that night, this shooter, who I later found out was this guy from Bessemer named "Joe Waters," didn't have one. However, it was enough to make everyone stop fighting and run out of the venue. Party over.

That night taught me two things: Bice would always be there for me if I ever needed him, and I needed to stop trying to screw with so many girls. At least temporarily.

That same night, before all the madness went down, I reconnected with this girl named Tamara. I had met her a few months before at the state fair, and even though we spoke a few times on the phone, nothing ever came of it. She was pretty, and there was something about her personality that drew me to her. So after that night, I started calling her again.

Tamara and I got to know one another on the phone for several weeks, but the first time I went to see her was at her friend Tonya's house. She would be there or at her grandmother's house most nights until her mom got off of work and came and picked her up to take her home. In the beginning, I didn't go to her mom's house that much because her mom got off so late, for one thing, and also because she would always tell me how strict she was.

A few things I really liked about Tamara in the beginning: she was smart and pretty. She made some of the best turkey sandwiches I ever had, and she was a virgin. Believe it or not, meeting a girl who was sixteen or seventeen years old who was still a virgin back in those days was rare. I guess it sort of still is today, huh? I thought I had hit the jackpot, but because she was a virgin, it would be the only thing I'd "hit" for awhile.

What really made me become closer to Tamara is she took care of me. After that fight at the Civic Center, Bice and I ran into a few of those same dudes on several occasions over the next few months. One night, one of those guys and I got into a scuffle that ended up under a parked car and I cut my back on something sharp. I needed stitches but I did what a lot of kids growing up in underprivileged neighborhoods did. Nothing. Let time heal it. However, Tamara saw it, and one of the few times I snuck over to her mom's house while her mom wasn't there, she took care of my wound by putting cold cocoa butter on it and covering it. It was a small gesture, but it was the first time I felt a female, outside of my mother, showing some genuine compassion for me. It was certainly appreciated and shortly after, I asked her to be my girl.

However, before things got super serious with us, I did one of the stupidest things I've ever done in my life. Something that could've ended up destroying several lives. I'm embarrassed to even put this here, but I told you this would be "Open Mike" and it's important for me to share this, if it might stop someone else from attempting to do something so terrible. The thing is, the girl involved probably to this day has no idea it even happened and I'm so happy she doesn't. I just ask that God has forgiven me for even trying it.

Chapter 4

AD-LIB

AT THIS TIME in my life, I was seventeen and I was pretty sexually active. I was feeling myself and I told you, after that incident with Jackie, I wasn't faithful to no damn body. Damn, I was so ignorant. Anyway, there was an ex-girl-friend who wanted to get back together with me. Now, while we were together, it wasn't always roses. She had no reason to trust me, and I damn sure didn't trust her. Especially after I found out she had been spending time hanging out with the boy who lived right next door to her. I never brought this to her attention, but I knew, and like an idiot, I hung on to it until it was the proper time to be petty. Told you I hadn't learned my lessons properly.

The ex met me at my boy Durand's spot. No one was there except me, her, and Durand. We started talking, and I knew it was about to go down, so I told Durand I needed to use his room. *I think you know what I mean when I say "it."* She and I did what we had to do, and she was emotional. She was wondering if this was what I wanted from her to get us back together. Now, I don't know what the hell took over, but it had to be the devil, and only God was my saving grace. My cockiness and my vindictiveness of what I felt she had done to me in the past met full steam, facing each other. And had it not been for the good grace of God, I could've been facing time.

She was still lying in the bed with her clothes off and crying. Practically begging me to get back together. I said, "Hold on." I walked out the room and I had a smirk on my face. I was drunk with power, and looking back on it reminds me why God shouldn't give any type of power to those not ready for it because they will abuse it. I walked to the kitchen, and I saw Durand.

He said something like, "You put in that work?" and I nodded. I then said maybe the most stupid, reckless shit that's ever come out of my mouth.

"Hey, man, she's still in there. She'll do anything for me. You can hit it if you want it." *Even as I'm writing this shit some thirty years later as a father of two girls, I want to stab myself. I feel absolutely disgusted that I was even thinking that way or that those words would dare come out of my mouth.*

Luckily for all three of us, God was in control, and Durand's response was, "Nah, bruh, I'm good. I wouldn't do that."

Imagine if he had taken me up on my offer. Imagine him going in there. Nothing good would have happened. What if she'd said no, but Durand had already made up his mind that she'd said yes? Or even if she had realized what happened later and felt dirty. We could've been charged with sexual assault. Rape. Imprisonment. She could've been psychologically damaged or who knows what else. Once again, even though this person never knew I made this offer, I am so sorry for that stupid kid I was from the bottom of my heart, and I ask God for forgiveness.

> *I have to be transparent and include this for that kid who thinks his sexual prowess or being The Mack makes him a man. I wasn't thinking, or I just thought that behavior made me cool. Doing this type of stuff is beyond dumb. My ignorance, lapse in judgment, ego, whatever you want to call it, could've ruined lives that day. DO NOT RUIN YOURS.*

I ended up taking her home, and no, we never saw each other again in that capacity. And there's irony in Durand being the one making the right decisions and not me, as you'll find out later in this book.

Things were getting a little better at home, but the upgrade still wasn't good. There was constant arguing, and I could tell the stress had worn on my mom. *Just thinking about it now makes me emotional when you consider everything this woman has gone through in her life just to get me and my brother to where we are today. I appreciate it.*

She's told me a million times she would've gotten two more jobs in addition to her job at the Social Security Administration to put me through college, but I had already made up my mind to enlist in the Air Force.

There are a few reasons for this. One, my cousins Main and Reggie were already in and I saw how well they were doing. They had brand-new cars and, to a seventeen-year-old with nothing, that's almost everything. Two, despite what she said, I knew college would put a financial strain on my mom. Sure, I could've gotten student loans, but I also knew

I needed the discipline of a commitment. Had I gone to college, I probably would've done what a lot of folks from my city did. Gone for a year and then just ended right back in Bessemer taking some odd job to make it. I've always felt there was much more for me.

After graduating high school, I spent that summer in New York before reporting for military duty in October of '88. My first night of basic training was crazy. As soon as we arrived at the airport in San Antonio, we had orders being barked at us. We got on this bus and I remember it being deadly silent. The bus pulled up to Lackland Air Force Base. We got to our barracks and I swear it was so still, you could actually hear hearts beating. If there was ever a time I felt the thickness of nervousness and anxiety, it was on that night. It was like that for what seemed like an hour before, all of a sudden, all you heard was *tap tap tap tap*. It felt like something out of a horror movie. The heartbeats increased and I wouldn't be surprised if someone pissed on themselves. All of a sudden, the bus door opened. Those taps got closer and then... "GET THE FUCK OFF THE G'DAMN BUS, YOU MORONIC PIECES OF SHIT." This little wiry white dude named Sergeant Henson with a tight uniform and a Mounty hat was going off on us. Guys started scurrying off the bus, where we were told to go into this cafeteria and given five minutes to eat. And when they said five minutes, they *meant* five minutes. Don't get me wrong. They had a good spread set up. It was steak and mashed potatoes, but have you ever tried to eat a steak and HOT mashed potatoes in five minutes? We didn't have time to blow on our food to cool it off. It felt like we were stuffing hot, yet sort of tasty, coals in our mouths. The roof of my mouth was damaged for weeks.

Next thing I knew, we were lined up outside and it was deadly silent again. After a few minutes, we heard another set of taps. This time, this slender black dude named Staff Sergeant Gibson was in front of us. His demeanor was cool but forceful. He told us to go upstairs. Find a bunk. Shit. Shower. Shave ALL facial hair. "NOW!"

Let me tell you something. It was absolute chaos. Guys were scurrying around trying to claim bunks. I understood the constant yelling from Gibson and Henson at this time, but why did some of these guys take the part of shaving off all facial hair literally? The training instructors meant beards and mustaches *not your damn eyebrows!* Yup, we had at least three guys who shaved off theirs. Comic relief for sure, and the only time I smiled that night.

Lights went out and you heard a bunch of eighteen- and nineteen-year-olds just crying like they had just realized they'd made one of the biggest mistakes of their young lives. I wanted to cry too, but for some reason I didn't. I just prayed that God would see me through those next six weeks and, as always, He came through.

I'm thankful for my time in the military. It taught me a hell of a lot. I'm not just talking about how to fold underwear in six-inch squares. *Yeah, they made you do shit like that.* But they also taught me the importance of time, discipline, and leadership. It also taught me that there are good people all over this nation, of all colors.

Now, let me clarify: my mom and family always taught me to love everyone, of any color, as long as they respected you. I also told you about the white lady named Betty from

Bessemer, who treated me as her own child, despite some in her family being suspect when it comes to race. However, even though there were plenty of white people in Bessemer (not as much anymore) when I grew up there, it was still pretty segregated. You rarely saw kids running in "mixed" company. We didn't think much of it at the time. It just didn't happen a lot. So when I joined the military, it was really the first time I was around a lot of white guys and we were sort of forced to live in close quarters with each other.

Here's what I realized. Once again, good people come in all sizes, shapes, and colors, but we are different in a lot of ways. I don't mean that in a disrespectful tone, but let's just keep it real. We can be different at times, so it was important for me to get to know them better and them to get to know me. That's still the case in society today. We don't get to know each other because we become comfortable with what is—and usually what is looks just like you.

I know we live in very sensitive, politically correct times, and I'm not saying that shouldn't be the case. It should! However, the military, especially early on, helped me realize that some people just don't know better.

The first example that comes to mind was when I was in basic training. There was this one white guy in my flight from somewhere like South Dakota who had *never* seen a black person in the flesh before he came to basic training. No joke. He was a super nice kid. I talked to him from time to time, and a few weeks into training, I guess he felt comfortable enough to ask me a question. Once again, very nice kid who had never seen a black person in person before in his life, but he walked up to me and said very innocently, "Hill, can I rub your nappy hair?" First of all, my hair has never been "nappy," but seriously, here was an innocent yet ignorant moment by a guy who was just curious. He wasn't racist at all. He just didn't know any better. And hell, no, I didn't let him rub my damn hair. I told him that, while I knew he didn't mean any harm, that that question was inappropriate and probably wouldn't go over well with another person of color. Hopefully, he's learned and taken my advice and not gotten the shit knocked out of him.

The second example happened when I was in military tech school in San Angelo, Texas. A guy named Charles Hill (we called him JR), who is now my best friend in the world, had a roommate named Ench. Once again, Ench is somewhere from "ain't no black people around this mug" USA, but he was cool. He hung out with us. He felt comfortable with us, and we did a multitude of things together.

Now, as you know, sometimes when people of a certain race or gender get together, they refer to one another by terms that no one else outside of that race should use. I'll leave it at that. I think you understand. And I think you know the term that black people sometimes use. I'm not saying it's right or wrong, but JR and I would use this term when referring to each other. The problem is, like it can become when certain white people hear this term of "endearment" used in rap songs, they can become too comfortable and feel like, "Well, I should be able to say it too." Ench did this. However, it was so innocent and actually done in the most respectful way a non-black person could ever use it.

I wasn't there, but according to JR, he and Ench were in their dorm room just shooting the shit when Ench just came out of nowhere and said, "Hill, can I ask you a question?"

JR said, "Yeah, sure, bro."

Ench then said, "Can I call you nigger?" Of course, JR was taken aback by this, but he remained cool because he knew Ench didn't mean any harm, he was just ignorant. There's nothing wrong with being ignorant. It just means you don't know any better.

JR told him that it would never be cool for him to say, and we never had any problems because of it. As far as we know, he never got upset about it. He just understood. Which makes me wonder why a few others in this country don't get it too.

As I mentioned, JR is my very best friend in the world. No disrespect to any of my other homies. I love them all. It's just that JR and I have gone through so much together that I really don't even look at him as just a friend. Ironically, we have the same last name, but it's almost like we share the same blood too.

It didn't start off that way. Ask him and he'll tell you that he actually resented me. When I got to tech school in San Angelo, I was made one of the squad leaders. There were only a few of us and we had to wear different color ropes on our shoulders. That's why we were simply known as "ropes." JR was this rebellious dude who didn't like authority, which meant he didn't like someone like me. We butted heads a few times, and we actually never became too cool until one night, about two in the morning, an emergency and confusion brought us closer.

It started with a bang on my dorm door. I was in the dead of sleep, and my first thought was, *I must be dreaming.* My second thought was the building must be on fire, but since I didn't smell any smoke, my final thought was, *Who the hell is banging on my damn door so hard this late?* I got up, still half asleep, and answered. As soon as I opened the door, there was this soldier who had just gotten to base and was on night watch, and he was in a panic.

"Hill. Hill. Hill...your wife is in labor. You need to come to the phone now."

Now remember, this is back in 1989 before cell phones, and when pay phones still were very much in existence. The young soldier was in such a panic that I rushed, grabbed some pants, and threw on a shirt. I put some slides on my feet, and I was running toward the common area where the pay phone was. I was still half asleep, but my heart was racing. Then, right before I got to the phone, I realized: "Wait, he said my *wife* is in labor. What the hell? I don't have a damn wife."

Then I started thinking, "Did I somehow get Tamara pregnant when I went home for Christmas?" Anyway, I got to the phone, said, "Hello," and the lady on the other end was screaming, "Charles, Charles, Rebekah's water broke. She's going into labor now." Now I was even more confused. Remember, it was two in the morning. I was kind of awake now and my heart was racing. Then it struck me. I'd been confused with the other Airman Hill. I was a bit relieved, I have to admit, and I explained that they'd grabbed the wrong guy, but then something took over. I wanted to help this dude and his family, even though we'd clashed in the past. So I ran up to his room pretty much in the same panic as the soldier that came and got me. He rushed downstairs and I went with him, just to offer support. When he got off the phone, I saw a multitude of emotions in this dude's face. Worry, panic, but at the same time strength, because he had to take care of business. He got back home to Kentucky, and I'm happy to say, his beautiful daughter, KC, was born three months premature but is a healthy, happy, beautiful thirty-year-old woman today.

God has a funny way of taking you through something to receive your biggest blessings. Despite the way we started, our relationship had completely flipped. We became inseparable. Almost doing everything together, and like I mentioned, he's my brother to this day. We became influential in each other's lives. Making major decisions based off of one another's experiences. He's the main reason why I got married so young.

When KC was healthy enough, she and Rebekah moved to San Angelo to be with JR, and they lived off base. I was basically family by then, so I was around them all the time. I was only eighteen, and JR is just a year older than me, but his family just seemed so beautiful together. Plus, they had an apartment and JR had a new car, a Nissan Sentra.

Side note. Looking back, it's funny how the simplest things influenced me. A lot of it had to do with living a better life, because remember what I had come from. Not having money or a home that had a man and a wife who showed much, if any, love toward one another. Plus, I grew up in that home as an only child, and I've mentioned that at times I felt out of place in Bessemer and never quite felt like I fit in. I felt lonely at times and I hate feeling lonely.

So up to this point, when I lacked something and desperately wanted it, I looked at how others had achieved it. I joined the military because my cousins had done so and they had new cars, clothes, and were out of Bessemer.

And so when I saw how great of a family JR and Rebekah were with their young baby, I wanted that too. Plus, I had just gotten orders to the Philippines and I really didn't want to go to a third-world country by myself. So I figured, *If he can do it and make it work, why not me?*

Here's a lesson. God made each of us unique. What works for him may not necessarily work for you. Also, most of the time, you only see what people want you to see and most of the time then, it isn't the bad shit. That's why they say everything that glitters isn't always gold.

However, I was eighteen years old. I was from the hood and hadn't ever really had much shit in my life. So if the military was going to pay me more money to have a wife, that was quite intriguing and might be worth it. Even with that said, while Tamara and I had gotten closer, it wasn't like we had talked about marriage that much before. Sure, we had been together for over a year, but before JR, I hadn't thought seriously about getting married. In fact, I wasn't even that serious when I asked her.

I had just gotten orders to go to the Philippines, and I was mildly depressed. Even though most of my job description had overseas assignments, I wanted desperately to stay stateside. So with orders and a packet talking about how great the Philippines was, I called up Tamara on the pay phone in the common area. The conversation went something like this. "Hey, T. I just got my orders. They sending me to the Philippines."

She said something like, "The Philippines?"

I said, "Yup. So you gonna marry me before I go?"

Now, this is something that's not going to make her feel that great, and I wouldn't blame her. Just remember, I was eighteen. I really had no proper guidance on a lot of things, so I was living life on the fly. Some *I'll figure it out as it comes to me* type of shit. So when I asked her that question, I was half joking. Remember, we hadn't seriously talked about marriage before and hell, I was eighteen years old. *I blame JR for this shit.*

Well, after our discussion, her reply was, "I don't know. I need to ask my daddy."

Let's talk about her daddy, or the man she referred to as her daddy. His name was Saxton Davis, but he went by ST. *Maybe the T was for his middle name. I don't know. It's Alabama. Shit is done differently down there.* Anyway, even though it wasn't her biological father, he was an ex-boyfriend of Tamara's mom and he helped raise her. Regardless, this dude didn't care for me that much, and he sort of let that be known every time I was around.

Anytime I would come over and he'd be around, he'd say, "Why you always around here, boy? Don't you have a home?" I heard that a lot. Maybe he had a sixth sense that detected my junior player bullshit and he didn't want me around the girl he regarded as his own child. Looking back, I don't blame him. I'd do the same for my kids. Well, I just knew he, of all people, would put a kibosh on any wedding plans, clearing me of my temporary insanity. So honestly, after I half jokingly asked her to marry me, I didn't think of it much after that. That is until she called me back two weeks later and said "yes." *Shit!*

What was I supposed to do now? Why in the hell had her dad approved of this? What got into him? Well, I'm not going to say, "Girl, I was just playing; I ain't ready to take on the responsibility of a wife." Nope. The ego actually kicked in even more. I thought about JR and how he was doing it. Plus, once again, there was a small part of me which did not want to take this overseas journey alone. *I know. I know. Selfish as shit. That was all me. Like a lot of eighteen-year-olds, that was my dumb mindset.* So let's do it. And less than two weeks later, Tamara's mom had booked the Botanical Gardens and arranged just about everything for our wedding, which would take place about a month and half later.

I had been in the military for about eight months at that point and had grown up quickly in that short amount of time. I didn't say matured—but grown up. There's a difference. I was on my own. I took on a lot of responsibilities and I would tell my mom and dad how much I appreciated them. However, I guess I also thought I was grown because I didn't ask them or my brother Preston if they approved of me getting married so young. I just told them I was, whether they liked it or not. They didn't resist much. Asked if I was sure but didn't fight back. I guess they thought, *Let's just pray that this fool doesn't fall into a huge hole, but if he does, we'll still have his back.*

I still don't know how a "wedding" got pulled together that quickly. Justice of the peace, yes, but not a full-scale wedding with out-of-town guests and everything. It was happening though. People were coming into town, including Tamara's aunt, who was married to this guy named Michael Hill, who happened to be a news reporter and a reason why I had dreams of doing the same thing. My grandmother flew down from New York, and I got my groomsmen together. My boys Vincent, Durand, this guy we called "Sleepy," and my best man, Richard. My stepdad. I still don't know why.

Bice was going through some shit at the time but was there, and my brother couldn't make it due to work. The cake was ordered, and everything seemed to be going smoothly until a week before the wedding.

I had just left Tamara's mother's house and as I was pulling up to my parents' house, I saw a man standing on the porch with my dad. As I was getting out of the car, I heard a very familiar, country voice raining down on me, coming from the man with my dad.

"Is dat Miiii-kah?" It was Tamara's dad, ST.

I said, "Hey, Mr. Davis, yes it is." Now, until this point, I had been home on leave for about three weeks and for some reason, had never even seen him until now. And come to think of it, Tamara never actually brought up his name since saying "yes." The next thing I heard shouldn't have surprised me, considering our history, but at this moment, it did.

"Let me tell you something, boy. You ain't marrying my dah-ta. She is going down there to that University of Alabama at Tuscaloosa, so you ain't marrying her."

So here we were, a week before the wedding. (*A wedding you approved of, by the way, because she told me she asked you and you said "yes," and now you have a change of heart? What the fuck, man?*) I wanted to go off on this dude, but I was still respectful, and I told him, "She said you said it was cool."

His response: "She ain't ask me shit!"

But she told me she had, and now he was saying that wasn't the case. Now he was on my parents' porch going off. I went to get Tamara on the phone to find out what was up.

"Tamara, your dad is over here saying we ain't getting married and says *you* never asked him, like you said you did." Pause. "Hello?" Next voice I heard was Tamara's mom Sandra (San for short), who was going off harder than ST ever could.

"Why is that man over there? He ain't her father in the first place. So he ain't got shit to do with her getting married." Now, this was directed toward him, but I felt the impact. San can be a sweet lady, but when she feels crossed, there's another side that comes out of both her and her sister, Kee, that would make the most evil of men feel a bit threatened. So when ST heard that wrath, he shut it down, and he left.

Now I know what you're thinking: "Bro, she lied about asking her dad, so why did you go through with it?" Ego, pride, and not wanting to disappoint anyone. Early in my life, those were a few of the things that stunted my growth as a person. Especially the disappointment part. I've endured a lot of stuff just because I didn't want to hurt or disappoint someone else, even if it meant I was hurting. I'm not blaming anyone else, it's just what I did. So even though my senses were saying *Don't do it*, I didn't want to hurt or disappoint Tamara or all the people who came down and/ or worked hard to put it all together. So a week later, it was wedding day.

Chapter 5

COMPRESSION

MAY 27TH, 1989, despite Tamara forgetting to bring the marriage license to the ceremony, which delayed the wedding by an hour, we got married. It was a nice ceremony, and thanks to Tamara's uncle and aunt, we even went to Disney World for our honeymoon. Our marriage, however, was no ride in the park.

When we got married, the initial plan was to have Tamara start school at the University of Alabama while I did my tour in the Philippines. I know what I said about being alone, but honestly—and frankly stupidly—I was just happy I was going to be receiving more money for being married. I knew this, and something tells me so did San.

Now what I'm about to say is not to try and disparage this woman. I'm positive she was looking out for Tamara's well-being. However, I also got the feeling that she saw a way to take some of the burden of a few of those student loans off of Tamara and herself.

The reason for this is her reaction at a cookout my parents threw for me and Tamara when we got back from our honeymoon. Once again, the initial plan was for Tamara to stay stateside while I went to the Philippines, but family members, including both our grandmothers, her aunt and uncle, and my mom kept telling us that would be a bad idea for newlyweds to be separated so soon. After a while, I started feeling the same way. Maybe it was the "Mike doesn't want to be lonely" gene popping out, but eventually Tamara saw it the same way, and relented. She'd come with me. Now we had to tell San.

To say she wasn't too pleased is a huge understatement. When Tamara broke the news to her, all I heard was, "That wasn't the plan. That wasn't the plan. Had I known this, I would've never let you get married." I didn't know how to take it at the time. A part of me was like, "Well, she's just hurt because her baby is leaving her." Another part was like, "Did she just think I was going to get married and not be with my *wife?*" It took several people to talk her off the ledge, but she finally came around a few months later.

I actually left for the Philippines by myself. Tamara needed a visa and it would take months before she could get one. When I arrived, it was the first time I had an *Oh shit, what am I in for?* moment. Even though I had been sort of fending for myself since I was seventeen, this was the first time I was totally independent. Even in basic training and tech school, there was some structure. When I got to the Philippines, I just had a job that I needed to be to on time. The rest was up to me.

Luckily, after I got past the initial time difference, I had several people who looked out for me. A few guys I hung with included these dudes named Damien, Mandel, James, and Brad. All good dudes with unique, outgoing personalities. Especially Brad. We called him B-Train. A tall, dark brother with a great spirit and funny soul that loved to dance, drink, party, and crack jokes.

There was also a guy who later was like a much older big brother. His name was Michael Burley. Burley was one of the funniest guys I had ever run into. He was different because he carried himself a lot more distinguished than a lot of the others. Part of that was because he was older and married. Burley was also the most militant brother I had ever encountered, and these days, he's a part of the Nation of Islam.

We all worked at the 6922. Double Deuce. *Oh, I forgot to mention: I worked in intel in the Air Force. I know! I still don't know how I got a top secret clearance with some of the shit in my and my family's background, but something slipped through the cracks.* My first day on the job, as I was coming through security, I heard one of the security police ask the guy checking my badge, "Ask him where he's from."

I heard him, but the guy asked me anyway, and my reply was, "I'm from Birmingham." Now, this is common for people from Bessemer to say when speaking to someone outside of Alabama because it's the nearest major city.

However, the voice boomed back, "He ain't from no damn Birmingham, he's from Bessemer!" I'm thinking, *Who in the hell is this and how in the hell does he know me?* As I was thinking this, out stepped this tall dude in a beret and security uniform. It was Anthony West, a guy from Bessemer, who was about five years older than me. I had gone to school with his sisters at Jess Lanier. Yes, halfway around the world stood two dudes from Bessemer. I didn't even know he was over here, but he and his wife Angela, who

I also went to school with, were my big brother and sister the entire time I was there, and a big reason why I survived.

However, the one guy who I will be eternally grateful to is this guy named Torin Ellis. What's crazy is, after I arrived, Torin was only in the Philippines for about two more months, but he immediately became my blood. This cat was from Iowa *(I didn't even know they had black people in Iowa then)* and was only a few years older, but without Torin, I don't think I would've made it through my first few months over there at all. This dude was and still is to this day super cool. He carried himself with grace, but was *not* to be fucked with. I'll just leave it at that.

Being in the Philippines was a challenge. Not because I was nineteen now and I had a job in a third-world country. That's not it. So how can I put this? Let's just say that if you're a guy (and you don't even have to be a good-looking guy) in the Philippines, there's *never* an excuse for you to go long without having sex. Here's my problem. I was nineteen. I was around a bunch of single guys, but I was now a newly married man, but my wife still hadn't gotten her visa to come and join me, and a brother was getting quite horny.

No, I didn't. At least, not for a while. I was approached by several women—locals and military women—but I would always reply, "I'm flattered, but I'm happily married." *Damn, if I would've just been able to keep that line and meant it on repeat, I'd have more of my money and less divorces right now.* However, I digress. I played it cool the entire time Tamara was working through her visa issues while back home in Alabama. I even turned down this one girl and said, "But hey, I'd love to introduce you to my wife when she comes over." I did, and they're still good friends to this day, thirty years later.

It's interesting remembering those days and my first marriage. I know what I said about the proposal. Her dad tripping and her mom opposing Tamara coming over. However, we were in it. Tamara was committed and I owe her a lot for making a huge sacrifice, delaying her education, to be with her husband. She deserves a lot of credit for overcoming our beginning and becoming a successful doctoral nurse practitioner. I'm proud of her because Lord knows my dumbass ways could've destroyed her.

> *Let me warn you now, I'm about to get into some seedy shit about my life, and although I'm sharing this, I'm not particularly proud of many of these moments. Once again, I'm sharing it because it's shaped who I am today. Even the terrible parts. I had to grow and learn on the fly, and while I'm still far from perfect, I think I've come a long way. Not that I deserve credit for that, but maybe someone else can see a little of them in what I've gone through and maybe this can give them hope that if I can change, so can they, and more importantly, will WANT to change.*

I was not a good husband to Tamara. I wasn't terrible, but I definitely wasn't good. Obviously we were both young and living in a third-world country, pretty much alone, so a lot of things were just hard or nearly impossible to figure out for two teenagers. However, when she finally got to the Philippines, after dealing with her visa issues for four months, life was good. At least in the beginning. I had my buddy with me, and it didn't take long for her to get acclimated with her new environment. We had fun together. The only thing funny about a honeymoon period, though, is when it's over, that shit is *over*. Ours lasted for a few months after she arrived.

One thing I want to do in this book is try not to lay too much of the blame on anyone else. I'm not going to say everything was all my fault, but I'm going to try and show you my side of the responsibility. So the issues that Tamara and I had in the beginning may have had a lot to do with the fact that she had deferred her college education to join me. When she got there, there really weren't any programs or college courses she could even take. You have to understand, she couldn't take "online" courses because this was before there even was an "online." She was away from her family and friends, and calling them cost so much then that it was rare she could even talk to them if she missed them. I know it was her choice to come, but it was my and others' influence that pushed her in that direction.

The first time I remember us having an issue that made me go "Oh shit" was actually playing a board game. Tamara is ultra-competitive. She hates to lose. Especially if it's a game involving intelligence. We would play Scrabble and she'd *always* win and she'd talk shit, but there was this one night I was actually winning. Of course I *had* to talk shit, and it didn't go over well. Before the game was over, she got so pissed that she swiped the game off the table. Shit went everywhere and she just stormed off.

Here's what I've learned about my life that I had to change. When someone shows me a different side that I don't like, I put up a huge barrier and I'm on guard. I know a lot of people are like that, but I had to realize that people aren't perfect, and I've always just wanted peace and perfection in my relationships. For me, it was also an excuse or at least a card to play later to justify my actions.

So Tamara's moment is one that just about anyone could have, but it was a different side I had never really seen in her. It made me question how much I really knew her, and doubt crept into my head. The devil is known to make a person do some evil shit due to doubt. It just started an avalanche. I started calling her "spoiled" and "little girl." She couldn't stand being called that, but once I knew it bothered her, I had her triggers and I pushed them often. I was building my case to find a way out. Then the night happened that started my downward spiral as a married man.

As I told you earlier, I was faithful to Tamara before she got there. Turning down offers left and right, but temptation is a bitch, man. The combination of that and any issues you're having with your girl can be disastrous. So when I went to this off-base club called The Green Toad one night with a few of my friends, I had my first taste of marital infidelity that honestly started my path toward a certain addiction.

It started off innocent enough. I was having a few drinks and talking with the fellas. Then I noticed one of my friends (I'm not going to say his name) talking to one of the "waitresses" and handing her pesos. Let's just say she was taking his order but not for stuff that's found on the menu.

Yes, The Green Toad was one of those infamous off-base Philippino spots. I was a little buzzed at that point, and pretty soon there were three women at our table surrounding me and my friends. They were talking and flirting, and the next thing I knew, they'd disappeared. However, they weren't gone. They had gone under the table. I felt something moving between my legs going toward my crotch. Now let me stop to explain something. My friend had paid for a game they call "smiles." The object of the game was to have guys drinking and shooting the shit while these women would go under the table and well, I don't think I need to tell you what they were doing. The first guy to "smile" was the loser and had to buy the drinks. I lost. I had no idea what the game was, or that I was even playing, so when this woman went for my crotch, I actually looked under the table to see what the hell was happening. Disqualified.

Here's what was going through my mind: *This is wrong, Mike. You're married. Get up and just leave before something happens.* That was followed up by, *Fuck that. She's here. You're here, and ain't nobody gonna know.* As I mentioned, I had cheated on girlfriends a lot, but now I was *married.* This was wrong on all levels, but I couldn't or wouldn't resist. Next thing I knew, she had my pants unzipped and it was out. And even though the temptation was overwhelming, the mind was still saying it was wrong, and it was not allowing it to cooperate, if you know what I mean.

So she went, "The snake is asleep. I need to wake it up." So right there under the table, this "snake charmer" works her magic. Next thing I know, we're in this back room, and she said, "Even though your friend only paid for oral, I really want you inside me."

At first I said "no," but she kept asking me as she gave me fellatio, and suddenly, I was wearing a condom and she was on top of me. For about thirty seconds. Not even a second after I released my ecstasy, guilt jumped all into me. I was like, *What in the hell have I done?* I pushed her off me, pulled up my pants, and ran out into the bar. My friends weren't there because they were with their own private snake charmers. I sprinted out of that bar like I had stolen something and I did not stop running full speed until I got to my house, which had to have been a good three or four miles away.

When I arrived in the house, Tamara was asleep, oblivious to what had just happened. I was so embarrassed. I was so ashamed, and my conscience was kicking my ass. I rushed inside and I dared not go toward Tamara. I went straight to the bathroom and took the hottest shower of my life. I wanted to burn the stench of this woman and my skin off. I got out and, still not feeling clean enough, I jumped in bed next to my bride. I just cuddled her and told her how much I loved her. She was pretty much in a coma, but I didn't care. I just never wanted to leave her side again. Once again, I had cheated on girlfriends before, but not on my wife. This was a sin. This was the ultimate betrayal. How could I have done something so reckless and dumb? I promised myself and God that I would *never* do anything like that again. Unfortunately for many of us, we lie to ourselves and God very often. I was addicted.

Working in the Philippines and the 6922 was a blur. Not much excitement that I recall. We had a lot of fun hanging out at the dorms and off base. Ask someone who's ever been based at Clark Air Base about the Nipa Hut and the banana lady. She had skills that I've never seen before nor do I think I'll ever see again. I was a pretty good football player for our team on base, and we ended up winning a championship my first season, but the majority of my memories in the Philippines were counting down the days until I could leave the Philippines.

I felt stuck there at times, and then there was this one night I felt stuck and helpless. We didn't have a phone in our home, so if I wanted to call back stateside, I had to go to the dorms. One night, Tamara and I were in the dorms, and I called back home and my mother sounded shook. She informed me that Richard was in jail. He had killed someone. He was at this lady's house. For what? I don't know and really won't speculate, but your judgment may be right. From accounts, he was chilling in her crib when the lady's boyfriend showed up. There was an argument. The guy went after my dad, who, as usual, was carrying a weapon. According to my dad, he feared the guy was threatening his life, so he pulled out his gun and shot him.

My mom said police raided her house and found numerous guns and left the house wrecked. She was shook. Her husband was in jail and I was halfway around the world. Once again, I was helpless. I felt much like I had felt as a kid when she was being physically abused and I was too young or too scared to stop it. I cried that night and prayed that God would protect her. Of course He did. Richard ended up getting off after it was ruled self-defense.

Tamara and I weren't doing too bad. After that initial transgression, I was pretty chill. Don't get me wrong, I was addicted and wanted to, but I just wouldn't put myself in certain situations that would allow me to act on it. We did have one incident that really shook us up. An earthquake.

The scariest thing about earthquakes is you don't know when they're going to happen. It's not like a hurricane, tornado, or something a weatherman can predict. It just comes and comes hard. Ask anyone who's gone through a big one; it's some of the most terrifying shit you'll ever experience in your life.

Tamara and I were at home one afternoon, and all a sudden, the earth just started rumbling. Literally. It was so intense that even though it happened nearly 30 years ago, it feels like yesterday. I had experienced a few mild tremors before Tamara had gotten there, but nothing like that. We were both in the living room and both off balance. It was like I was dizzy, but I noticed the fear on Tamara's face too. She screamed, "Michael, what's that?"

I answered, "It's an earthquake."

"What are we supposed to do?" Tamara asked.

I screamed, "Hit the floor and get under the table."

I can laugh at it now, but when I told Tamara to hit the floor, she *really* hit the floor. Hard! She just let her body fall, and for some reason tried to slide under the couch instead of the table. Meanwhile, my dumb ass was more concerned about material stuff, instead of my own safety. I was busy making sure the new 27-inch TV I had just bought didn't fall and break. Like I said, it was a horrifying experience. That earthquake in July of 1990 registered a magnitude 7.6 and was centered about eighty miles northeast of the base. More than two thousand were killed and a million were left homeless.

We were already in a third-world country. So imagine being in a third-world country devastated by an earthquake. We had the "luxury" of the base and US support, but we saw so many of the locals who didn't. Looking back, God has always put me in situations, good and bad, that I could learn from that would shape my life. Seeing the poverty there helped keep me humble. I'm not saying I haven't had a few "cocky moments" (more on this later) but it's given me an appreciation for what I have. It's a lesson that I still carry in my life.

My overall Philippine experience wasn't too enjoyable. Some of the locals were great. Socializing on and off base was great, and some friendships made there are still strong today. That was the good part, though. I just couldn't fully enjoy it. I was homesick. I was trying to figure out a new marriage. There was also a sense of fear because a lot of Americans were targets of terrorists called the NPA, and the base had many restrictions. And now, after this earthquake, there was sadness. I just wanted to leave. I definitely wanted my wife off that island. Here's my truth, though. Mainly for her safety, but partly because I wanted to act like I was single again.

I was supposed to do a three-year tour at Clark AFB, but it turned out to only be a little over a year and a half. Because of the earthquake and downsizing, many of us got to end our tour early, so I was off to Hawaii.

I got stationed at Wheeler AFB but worked at a place called Field Station Kunia, or the Tunnel. They called it the Tunnel because the station was literally a tunnel built into the side of a mountain. The shift work was a bitch, but we had fun. I was working with these guys named Myron and Kui Pai, who was a Hawaiian native who had joined the military. We'd always crack jokes, many times just repeating what we had heard on The Def Comedy Jam with Martin Lawrence hosting that had just come out.

Now this was back in 1991, and we said *everything* the comedians said. Little did we know it wouldn't be a laughing matter for long. There was this woman named Laura on our shift, a pretty white woman that our supervisor, Patrick, was "fond" of. Patrick was married (and a prick, by the way), but that's not the point. One day, because Laura didn't get her way with something, she went and told Patrick about our comedy routines on the ops floor. I had never heard of "sexual harassment" until that day. Of course, it became a household term later that year with the Anita Hill/Clarence Thomas situation, but here, months before that, we were being accused of it and trying to answer those accusations.

"What? She said what?"

"Well, yes, we used those terms, but we were just repeating what Joe Blow comedian was saying."

"Doesn't matter?"

"It's wrong?"

"We didn't know that."

We got written up and had to apologize to this woman. Looking back, yes, we were wrong, but this was the same person who had a mouth like a sailor and told sexual jokes of her own. However, Ms. Entitlement didn't get her way, and we all know that one white, entitled, pretty woman who the supervisor wants to smash will win out over three minority dudes most days.

Tamara and I moved to this small, overpriced two-bedroom apartment in Waipahu, furnished with the handmade furniture we'd bought in the Philippines before we left. Life was cool. We were getting along for the most part and hung out a lot with Myron and his wife, Tracy. They were both from Indianapolis, and when I tell you that damn Myron was a fool, it's an understatement. Always cracking jokes, and his wife Tracy seemed to be the butt of a lot of them. I'm talking about salacious jokes about how she gave fellatio and what she would say during sex. Look, I ain't gonna lie, I laughed, because yes, I was just as immature.

One thing I learned early in my marriage to Tamara, though, is she didn't always take jokes well. And if we were drinking (she blamed me for getting her started), sometimes things would go sideways.

One night, Myron, Tracy, and another couple whose names escape me were all hanging at our apartment, playing games and having drinks. I don't really recall what started it, but things escalated quickly. I, more than likely, did or said something that irritated Tamara, and she was heated. I could've defused the matter, but unfortunately, back then, if there was drama, I was going to turn up the heat. At least the rhetoric. If I recall, this particular night, I kept calling Tamara "little girl," which she couldn't stand. We were all in the living room, and suddenly she stood up in my face. I might have laughed and dismissed her, but suddenly she actually charged me. She backed me up so quickly and so aggressively that before I knew it, my back was literally in our china cabinet. I heard all kinds of glass breaking. I really thought I was all cut up. So as soon as I heard it, I reacted. I grabbed Tamara and took her to the floor. I was holding her down and all of a sudden I heard Tracy yell, "Mike, don't hit her. Don't hit her." Everything in my being today maintains I wasn't going to hit her, but I probably wanted to. I can't lie about that. I was mad and at that moment scared, and my actions were out of instinct. However, after seeing my mom endure beatings from a man, how could I possibly ever violently put my hands on a woman?

I'm not going to sit up here and write a book called "Open Mike" and not tell you my truths. Therefore, I'm not going to lie and say that we've never gotten close to throwing blows. Once again, I could never close my fist and hit a woman. Never. However, there were times when it got physical. We'd argue. She'd point her finger in my face or vice versa. The other would slap that finger away and there would be some mild pushing. I'm not trying to sugarcoat it. Even if it's just a little pushing or shoving, it's still wrong, and I'm sorry for ever participating in it.

Once again, the only advice my biological father gave me that really made sense that I try to apply to my life today was: if a woman gets in your face and wants to start something physical, take a walk. Now that I have two daughters, all I know is that when they have guys in their lives and things get heated, those guys better walk themselves if they want to be able to later.

I may act all hard, but those who really know me know I can be a very emotional person. Maybe I wouldn't allow my emotions to go full bore when it came to falling in love (because, like I said, I was too afraid to be hurt). However, there have been times when I've cried in front of a woman. Sometimes I'd cry in a movie, if it's really good, but I could always play that off in front of a girl.

The first time I couldn't play it off in front of Tamara happened on November 8, 1991. It's not the date of a death in the family, but the day Magic Johnson announced he had to retire due to HIV. Magic was and still is my favorite basketball player of all time. I just loved everything about him, and one of my biggest thrills in life was later getting to interview him, eventually working with him, and the two of us becoming pretty cool. So the day of that announcement, I was overwhelmed. Back then, if you said HIV, it was a death sentence. *My favorite player is about to die!* Of course, he's still going strong to this day, but that was the assessment back then. I cried like a baby. I'm talking snot and everything. Tamara didn't make fun of me or make me feel lesser of a man. She held me and let me know it was all going to be all right. I appreciate her for doing that, but obviously not enough.

Chapter 6

HOOK

AS MEN, WE sometimes view life very differently after we become fathers, specifically to daughters. Many of us would never want a man to treat our daughters the way we've treated women in our past. You can't see me, but I've got both hands raised right now. This is why I've constantly apologized to many women over the years. Especially to Tamara. She went through it with me. About two years into our marriage, she still had no clue about my infidelity in that Philippine bar, or women I was talking to in an inappropriate manner. She may have suspected it but had no proof—at least she never brought anything to me at this point. Someone else did, though.

Once again, I was flirting and being inappropriate verbally, but after that initial transgression in the Philippines, I hadn't committed adultery. A lot of that had to do with opportunity. That changed with this one girl in Hawaii. Well, at least the opportunity to try did.

I don't remember much about her except she was pretty, she was in the military, she had a baby, she knew I was married, and oh yeah, she was dating this dude in the Navy that I'd run into and play ball against every now and then. That didn't stop her from finally inviting me over to her crib after weeks of me talking some hardcore game.

I remember being over there and we were watching TV on her mattress, which was literally on the floor. No headboard or railings. We were talking, and honestly, I was a little nervous but playing it cool. We started kissing, and next thing I knew, clothes were being removed. At this point, I was into it. The nerves were gone and I was *ready*. However, as I was about to go in (literally), she stopped me and said, "Un-un, I ain't yo wife. You better go put a condom on."

Fellas may back me up on this. When your head on your shoulders gets messed up, it can have an effect on the smaller head below. That's what happened to me. As soon as she said, "yo wife," an image of Tamara popped into my head and it seemed to take the air out of me. Well, in this case, the blood. Yeah, I was deflated and in the worst kind of sexual way. I tried to play it off. I went to her bathroom where she said she had some condoms, but that just gave me more time to think and I was—or should I say *my friend*—was done for the night. Yup, the snake was sleeping again and this time, there would be no snake charmer to wake him up.

I tried to wait it out, but after a few minutes, the moment was gone for her, and she just said, "Well, I gotta get up in the morning; you should leave." I was embarrassed, but I think a part of me was relieved. Of course, when I got in my car to drive home, I was all of a sudden so stiff I could've driven the car with no hands the rest of the way.

I never saw that woman again, but it didn't necessarily mean I was done with her. Remember when I said Tamara never brought drama to me to this point, but someone else did? Well, that drama came directly to my front door and it was because of her. Well, me technically, but still "because" of her.

My mother in-law, San, was in Hawaii visiting for a few weeks. (Yeah, it's about to go down in front of HER.) It was late at night. I don't know the exact time but late enough that we were sleeping. There was a knock on the door and San went to answer it. I was still asleep, but I heard her say, "Michael, it's for you." I came to the door, and remember when I said that woman I couldn't have sex with had a guy she dated in the Navy? You guessed it. It was him. He and I didn't have this sort of relationship, so why was he here? Well, apparently she'd wanted to make him jealous and told him I was either trying to holler or had hollered, and so he felt disrespected. He had every right to feel that way. We weren't that cool, but I knew him and knew they were dating, so I had violated man code. Well, mainly I'd violated the sanctity of my marriage, but he didn't give a damn about that; he came to deal with part of my disrespect.

San could tell something wasn't right, so she stayed by the door until I got there. When I arrived at the door, I saw him and said, "What's up, bruh?" because his reasoning for being there hadn't dawned on me at this point.

"You know what's up," he replied. "I know you been messing with [her name]. Come and deal with it."

Shit. *Mike, you really fucked up now. Your dirt has tracked you to your home, and you're going to be exposed in front of your mother-in-law and wife.*

A few emotions were going through my head. I was pissed. I wanted to beat his ass because he was doing this shit in front of my family. I was nervous. I'd just been busted—or at least had raised suspicions about my behavior in front of my wife and mother-in-law. I was scared. I didn't know what he had, what he was capable of doing, and I could see that he had back-up in the form of this big-ass dude that I also knew. So I did what any man would do in that situation. I lied. "Dude, I don't know what the hell she told you, but I ain't messing with your girl." Imagine that being said in a mad, nervous, scared kind of way. That was how I said it.

I give San credit. She stepped up. One thing about her is, when she goes off, she *goes off,* and off she went. "Don't bring that shit here. Y'all better leave." Whatever she said, she said in such a way that you knew she meant business, and instead of rushing inside the house to drag me out, they backed up as we closed the door. Now they were still outside in the parking lot, screaming for me to be a man and not let my momma protect me. So of course, I went into shit-talking mode. Even though I was still scared as hell, you ain't going to sit up here and snatch my pride. So I had to be big and bad and talk bigger and badder. I went into the kitchen and got a knife and said, "I need to take care of this." Once again, thank goodness for San. I think she knew I *really* didn't want to go out there and that I was just trying to save face or at least play off my guilt. So she stopped me. "You ain't gotta prove nothing. Don't go out there." She eventually told them that if they didn't leave, she was going to call the cops. They left soon after.

This all went down just a few weeks before I left Hawaii. Those guys sent word that they would eventually catch me in the street or at the gym, so I stayed pretty low key and I never saw them again. However, the impact would last a long time and maybe even still to this day for Tamara and her mom, who by the way, didn't trip that much about it right after. Now you would think that incident was my wake-up call. *Straighten up and act right, Mike Hill.* No, of course not. My foolishness was *just getting started.*

It was 1992, and I had gotten orders to work at Fort Meade in Maryland inside the National Security Agency. I still don't know how in the hell I got a top secret clearance from the government with my family's background.

Before going to get settled in Maryland, I took thirty days of leave for the summer in Alabama. Being away for a while and then coming back helped me to see Bessemer a little differently. It was even worse than I had remembered it. I swear, I'm not trying to completely shit on my home, but it could be downright depressing to be there at times. It was and still today is a very dangerous place to live. So much so that my dad felt I needed to protect myself. So while I was home on leave, he gave me a gun to carry.

Looking back on that, I can only imagine what would've happened had I been caught with it. It was not registered in any way, and who knows who had used it in the past and for what. I could've caught a case just by having it. At the very least, I could've found myself in hot shit with the military.

Also, I can only imagine what would've happened on one particular night if I had been carrying it. The night I was in a drive-by. *Yup, that happened.*

Growing up, I lived right across the street from these kids Patrick and Dregus, who lived with their grandmother and grandfather. They were several years younger, but I always treated them like little brothers and was always over to their house. They were good kids, but by the time I had gone off to the military and come back, they had taken a wrong turn.

So one night, when I was home on leave, I was across the street talking to them on the front porch of Dregus' sister's place, which was right next door to where they grew up. There were several guys there, and I was telling them how life could be so much better, and whatever they were into didn't have to be the road they had to travel down. They were present, but you could tell they weren't really listening. Suddenly, Dregus noticed a car down the street and one guy said, "Oh, they trying to start some shit." Next thing I knew, that car took off, screeching down the street in our direction. Everyone on that porch took off. We knew what was up, even though I had only seen something like this in a movie. Several people ran in the house, but I ran on the side of the house and toward the back. I heard a few pops, but I didn't look back. Suddenly, as I was getting to the alley behind me, I saw a guy approaching me, and he had a gun. My life flashed in front of me and there was immediate panic. *I'm about to die.* At least, I thought so. The kid with the gun said, "Who are you?" And I said, "I ain't nobody, man. I just live across the street," and he ran past me.

Come to find out, those guys were looking for one guy on that porch, but because he was around us, all of our lives were in danger. That's why it's important to hang around the right people because you never know the type of shit the wrong people will bring around you.

Now, my boy Vincent had left the state and was doing well for himself. I couldn't or wouldn't hang with Durand much because he was hanging with the wrong crowds. Doing and selling drugs and getting into trouble. But even though Bice had gotten into the drug game, I continued hanging with him. He was my dude and he had always looked out for me, so I felt like now it was time for me to return the favor. I wish I could've been there when he needed me the most though. *More on all of this later.*

Also at this time, Bice had pretty much moved in with my dad because my mom had moved out. It wasn't official yet, but it was only a matter of time before it became permanent. She had gone to New York to take care of my grandmother, who was sick. She had been there for a few months and even got a temporary transfer for her job at Social Security, and after a while, you just knew she wasn't coming back.

She may have done it under the cloak of nursing my grandmother back to health, but she did it. Honestly, no one in their right mind could blame her. I mean, she had left a few times before but always came back. Partly because of me. Later in life, I felt guilty because I sincerely felt like, and still to this day, feel like my mom endured the abuse and brutality of that relationship because she wanted me to finish school there. As bad as life was in Bessemer for her, it might have been worse for me somewhere else. Even back in New York. So for years she toughed it out, but now she had finally escaped.

As I've mentioned, I always had a fear/respect kind of relationship with my stepdad, but now, here I was, a grown man. All of a sudden, it was like I was more the father and he was the son when we had conversations.

He had always been a guy with this super tough exterior. And even though he was this badass with a sketchy past, you could tell he had a good heart. He kidded a lot. He loved to laugh, and kids loved him. I also knew without a doubt this man loved me. And I ain't even going to lie, I loved him too. I just didn't love some of his ways, and he knew it.

I was straight up with him. When my mom left, and we both knew she wasn't coming back, we had a sincere talk. He tried to blame her for leaving because he felt she had deceived him by using her mom. I told him it didn't matter how she did it. He should take responsibility for why she HAD to do it. He hadn't been a good husband to a good woman. Maybe those words started to really sink in, because suddenly it hit him. All of a sudden, for the first time since he'd been in my life, I was watching this man actually cry. Seemingly begging for one more chance to get it right with my mom.

Now, perhaps the right thing for a son to do when his dad is hurting is comfort him. Put his arm around him and tell him it will be all right. *Nope*. Not me. Even though I can be a compassionate person, I told him, "Don't cry now. Come on man, you got to pull it together."

Looking back, that obviously was dumb as hell for me to say to a person who was hurting. However, I know I did it back then because I felt that's how he would have wanted me to handle it. Be a man! It's an issue we have in society. Especially among black men. Afraid to show those emotions through tears, especially around another man, because we're too afraid of being labeled soft by society. It's wrong, and it's got to stop. However, in this instance it worked, because he straightened up right away. We continued to talk, though, and even though he probably still had a heavy heart, he was about to lay some heavier shit on me that instantly made my heart race.

Obviously, I knew certain things about him already: he was a dude with a dangerous reputation. Remember, this is the guy they called "Crazy Richard," and yes, he lived up to his reputation. He was physically abusive to my mom. I told you earlier about how he stabbed her and pretty much left her for dead. And you'll recall that he killed a man but got off because it was ruled self-defense. Well, apparently it wasn't the first person he'd killed, because during this particular conversation, he revealed to me that he'd carried out "hits" in the past.

For those of you not familiar with a "hit," it's when someone pays to have someone killed. Therefore, the term "hit man." Even though I had overheard him talking to friends about hits in the past, it was always about some guy who might have had a bounty put out on him. Something like, "I heard so-and-so got a price on his head" or "There's a contract on this dude." I had even heard a rumor about him (Richard) allegedly paying someone to take care of a former co-worker that had gotten a promotion over him. The guy, who actually used to be a close friend of Richard's, was shot (in the ass), but escaped death. Yup, I had heard all of these things before, but now he was telling me HE carried out hits himself?

I think I was in a bit of shock when he told me, and remember, this is right after he was emotional about my mom, so there was a wave of emotions. I don't even think I asked him why, who for, or even when. Then again, maybe I wasn't too shocked because it was "Crazy Richard" telling me this, and so I just brushed it off. Even if today that moment still feels like a dream, I know he told me this earth-shattering news. And even though I don't have actual proof, I have heard confirmation from a few who knew him, and I truly believe he wasn't lying. One thing about Richard: he was capable of just about anything, as you'll read about later in this book.

I was excited to be living in Maryland and working at NSA. I still love that area to this day, and it's where my exes and two kids reside. However, my time there catapulted my nonsense to a different level. I don't know if it was just being back stateside and having opportunities to get into stuff, but I found a way to do so.

Tamara and I moved into this city called Odenton and lived in some apartments right across from the base. We actually had some good times living there too. We would have our own karaoke night with friends, where you actually had to get into character. One night, I was Prince, and if that tape ever leaked, it would be a wrap for me. Come to think of it, if they had ways of recording people back in '92 like they do today, it *really* would've been a wrap for me during my Maryland days.

I was really feeling myself. I was getting a lot of attention from women, and I got buck wild. I'm not going to talk about all the inappropriate things I did while I was there because that alone would make this book larger than *War and Peace*. Because of my shenanigans, though, War and Peace is a way I could describe my marriage too. I was beginning a major war with my wife because I was out there trying to get a piece of ass.

I've said this many times while writing this already, and I'll say it plenty more before it's complete, but I was so damn dumb and reckless. I got so cocky that I had an "I don't give a fuck" attitude. I had an all-out affair with this girl who lived in the dorms and I was with her *all* the time. I spent more time with her than I did with Tamara, going to the movies and dinner.

When your male friends start looking at you like *What the fuck are you doing, dude?* because you're holding hands with your mistress as you're walking her back to her dorm room, you've probably gone a little too far. I had! I just didn't care.

To be clear, I'm not putting the blame on her at all. I was lying to her, making her believe that my marriage was on the rocks and it was pretty much over. I just needed time to get a divorce. I started to say it so much that maybe I even believed it myself. Problem is, I never told Tamara it was over. Once again, like a lot of people still are, I was doing some low-down, stupid shit.

That woman finally realized I wasn't going to follow through and tried to let it go. I tried to hold on. I even did stupid shit like invite her to my basketball game when I knew Tamara was going to be there too.

The last time I saw her scared the shit out of me, though. I hadn't seen her for a while and she had gotten out of the military. I was in a restaurant with Tamara and her family, and guess who came over as our server? My heart dropped. Tamara and her family had no clue, but of course, she knew. Let's just say that day, I wasn't that hungry anymore and I don't think I drank or ate *anything* she was going to be serving us.

I kid when I say that because I seriously doubt if she was vindictive. She was such a sweet person who wouldn't harm anyone and always felt terrible about what we were doing. That's why I need to apologize to her as well. I was in a dark place, and I manipulated so many. She was just one of those victims.

I enjoyed working inside NSA. The work was easy, and I pretty much had a Monday-Friday nine-to-five job there, which isn't always the case for someone in the military. However, I knew the military was just a means for me to pursue something else. For years, I'd wanted to be a newscaster. The question was how could I do that while being married and working full-time? Well, I had to figure it out.

It was discouraging as hell, and at times, I have to admit, still is. I met this prominent New York news director (who I won't name) who was nice and nasty. I mean, she was nice enough to hear my dreams, but she straight-up shit on them afterward. I was in the military, but I didn't have a college degree, and that's all she heard. She told me, "You don't have a degree, so I wouldn't even waste my time with you." I can understand someone feeling that way. A college degree is very important. I get that. So it wasn't what she said, just how she said it. It was dismissive and made me feel low. It wasn't like I was sitting in my momma's basement after I got my GED; I was serving our country. I was learning a lot while serving and growing up quickly. Her final words to me were, "Talk to me again when you've got that paper." I wanted to say, "I ain't asking you for a job. I appreciate the advice, but damn, your words of wisdom just aren't encouraging."

Maybe I was being sensitive, and maybe I'm being petty now that I make sure to speak every time I see her. Yup, 25 years later, 20 of those at a network or Top 10 market, and still don't have that degree. God is good.

Chapter 7

SIGN ON

I DID GET good advice from Tamara's uncle, Michael. He was a news reporter, who by this time was working in New York. He was always encouraging and telling me I could do it. He was honest about my speech too. Remember, I was from New York and Alabama, and you could hear those dialects clearly. Especially the Southern side of me. He said I needed to fix that, so I did. I basically retaught myself how to speak all over again, where my i-n-g's were clear and my words beginning with t-h didn't sound like they began with a d. Twenty-five years later, it's still a work in progress, but back then, I damn near needed subtitles when I talked.

I had talked about being on TV for years, but talk never does shit for you. Action moves things. So once I really focused to get that career started, I was determined to make it happen and let nothing stop me. I did my own research and took whatever classes the military offered. I made calls to the local TV stations asking if they needed assistants or interns.

One of the calls I made was to this Baltimore anchor named Stan Stovall. I left him a message, and to his credit, he called me back. I was so green, nervous, and honestly, I was fake. Not fake in the sense of not being truly who I am, but not sounding the way I truly sound. Black people sometimes put on what we call our "white phone voice" (WPV) and my WPV was in full effect with Stan. Here's the kicker. Stan is black himself, but he was a "clean-speaking" black, and I felt like I had to match his tone. He didn't have any positions to offer me, but he gave me some of his time and so I'll always appreciate him for that. It's one of the reasons why I always try to give my time to anyone who truly needs it today. You never know how that will impact someone's future.

However, the woman who was the first guardian angel of my career was Annette Stenhouse. Annette worked at WBAL Channel 11 in Baltimore as a producer. When I was making my calls inquiring about internships and such, I somehow got put in touch with her, and even though this woman had never talked to me in her life before this call, she treated me like I was her little brother. She was so warm, pleasant, patient, and informative, placing me on my initial path. Even though I would need to be getting college credit to get an internship at her station, she told me about this other station down the street that didn't require it: Fox 45.

I called Fox 45 and talked to this guy named Max Morgan in the sports department. Max was a big black guy, with a very clean-spoken country drawl, and he's another one of my career angels. He told me I needed to be getting some sort of credit to get an internship, but told me about this local broadcasting school I could enroll in that would meet the requirements. I enrolled, and my first internship had begun.

The first day I showed up, I was dressed like I'd just come from church with my Sunday best on. Hell, it was an internship. I thought I was supposed to be dressed super professional. Suited and booted, right? Not in a newsroom. Everyone got a good laugh out of the overdressed, uninformed rookie, and Max later told someone, "I think his ass thought he was going on air tonight." It was all in good fun, and it didn't take long for me to realize I was going to like it there and learn a lot.

The first show I worked on was the station's half-hour Sunday night show, "Sports Unlimited." Max introduced me to the producer, Alex, and I learned how to edit that night. Fox 45 was a non-union station, so I got to touch everything. In fact, they actually had me edit a highlight package for that night's show, and when I saw my name on the credits at the end, I was in heaven.

Once I started interning at Fox 45, my social life was pretty nonexistent. Hell, I didn't have time. Between working at NSA, going to broadcasting school at night, and the internship, I was swamped. However, I still found time for my debauchery and my ass stayed in hot water—like that time I lost my wedding ring because I misplaced it on one of the many occasions I slipped it off my finger to try to talk to a girl. Or that time I decided to be an amateur stripper.

Oh damn. Yeah, I have to admit it, that actually happened. The more I write this, the more I'm thinking Tamara could have just killed me and gotten off on a temporary insanity claim because I'm sure my behavior drove her absolutely bat shit.

I was on leave and went to Bessemer without her just to hang out with friends. Bice, a friend named John, Stan, and I went to see Martin Lawrence in concert at the Boutwell Auditorium. The concert was great, and we got extra saucy that night. After the concert, we ended up at a night spot in Birmingham called Tee's Place.

On this particular night, they were having an amateur stripping competition and were looking for contestants. Top prize was $250, and of course, any tips you got. One guy was overly eager. Like he had been waiting for this moment to sign up all month. Another guy walked out soon after, and then the DJ was asking for the third and final contestant. "Come on, fellas. Show those moves. Get that money."

Now at first, I wasn't even thinking about it. Yeah, $250 was a lot of money to me back then, but I hadn't been drinking "that" much. Also, I can't really dance, so I was kind of stiff. And by the way, need I remind you I was married. *Here's a lesson for you, though. Your ego is a powerful tool that, in the wrong mind, will easily destroy.* With the crowd having already formed a circle around the first two contestants, Bice and John playfully shoved me out to the middle with those two guys. I was only out there for three seconds before I ran back into the huddle of people, but I heard some ladies lose it. *I may have been slightly cute and a little sexy way back then, but I digress.* Bice and John tried to push me back out, but this time I was ready, and I was resisting. However, a lady standing next to us said, "Baby, get in it. If you don't win, I'll give you the $250 myself." In my head I was like, "Lady, I don't know why you have so much confidence in my non-dancing ass, but you got a DEAL," and I walked out as contestant #3. I was now in it. I don't know if it was to win it, but at least I knew I was gonna get paid.

The first guy went out. He was just acting stupid. At the end of his dance, he took his boot off and playfully acted like he was going to hit this girl with it. The second guy went and did his thing, and the girls seemed to like him. So now, even though I felt like the money was guaranteed, my ego and competitive spirit kicked in. I HAD to win.

The music came on. I did a few dance moves, keeping it simple for the most part. A few hip gyrations and pumps here and there. Let's just say the movie *Magic Mike* was NOT inspired by me or my moves, but I wasn't doing so bad. I heard the women screaming as I was taking off my clothes down to my special "jungle-inspired" boxer shorts. I was getting hella tips, but I needed to take it up a notch. Then I saw this one lady in the crowd who looked at me like a fat woman looking at some moist chocolate cake, and I knew I had my opportunity. I went over to her and started grinding on her a little. The crowd went crazy. And then, I absolutely took it to the next level. However, instead of going up, that next level was to actually go down. *Hell, y'all grown. You know what that means.* I wasn't actually doing it, but just the simulation of the act made the crowd explode. They weren't making it rain. It was a damn monsoon.

I knew I had won this contest ($250 plus close to $70 in tips), so I was happy...briefly! As I was picking up my tips, I happened to look up right into the eyes of this woman named Tanya. Tanya happened to be Tamara's best friend. Of course, I had no idea she was there. As you can imagine, she was unhappy to see me. I was about to really be exposed.

I expected Tanya to be on the phone with Tamara right away, so I was a little surprised when I got back home to Maryland and my shit wasn't on the street. I did give Tamara one of those stories where you sort of tell on yourself, but don't reveal the whole truth by telling her I won a "dance contest," but definitely not about the stripping. A few weeks later, I still hadn't received any flack, but that soon changed.

One day, I was hanging at the dorms and called home. Tamara answered and I asked what she was doing. She said, "I'm talking to Tanya." My heart dropped, but she said it so calmly that I was thinking, *Okay, maybe she didn't snitch on me.*

I told Tamara, "Oh, please tell her I said hello. I was just checking on you."

Tamara said, "Okay" and clicked back over to the other line.

Five minutes later, the phone rang, and guess who it was from and guess for who? Y'all smart. I got on the line and for the next two minutes or so I heard Tamara raw and uncut. It was so brutal that after a while, I was picking up just a few key words or phrases. "Embarrassing." "How could you be so stupid?" Curse word this. Curse word that. "I should've known it wasn't a dance contest, 'cause yo ass can't dance." I just had to take it because, once again, I deserved it.

Despite the heartaches I gave her, Tamara still believed in me when it came to my broadcasting aspirations. She was super supportive, and so were Michael and Kee, her uncle and aunt, who actually loaned me some money to pay for this broadcasting school I was attending. She was also very understanding about the long nights I was spending at the news station. *By the way, those long nights at the station were "legit" work nights. Not an excuse for my tomfoolery.* I understand if your mind would lean toward wrong-doing based on what I've already told you about my past.

Those long nights at Fox 45 paid off for me and many others. The sports department there has become a major factory for developing key talent in the broadcasting world. Too many to list here, but Kevin Frazier, Guy Rawlings, Brent Harris, Keith Russell, and Rob Carlin were some of the guys working as either interns or sports reporters when I was there. Every Sunday, after the thirty-minute show, this group, along with this guy named Nate, and Alex Parker would work on our resume reels. We even gave ourselves some corny nickname like "The After Hours Club."

The great thing about Fox 45 is that it was a non-union station, so we got to run all the equipment. A few would be on cameras. Someone would be loading and playing tapes. One would play director. Another would be the technical director, and of course, one got to sit at the anchor desk, using the scripts and tapes from a previous sportscast. We'd all rotate until everyone got one or two tries at the anchor desk.

It was fun, but some nights, we'd be in that station until two or three in the morning, and remember, I had to work at the NSA the next day. It's one of the reasons why I get upset when I see kids thinking a career should be handed to them. I always say you have to work to get work in this industry, and once you get the work, work harder.

A few months into my internship, I was doing some on-air sports updates for this radio show hosted by this guy named

Stan the Fan and a high school public access show that another intern named Jefferson Slade had produced. Thanks to that, the After Hours Club, and going out with Guy Rawlings in the field, I had enough material to put together my first resume reel, and it was bad. Not terrible, but far from good or even fair.

The sports director, Bruce Cunningham, was and is still to this day my sensei. From day one, this guy treated me like a son. That's why I call him "Poppa" Bruce. He was someone I had seen on television earlier in my life when he worked in Birmingham, and he has always had a good spirit about him. He pushed me when I needed to be pushed, but also knew when to just sit me down and give me good advice. He also saved my career way before it got started when he actually took me out of the station and drove me to his house when he knew I was about to beat the hell out of this one guy who worked in the sports department. He also was the first person to let me know it was okay to be MYSELF. In fact, it was like he demanded it.

Now, just to give you an idea of my so-called style at this time: I was white. At least, when I was on the anchor desk or practicing in the field reporting, I was using what a black person would say was my "white voice." It was what I thought I *should* sound like. It was proper, and there's nothing wrong with that, but it didn't sound like me. A guy named Weidong (pronounced We Dong Ho) changed that.

He isn't a household name. Not a major sports superstar or a celebrity, but I'll always remember his impact on me as a sportscaster. He was a player on the Chinese national basketball team. One night, during an After Hours Club session, we had to do a highlight of one of their games in the FIBA World Championships. I had already done one round that I thought was good or a "keeper," so I was just going to have fun the second time through. So during the highlight, Weidong made a spectacular play, and I read the highlight just like I was talking to one of my best friends in a sports bar. "Check out *my man* Weidong putting in work on these players." As soon as I said it, I heard the guys behind the camera cracking up, and afterwards, the guys in the control room couldn't stop talking about "my man Weidong." A few days later, I showed Bruce the tape, and he said directly, "You hear what you did there? That's you! That's the Mike everyone knows. That's the real you. Do that and you're on to something."

At that moment, it was like a light bulb had gone off. I wasn't going to try to be or sound like a sportscaster anymore. I was just going to be me. It's still the advice I give people coming up in the industry. Don't try to be a sports-caster. Just be yourself and the rest will come naturally.

Over the years, people tried to compare me to the legend-ary and dearly departed Stuart Scott because of his style. I can understand some of the comparisons, and it was an honor to just be in the same breath as him. However, I've never tried to sound like him or anyone else. Maybe Stu's style gave me more license to be me, but if there's anyone that deserves the credit or blame, however you want to look at it, for me sounding and acting the way I do on air, it's Bruce Cunningham and of course, *my man* Weidong.

My other memorable moment with a "Dong" as an intern happened during a charity basketball game. Muggsy Bogues, then a player for the Charlotte Hornets, was holding a game in Baltimore where he grew up. Fox 45 sent me out to get interviews in the locker room afterwards. I remember players like Anthony Mason, Larry Johnson, Reggie Williams, Alonzo Mourning, and Dikembe Mutumbo all being there.

The game was being held at the Baltimore Arena. It was much smaller than a normal NBA arena, and so the locker rooms were extra tight. Imagine, if you will, big basketball players being surrounded by a swarm of media members in what amounted to a closet. Extra tight and space is at a minimum. Anyway, we were interviewing Anthony Mason at the time, who was actually sitting down on a folding chair with his feet in ice water. Since it was super crowded and he was sitting down, in order for me to get a spot near him, I actually had to kneel right next to him to get the microphone close. We wrapped up the interview, and since it was so tight, I couldn't really stand, so I pivoted while I was on one knee. As I turned around, *whack!* I felt an object hit the side of my forehead, and in a horrified, nervous, and shocked voice, I went, "Ah damn!"

Now this is one of most embarrassing moments of my life, people, but it's OPEN MIKE, right? So I'm going to tell you what that blunt object was. You ready? It was the penis of a super tall basketball player. I'm not going to say who it was, but I guess you could say we went head to head. Even when I see him today, I refer to him as Snuffleupagus, Big Bird's imaginary big-nosed friend on Sesame Street. If you look at a picture of Snuffle, you'll get my reference. His reaction was, "Ohhhh, I'm so sorry." My reaction was, *I need to go and scrub my entire face. Not just the small corner of forehead that's been violated.*

In 1994, I was sending tapes out left and right looking for that first job in broadcasting. I wasn't having much luck, but I could still use my job search and NSA to do my dirt. *Here comes another "Mike's a creep" moment.*

So I met this girl while I was hanging out in Atlanta. *I don't know why I was in Atlanta at that time, but that's not the point.* Anyway, she looked like the actress Victoria Rowell, and even though I met her in Atlanta, she lived in Indianapolis. She knew my situation, but as usual, I made things seem worse than they actually were, and we talked often. Other than the first time I met her, I hadn't seen her, so we needed that to change. But *how* did I tell Tamara I needed to go to Indy where I knew absolutely no one? The reason I gave will go down in the creep squad hall of fame of all-time lies.

Since I worked at the NSA, I had a top secret military clearance. That place was a fortress, and if you didn't work there, you really had no idea what was going on inside. That's why, if you worked there, you could make outsiders feel like you were some deep cover, James Bond type of shit. That included your spouse, if need be. So my warped mind came up with the clever idea of telling Tamara I needed to go out of town for the weekend on a mission, but this mission was "hush hush top secret." I was like, "I have to leave town this weekend, and I'm not supposed to even tell you where I'm going." To make her less suspicious, I eventually told her it was going to be in the Indiana area, and that while I was there, I was going to visit a TV station if "my supervisor gave me some down time." She was smart, but I was a really good actor, so she went with it. She even dropped me off at the airport. I was off to Indianapolis to see this girl.

I was only there for the weekend. We had a good time. We went out to eat. We talked. We were...well, ya know. This girl was feeling me, and every now and then, she'd talk about how she wanted this permanently. I knew that wasn't going to happen for a while, but I wasn't about to give her any hints. So when she asked me to leave the out-going message on her answering machine because she lived alone and wanted it to appear a man lived there, I didn't hesitate. I even left the *same exact* message I had on my own voicemail at home. I just changed the number.

> *Now let me explain something to you youngsters born after 1990. Home answering machines weren't like the voicemails of today. Everyone could hear the outgoing and incoming messages loud and clear if you were in the house.*

So that Saturday, I was in the shower with this woman. The phone rang, and since I'm Captain Obvious, I said, "I think your phone is ringing."

She replied, "Don't worry about it, baby, they'll leave a message if it's important." It was! When the phone stopped ringing, the answering machine picked up and you could hear my voice.

"You have reached [this phone number]; no one is home right now, but please leave a message...BEEP!" We were still in the shower, but when I heard the caller's voice on that answering machine, I was all of a sudden in a different kind of hot water.

"Ummmmmmm, this is Tamara Hill. I'm trying to reach Mike Hill. I know he's there because this is his *voice* on this answering machine."

I really couldn't tell you what else she said after that because I think I temporarily died, only to be resuscitated by the screams of this woman I'm in the shower with.

"Oh, my God! Oh, my God! Why is your wife calling here? How did she get this number?"

Of course, I had no idea at this point, and I was really in no hurry to find out, but I knew I had to. After receiving some very unpleasant but well-deserved calls from my mom and Tamara's Aunt Kee, I finally got the nerve to call Tamara back. Obviously, she was livid.

"You son of a bitch, I'm throwing all your shit out. I can't believe you. You ain't shit." Looking back, she probably didn't say enough, but my reaction tells you exactly how I thought and what kind of person I was at that time.

"You ain't gonna do a damn thing. I can't believe you got my mom and your aunt calling this woman's house acting crazy."

Yeah, I told you, my mind was warped back then. We went back and forth like that for about an hour, and then I finally hung up.

Meanwhile, the woman I was with was acting nervous, telling me I should probably leave, and I agreed. However, as I was trying to make arrangements to go back home early, her mood and attitude changed out of nowhere.

"I'm sorry you're going through this. Don't leave. Just make love to me."

Yeah, readers, my reaction was exactly like yours. What the fuck? Woman, do you think that even if I wanted to, I could right now? But somehow, I did.

A few hours later, things had calmed down a bit. The phone calls from my mom, Kee, and everyone else Tamara knew had slowed, and Tamara called me one last time. This time, her tone was totally different. She was calm, loving, and weirdly compassionate.

"Just come home. We can work through this. I love you, and I want to make this work."

Now, mind you, when she was going off, my attitude was almost as hostile as hers. Very defensive. Now that she was calm and loving, when I tell you I got nervous as hell, that was an understatement.

I eventually flew back the next morning. My boy Q and his wife picked me up from the airport. Tamara and his wife were cool, so you can imagine what her attitude toward me was on that day. I was in the backseat, and I remember Q kept looking at me in his rearview with a halfway smirk, just shaking his head and basically acknowledging that I had really screwed up.

When I got home, there was no arguing. There were no threats. I felt bad for Tamara because she had obviously been crying. We talked about the situation here and there, and nothing ever got out of hand, but inside the warped mind of this creep, ironically I could not trust *her* because she was being too nice. So for the next few weeks, I chose to sleep in the guest room with the door locked and a chair under the knob because I was too afraid of what she might do while I was sleeping. *I know. I got some damn nerve, huh?* I actually wish she would've killed a part of me. Unfortunately, she didn't.

I later discovered that Tamara had received an anonymous call saying, "If you want to know where your husband is, dial [the number]." Of course she followed through. Come to find out, the woman in Indy had a friend of hers call my house and leave that message that Tamara received. She figured if Tamara called and heard my voice on that answering machine, it would expose us, force Tamara and me to break up, and then I could be with the woman in Indy. It didn't work that way, but the damage was certainly done.

I'm pretty sure I nearly broke Tamara then. It's amazing how strong that woman was over the years. She's a testament to truly overcoming being in an abusive relationship. No, I never laid hands on her, but mental abuse isn't much better. When you put your wife through the embarrassment of having to go and get an STD test based on *your* foolishness, you're an abuser. *Fellas, think about what's going through her mind while waiting for the results. That's the only positive thing you never want from someone.* Thank God her results came back negative. It's too bad the results of my future behavior turned out to be the same.

Grandma's Hands:

A TRIBUTE TO LILLIAN GILLIS

IN MANY WAYS, my grandmother was more influential in my life than my mother.

Everything I do is to make her proud. She is the woman I admire most in my life. Inviting and warm, her home was always filled with people and laughter. Her sweet spirit was magnetic and drew people near to her. Her love for entertainment often resulted in me and my brother being called front and center to the living room to dance and perform for company. Maybe we reminded her of her hay day when she was a dancer. Grandma smoked, drank liquor, and relished in the simple pleasures of life. There was never a time that she didn't have a smile on her face. She was a class act and believed in giving those around her the very best of what she had to offer. She would often say "If I have the money, then I'm going to get top of the line." Her sentiments reflected in her selection of furniture and the way she appointed her home. She was such a lady. Even the way she smoked her cigarettes showed her finesse.

My love for her was never-ending for many reasons, among them being that she often saw things in me that I couldn't see in myself. As a teenager, I would sit in her room and we would just have talks. She would teach me about God and give me life lessons. She taught me to want more from myself and those around me. She was a prophet who saw the vision for my life well before I did.

One summer I accepted an offer to earn some extra money by helping my dad, who worked for the water company, dig ditches. I had a shovel and I was tasked with chopping up rocks while he used a backhoe. After all of the hard labor, I can recall receiving like $75. By the time I got back to my grandmother's home, everything on my body hurt. Prior to that day, I had never been assigned hard physical labor. My grandmother took one look at me and said, "Baby, this ain't for you. You weren't made for that. Your job is not physical labor whatsoever. Using your mind is what you are to do." I was shocked by her words because I wasn't complaining about the work, and I was not aware that I demonstrated in any way that my body was sore. She just knew. "Use your mind. God's got something better for you," she said.

Eventually, she took ill and we all knew our time with her was limited. There were so many times as a young boy that I could have been outside playing, but instead, I was at her feet, watching the motions of her hands as she taught me and poured into me. I had cousins that were on drugs, and she taught me to make different choices for my life. She would ask me if I wanted to put my mom and her through what the family was experiencing with my cousins.

The last time I saw her, I felt deeply connected, more than I ever had. On this day in particular, both my Aunts Gladys and Arlene were sitting at her bedside. After spending a substantial amount of quality time, I stood up in preparation to leave. Just as I began walking toward the door to slip out, I heard her softly speak my name. When I turned to face her, she said, "Don't let no broad run your life. Always be happy." Although I heard the words that she spoke, I could not help but to notice that her face was illuminated. It was as if she was already an angel. In that moment, time stood still. I left with a heavy heart as I knew that it would be the last time that I would see her face. I knew that I would be left only with the words she had spoken and the memories we had created together.

About a month later, she was scheduled for a small medical procedure that she would not sustain. Although we were all aware of the possibility, nothing can prepare you for the departure of the ones you love and cherish. She departed from the physical body, but I know with certainty that her spirit lives on in me. I am so much like my grandmother in so many ways. From the day that she passed, my solemn prayer was to make her proud.

In retrospect, the theme of all of my talks and special moments shared with my grandmother was of love through accountability. It is because of the unprecedented strength that she so effortlessly transferred to me that I can tell my story. Her words now hang dearly in my heart, and I am a living witness of the ways in which they manifest each day. Today, I can only pray that she is as proud of me as I was of her all the years that she lived. I am all that I am because of an awe-inspiring woman known to the world as Lillian Gillis, but eternally known by me as Grandmother. Her hands molded me.

Chapter 8

SEGUE

MEANWHILE, I WAS making some strides trying to get into broadcasting. Because of my internship and TV ties, I crossed over and started working in the NSA TV studios. I was one of the main anchors providing classified reports that went out to NSA offices and all the different government agencies, including the CIA, FBI, Pentagon, and White House. My internship turned into a role at the station. I was a non-paid PA, but I was overwhelmed and grateful for the experience.

I finally had what I thought was a solid résumé reel. So I was sending out tape after tape. Dub after dub. It was $3.50 a pop for priority mail postage. I did my research on each station and city and sent out custom cover letters to prospective employees, making little references here and there to ensure they *knew* I knew about that station or community.

In all, I sent out 74 résumé tapes. *Seventy-four.* I got 71 rejection letters. I remember the first one I got something back, I was actually excited to get it. It was an EOC form—a form sent from the station's HR department just to let you know they got your application. That first one came, and I was juiced because it had the station's letterhead on the envelope, so I didn't know what to expect. Soon, after getting about fifteen of them, I realized it was just their way of saying, "We got your résumé, but you might as well resume your search, because you won't be working here." Needless to say, my excitement began to dwindle when I received mail.

I'd follow up with calls here and there. I got yelled at by a few news directors who didn't want to be bothered by some punk kid looking for a job in their sports department, while a few others were nice and would just tell me the position was filled.

Once again, of those 74 stations, I got 71 "rejection letters." To this day, I keep every last one of them. It served, and in some way, still does serve as motivation to keep going or a reminder of how far I've come. I have to admit, at the time, there were moments when I didn't think this sportscasting thing was going to happen for me. I'd get upset. Frustrated. Downright pissed. I don't know how many times I'd punch the wall or throw my briefcase across the room when I was told "no." However, here's the one lesson I learned from this, and something I share with people all the time. In this business, you can and *will* receive many no's. However, don't get too far down on yourself. Despite all those no's, all it takes it one *right* yes to change your life.

Seventy-four stations. Seventy-one rejections. That means three stations actually responded to me. One was from a lady in Grand Junction, Colorado. *Yeah, y'all, I was sending my tape everywhere. I even tried to get a job in Montana.* The lady in Grand Junction was nice—nice enough to start off with, "Hi Mike, you're not getting the job, but I just wanted to critique your tape." I actually thought that was nice, and she gave me sound advice.

Another callback came from a sports director in a city in North Carolina, who also told me I wasn't going to get the gig, but he and everyone in the sports department loved—you guessed it—"*my man* Weidong."

The last call I got was from a guy named Bob Borngesser around late 1994, early 1995. He was the news director for this station WHAG-TV in Hagerstown, which was just 75 miles away from where I lived. He had an opening for a weekend sports anchor gig and wanted to know if I was interested. Uh—hell yeah! So we set up a date for me to come to Hagerstown for an interview. The day came and Maryland was having a crazy-ass winter storm. Snow and ice covering the roads and the authorities were telling people that if they didn't have to be outside, stay inside. However, one thing you should know about my crazy life is, no matter what, God has always found a way out of no way for me. By His grace, I had purchased a 4x4 truck and so I was going to make it to my interview on this day. It took me three hours to drive 75 miles, but I got there and got there ON TIME.

The station was pretty much an office building in the middle of the street. When Bob saw me, he said in that deep voice of his, "I'm sort of shocked. I didn't think you were even going to show up." Like I said, I wanted this and nothing, not even Mother Nature, was going to stop me from getting there. Bob showed me around. I met a few people, including Matt Pencek, the current sports director. Had a good conversation. Left and I heard...nothing.

February 28th, 1995. It was discharge day. I was getting out of the Air Force after serving for six years. I was getting my discharge papers and the 1st sergeant asked me, "So what are you going to do now, Hill?" And that's when it hit me. Man, I didn't have a damn job. I was officially unemployed. What WAS my plan?

Tamara and I were living with Q and his wife because the movers had already come and packed up our apartment and moved the furniture into storage. One plan was to move from Maryland down to Virginia with my brother Preston and his family for awhile until I could get a job. At this time, I was banking on a broadcasting job. Thing is, because of my top secret clearance, I could've taken a job in the corporate/private sector with a starting salary of about 85K a year. A lot of money for a 25-year-old back in '95. *Hell, who am I kidding, it's still a lot for a 25-year-old now.* However, I didn't want that. I wanted to pursue my passion and my dream. I wanted to be a TV personality. I wanted to have fun. I wanted to be happy. I wanted a JOB, but until this point, none in the TV world had become available to me.

Can I tell you just how amazing God's timing is?? If not, you'll find out anyway if you keep reading. After I got my discharge and had to give my 1st sergeant some lame answer to his question, I went back to Q's house and I was mildly depressed. I'd truly believed that I would have a sportscasting job by the time I got out of the military. Surely, I'd get lucky with ONE of those 74 tapes I sent out.

Depression just makes you want to sleep, so I went and lay down, but before I did, I asked God to help me figure it out. "Lord, let Your will be done, whatever that is. Just give me the answer." *Despite my transgressions, I've always considered myself a nice guy, who's strong spiritually. My mom, Grandma Lillian, and Richard's family always kept me close to God. Lord knows it's been tough, and I've done my share of backsliding, but He's always looked out for me.*

After my prayer, I lay down and fell asleep. About an hour later, the phone started ringing and since Q was home, he answered. He called upstairs and said it was for me. I came downstairs, thinking it was Tamara, but it wasn't.

"Hello," I said.

"Hi, Mike, this is Bob Borngesser from WHAG in Hagerstown, got a moment?"

At this point I wanted to scream, "Hell to the yeah!" but I played it cool. "Yes, absolutely."

Bob continued, "Well, we still have this opening for a weekend sports anchor/weekday reporter and we'd love to have you if you're still interested." I honestly forget what I said afterwards. I was overjoyed, but obviously I said "yes" and I told him I could start in a few days.

YES! Two hours after getting discharged from a six-year stint in the military, God had answered my 1st sergeant's question and my prayers with one phone call. I was about to be a full-fledged, legit TV sports anchor. How about that for God's timing? On that point, when I look back, it's actually good that I didn't get a job offer with some of those early tapes I was sending out. Think about it. I had been sending out tapes for about eight or nine months and I was still in the military. While you're in, it's a commitment that they take seriously and hold you to. There are certain circumstances that they would let you out early for, but for the most part, had I received a job offer, I likely would've just been S-O-L, unless I'd gone A-W-O-L, which could lead to J-A-I-L. In other words, had a job offer come too soon, I would've just taken an L.

Momma, I made it!! I'm on TV now. I'm a superstar. Adoring fans asking for autographs and we're going to the front of the line wherever I go. Shhhhhhhhhhhhhhhit!!!! Okay. That STILL hasn't happened. Well, sometimes, but my early TV career was ANYTHING but glamorous.

First, let's talk salary, which I actually failed to do when I accepted the job from Bob Borngesser because I was too excited to even ask. I didn't care, but damn, a brother gotta eat, right? Remember that 85K salary I said I could've probably gotten because of my top secret security clearance? Let's just say my first TV salary was a little bit less. Guess how much?? No, go lower. LOWER. MUCHHHHHH LOWER. I was getting paid six seventy-five!! Oh, hell nawl. Not $675 a week. $6.75 an HOUR. If I wanted to, I probably could've applied for and gotten food stamps. I didn't, and it was tough, but I was so happy.

It's what I tell kids all the time now. Follow your passion. Follow your dreams and not just the money. If you're happy on your job, you're likely going to be good at your job. If you're good, people will see it, and your opportunities for advancement will come often and quickly. Sure, had I taken that private sector gig out of the military, I would've made good money, but I could've also ended up hating my job, which would have made me miserable. At the end of the day, it's best to choose happiness and enough money over misery with a lot of it.

I laugh thinking about how we worked at WHAG. We put a good product on the air. No doubt about that, but there were no bells and definitely no whistles. When I first arrived, we worked on typewriters *(no, not computer keyboard joints... I mean actual typewriters)*. We'd turn in our scripts to a P.A., who would tape them together and feed them through a prompter machine that each individual anchor would move with a foot pedal. They eventually got a computer system a few months after I arrived. However, the entire time I was there, we couldn't go live.

My first report at WHAG was covering some local high school basketball playoffs. We hadn't gotten our furniture yet, so the first time I was on TV, I actually watched it on this little 8-inch portable joint on the living room floor. That moment still brings a smile to my face.

Even though I wasn't making much money, I was happy. God provided and Tamara and I were doing pretty damn good. Sure, we lived in a terrible one-bedroom, one-bath apartment. And who cared if my truck was stolen in the complex's parking lot and stripped a few months after living there? We were actually pretty good, and most importantly, I was behaving. We even received a financial blessing/boost when a post Air Force examination determined I had some service-related ailments. I got 50 percent disability for various things (I ain't sharing EVERY damn thing with y'all) I went through while in the military. Therefore, I was rewarded 50 percent of my military salary for the rest of my life. God is good.

Once I got my first job, I appeared to be on the fast track to success. I was receiving accolades from my co-workers. One of the main news anchors named Sue was really the first person to tell me, "You're going to be on that ESPN" one day.

He's passed away now, but I will forever be indebted to Bob Borngesser. Bruce may have started it, but Bob encouraged me to be ME even more. My style was best described with three words: A Damn Fool!!! I was nuts. I would wear baseball caps. I'd sing. One time I wore those little nose strips on air (my friend Bill stole them...shout out to Bill). They didn't care what I did, as long as I didn't curse. I even gave my sportscast a title, *"Sports Time 25"* and most people LOVED IT. After just 3 months working there, the sports director Matt Pencek took another job in Pennsylvania and I was promoted to sports director. I got a raise and everything. About $7.80 an hour. *I know, BALLING!!!*

All the frustrations of getting those rejection letters and long nights with the After Hours Club was paying off, even if not "literally" paying off yet. Since we were so close to the Washington, DC area, a few people who worked in TV there got our broadcast, including a news director for WUSA-Channel 9 there named Dave Roberts. He'd seen me on air and reached out inquiring about my status. I think once I told him I had only been in the business 4-5 months, he knew I wasn't ready to be seriously considered for anything there. Funny thing, Dave and I would cross paths years later at ESPN, and he was instrumental in my growth there.

Once I got that phone call, though, I was curious and just wanted to test the market, so to speak. I sent out four tapes. Now remember how I told you I got three responses to 74 tapes previously? I got two responses on these four that I just sent back. One was from a station in Detroit, but I didn't like what was being offered and really didn't want to go to Detroit. *Nothing against The D...I don't want "The*

D vs Everybody" coming after me. It just wasn't right for me at that time.

The second call was from this guy named Eric Hulnick, news director at KSEE24 in Fresno. He had a weekend sports anchor job opening and asked me if I was interested. I was, even though I had no idea where Fresno was in California. He asked me a few questions about myself and hired me right there over the phone. Two-year deal, 28.5K the first year. A solid 30K the next. That felt like a lot to me at that time. Remember, I was making 7.80 an hour.

Seven months after getting my first job, I was hired for my second. I went from market 198 to market 56, which is a huge jump for just about anyone, but I was ready for it. Or so I thought. I was good but still very green. Remember, they had no live capabilities at WHAG, so my first-ever live shot came in Fresno at a hockey game, interviewing a player on the Russian national team through an interpreter. That was dicey. I did corny stand-ups, and my fashion gear was terrible. I remember I didn't have a clothing allowance, but they had a barter deal with this one store, and I got two sports coats. One was red, the other green.

Like in Hagerstown, I was allowed to be myself. I even did this Sunday segment called Big Board Sports, where I did my sportscast in front of the weather wall, so I had all these cool graphics and video behind me. On those days I couldn't wear my green jacket, though. *Most weather walls you see on the news are just a big green wall which production superimposes graphics on. If you wear green, somehow it's like YOU become part of the wall and that part of your body disappears. It's weird as shit.* Anyway, Big Board Sports was a hit. This great director named Manny Lujuan, who's still a great friend to this day, put it all together for me complete with rap music *(that we'd be charged up the ying yang if we used today)*. I was growing and starting to get recognized. That in itself is like a drug that you have to be very careful with and not abuse. *Don't worry, I'll talk more about this later because I overdosed on it later in my career. Stay tuned.*

I worked under this guy named Orin, who, like me, had been born in New York, so we had that and our love for the Yankees in common, but nothing more. He was helpful and actually had some skills. I'll give him his props, but in his mind he thought he was the best sportscaster in the history of mankind. Nothing wrong with believing in yourself, but there's a fine line between smug and arrogance.

Orin had been in Fresno for awhile, and yes, he wanted to go to a bigger market. There was only one problem, in his opinion. He was a white man and couldn't get the opportunities he deserved because they were all going to people of color or women. Yep, it's my first encounter with…I'm not going to say racism, because I truly believe Orin, who was Jewish, didn't have one ounce of racism in his body… .I'll call it utter ignorance or entitlement that many suffer from in this country.

He wasn't and still isn't alone. There was a reporter at our station named Michael who felt the same way at that time. Now, I understand the business. Sure, there are jobs in mostly every industry where they are specifically looking for diversity. Usually, it's because it's NEEDED. However, when Orin and Michael would give me a backhanded compliment by saying things to me like, "Yeah, Mike, you'll make it to a top 10 market because you're an African American," I

used to think, and still do think, it's some of the most ignorant shit ever to say. Like I could just go to a station in a
top 10 market and say, "Yeah, I'm not really qualified or a
good candidate for this job but I'M BLACK. That should
automatically make me a finalist, right?"

In my earlier years, comments like this would start an
argument. However, the military helped me deal with
putting out minor fires before they became blazes. When
they would make these "You'll make it cuz you're black"
remarks, I'd retort with, "You're still more likely to make it
than me because you're white, so what else is holding you
back?" I know!! It's childish and maybe I shouldn't have
engaged, but I did.

Meanwhile, I was really struggling financially. Even with
my military benefits, 28K just wasn't cutting it for me and
Tamara. She was volunteering at a hospital but really wasn't
working. It wasn't her fault. I was the one moving around
and so she sacrificed a lot for us in the beginning. I was in
the business but didn't know anything about business early
on. That included knowing you could actually negotiate a
contract and not just take the first offer.

Once again, I was so happy to be receiving a new job
and that 28K that I didn't negotiate with Eric Hulnick for
moving allowances or possibly even more money. Therefore, I had to pay for that move myself, which wiped out
the little savings we did have.

I was so broke when I first got there that some days I'd go
without eating because I just couldn't afford it. I was cool
with a group of guys who lived together, two dudes named
Greg B, Greg C, and Manny, who I told you about. I'd go
by their crib and PRAY they had cooked or grabbed some-

thing and were kind enough to offer me some. I never let on to anyone about my finances because pride got in the way.

It may have been a struggle financially, but not so much at home. Things were actually going quite well with me and Tamara. Of course, we'd have our occasional argument but nothing major and guess what, I was staying "cheat" free. Not that any married person deserves an award for that, but it was an accomplishment for this addict. *Honestly, I rarely went anywhere in Fresno because there was just no place to go.*

However, the one place I did go when I had an opportunity to was Los Angeles. The first time I went there was around Christmas of '96 with Manny and another friend named Ryan Tyeska. We were just hanging out and ended up at this Christmas party, somewhere in the Valley, I guess. It wasn't just any party, but a lot of black Hollywood was there, including Tisha Campbell and Tichina Arnold. I've always been a huge fan of that show "Martin" and since they were two of the stars, I was super stoked when I saw them, but I've always kept it cool on the outside and never fanned out.

I remember the dude that played Big Red in the *Five Heartbeats* movie was also there, but the person I got most excited about this gorgeous actress who I had an enormous crush on. In fact, any heterosexual man in his right mind would have had a crush on this woman. I was actually sitting on a couch with her and a few others and really didn't know it was her at first. Actors are sometimes shorter in person and without makeup can look different, but she was still beautiful. As I was getting up, I had to pass by her and accidentally stepped on her foot. I remember saying

"Sorry" and she said, "It's quite all right, baby" (at least that's what I heard). So we had a "moment" and I was in love. *Of course, I'm only joking, so no disrespect to her incredible husband, who I've actually become cool with over the last year or so. Then again, I'm not using her name so you can have fun just trying to guess who it may be.*

However, I'm not telling this story to tell you the moment I fell in love with Ms. ?? I'm telling this story because that was the night I fell in love with L.A.

During the party, I just went outside for a moment. Let's just say the house was a little "smoky" and I wasn't partaking at the time. I went to my car, but instead of getting in it, I just lay down on the hood and looked up into the sky at the stars. As I did, I swear God talked to me. *No, it wasn't weed. I told you I wasn't smoking anything that night and wasn't around long enough for a contact.* I swear, I heard God tell me, THIS IS WHERE YOU NEED TO BE. THIS IS YOUR HOME AND ONE DAY IT WILL BE YOUR HOME. I'm telling you, God spoke those words right into my heart. It had nothing to do with the celebrities on the inside or the lifestyle I saw them living. Maybe in a way it did because being around actors and getting into acting was my destiny (more on that later) but it was more about a comfort. I had never been to L.A. before this day, but I knew it was my home and every time I ever came back before eventually moving here, I felt the same way I felt that night on my car. Listen to God. He knows where you're supposed to be.

Believe it or not, by this time, Tamara and I had been married seven years. Things had been steady financially after a few months, and we decided it was time to start a family. When she told me she was pregnant, I was just so overjoyed. I was going to be a father. I couldn't wait to see a human being that I'd helped create. Of course I was going to spoil him/her to death. I always said growing up that when I had my own children, I was going to give them everything they needed and pretty much most of what they wanted. I'd teach them to appreciate it, though, and not feel entitled to it, but because of some of the things I'd had to endure in my childhood or some of the things I didn't have because we couldn't afford it, I was going to make it my mission to have for my own. I was ready. Tamara was ready. God wasn't.

Chapter 9

STEREO

I WAS AT work on a Saturday getting ready for my sports-cast when I got a call from Tamara. She was upset, and so I was immediately concerned. She told me she was spotting. I was scared as hell, but I tried to remain as calm as possible so as to not scare Tamara even more. I left work and took her to the hospital. When they did the ultrasound and the doctor told us there was "no sign of pregnancy," it was like someone had kicked me in the nuts and punched me in the gut at the same time.

She was just a few months pregnant, but we were so excited that we had basically told everyone. That made things harder because we had to explain to everyone what had happened every time someone would ask about the pregnancy. We later found out that miscarriages are quite common early in a pregnancy. It's just that not many people talk about it, and it's a reason why many won't even announce a pregnancy until after at least the first tri-mester. Hard to believe our baby would have been a grown man or woman today.

Because of the miscarriage and the fact that we were super homesick, I asked KSEE24 if I could break my contract and move closer to home. I was in the middle of a three-year deal, but they surprisingly understood and gave me their blessing.

It was time to send out more tapes. However, this time, I wasn't sending them out. I had an agent that my mentor Kevin Frazier had connected me with named Kris Kellam. Kris told me about two openings she wanted to submit my tapes to. One I believe went somewhere in North Carolina and the other to WKRN-TV 2 in Nashville. We heard back from WKRN almost immediately.

From what I can recall, hearing about Nashville was my first sign of getting cocky or full of myself as a broadcaster. Obviously, if I could go from one legit response out of 74 tapes to two responses out of four to now one out of two in less than three years, I must be the shit, right? Plus, I now had an agent and WHEN I got this job offer, I'd have the chance to jump from market 198 to market 31 in less than three years. I even remember telling Kevin, "I don't really want to go to country-ass Nashville, but if they're going to fly me in and wine me and dine me, I'll listen." *Damn, I sounded like a prick. I wonder if Kevin remembers that?*

It was February of 1997, and as we were about to land, I just remember looking out the window and thinking, "This is some country shit," like I hadn't been raised in Alabama or something. *What a douche.* I arrived and it was one of the rare occasions that it was actually snowing there and the sports director at the station, John Dwyer, was driving me around on these ice-covered roads in a small-ass but nice convertible sports car.

The station looked like an old warehouse and the studio was right in the middle of the newsroom. However, the people were so nice and when I met and sat down with the news director, my attitude changed. Matthew Zelkind, or Z as everyone called him, made you want to win for him. He was so cool and even though WKRN wasn't doing great in the ratings there, he made you feel like it was going to turn around quickly. Most importantly, he absolutely loved sports and he wanted me to be ME.

Z and the tour John gave me of downtown where they had just built this new arena had me sold. Complete attitude change. I was ready to move to Nashville. I even told John how much I looked forward to working with him and couldn't wait to get started. I was still a little cocky because John so kindly reminded me that I actually hadn't been offered the job yet before he took me back to the airport.

Whoa!! I thought I had blown it. Had my cockiness cost me this opportunity or would John just look at it as excitement and not go back and tell Z I wasn't the right guy? It was the latter. Three years after I began my journey in Hagerstown, I was off to Nashville.

Fifty K year one. Fifty-five K year two. In addition, I was getting a moving allowance. I was loving life, and my career was starting to take off. Tamara and I rented a townhouse in this section of Nashville called Bellevue, and I jumped right into work. She and I were also doing great. For now.

The great thing about coming into the Nashville scene at that time is it was the beginning of professional sports in the city. The NFL's Oilers (later changed to the Titans) were moving from Houston with their star players Steve McNair and Eddie George, and Nashville had just been awarded a hockey franchise, which would become the Predators.

I was soaking it up and becoming a little recognizable. I was getting asked to speak or MC events. At one particular event, which a few of the Titans were part of, I met these guys, Charles "Chuck" Sueing, Donnie Hatcher, and Jerome Davis, or JD. We instantly clicked and it became my crew.

We did a lot together. Too much. *Yep, you can just use your imagination here because Nashville is where I really fell off the wagon and never quite recovered.* Donnie and JD ran this event called *First Fridays* and it was always a "nice look." We'd either be there or in this club called *"Sumtn Live,"* and I was up to no good again.

Nashville was the first time I had been in a nice African American community since I left Bessemer. It also provided me with a dangerous mix. A platform that made me a little bit of a local celebrity and plenty of opportunity. I started getting recognized A LOT. That made it increasingly easier to meet and talk to women and, for this addict, that wasn't safe.

Man, I was really caught up. I had people recognizing me and women I was fooling around with, but then The Source magazine took my head to the next level. The Source was a national hip-hop publication which did a sports issue. In one of the issues, they talked about this local sportscaster in Nashville with flavor who reminded them of Stuart Scott, who was now pretty popular at ESPN. Even though I HATED being compared to Stu, shit, this was a national magazine and they were talking about me, and in a good way. I MUST be the shit!! I acted like it.

John Dwyer was great. Kind of smug but always shared the spotlight with me and always tried to keep the peace. Because my head was becoming so large, I was probably becoming increasingly harder to work with. I was still nice for the most part, but I really had my days.

One sportscast, I had what we call in the business an "abortion." Everything went wrong. All my tapes were out of place and if it was the right tape, there was something wrong with the edit. It was just a terrifying 3 1/2 minutes. What made the matter worse is my sports producer, Tim, the one who was usually in my ear or at least in the control room in case shit like this went wrong, wasn't there. He'd decided he was going to just sit this one out. I WAS PISSED and after the show, I told him I was. His response was, "Dude, why are you so mad? You're such a f***ing prima donna." I went ballistic. I started slamming shit and screaming at him. I had a basketball in my hand for some reason and when he called me a prima donna, I started to throw it at him. He crouched into a ball to shield himself, but I just slammed the ball to the ground and ran outside. It was pouring rain, but I had to get away or I felt like I would've hurt someone. I went out to the parking lot, and as the drops of rain drenched my body, I screamed at the top of my lungs.

I was wrong. Sure, some of the blame goes on the tape operator or even Tim for not being there to restore order in that control room, but I could've and should've handled things much better. However, hindsight is always 20/20, and it was too late. That incident cost me dearly. First of all, my reputation. I had always been known by my colleagues as being the "nice guy." Some in the building that night saw a different side, and it was embarrassing. It really hit home when our meteorologist, Lisa Patton, a lady I had a lot of respect for, told me she was "disappointed" to see me act that way. The look on her face is one of the reasons why I now do my best to not allow anyone or anything to take me to that place. In this business, your reputation is everything, and my name is super important when it comes to my character. However, outside of Lisa's disapproval, it could've been worse. I got suspended without pay for three days, but according to Z, the general manager at the time, this guy named Mike Seichrist, wanted me fired. Z fought for and saved my job. *One of the many reasons why I'll always have love for that guy.*

Unfortunately, Z wasn't a marriage counselor because there really wasn't any saving my marriage. I was wilding. No need to go into detail, but I was completely out of control. Tamara had begun working in a hospital and had to get up early in the morning. If I went out, and it was pretty often on the weekends, I'd creep back in the house sometimes at three or four in the morning—and Nashville shuts down at two. I started noticing a pattern, though, when I came home this late. *I'm about to take you inside the twisted mind of a devious bastard here.* I could come in, take off my clothes, and even brush my teeth, and Tamara would not budge. However, as soon as I pulled back the covers to my side of the bed to get in, she'd wake up immediately. When she did, the very first thing she would do would be to look at the clock. Even though she'd still be in a half-asleep trance, if it was three or later, she'd say, "Are you REALLY just getting home?" And she would have an attitude for days. So I fixed that.

One of the skills the Air Force taught me when I was an analyst was to pick up trends. I noticed that was her trend, so I had to improvise, adapt & overcome. *Hey, I know that's the Marines' slogan and I was in the Air Force, but work with me here.* I knew she'd usually be in bed really early on nights where she had to work the next morning. So that meant she'd be asleep for hours when I was getting back in late from the club. On those nights, I'd creep into the room and BEFORE I got in bed, I'd go to her night-stand where the clock was and I'd turn the clock back to a decent hour. So let's say I got in at 3:30, I'd turn it back to 2:15 or so. When I did that, I'd get in bed and like clock-work (no pun intended), she'd pop up, immediately look at the clock, see that it was a "decent" hour, and go right back to sleep. Of course, when she went back to sleep, I'd get up and reset her clock to the right time. No drama. No issues for weeks. It was wrong to do, I know, but back then I'd get a peaceful night of sleep and better yet, PEACE for weeks to come.

I told her what I had done years later, and she was beyond pissed. I can't blame her. The more I write this, I realize how strong that woman is to have overcome everything my dumb ass was doing. *Oh, there's more.*

I was becoming more popular in Nashville. I ain't trying to make it seem like I was some sort of huge celebrity, but at that time, I was getting recognized by many people in the area. It's something that, of course, went to my head, but something I believe Tamara grew tired of. She told me several times, "I'm tired of being Mike Hill's wife," and it always bothered me. Now I know she meant it like, *I want my OWN identity*, but in my twisted mind, I'd make myself believe she was telling me she didn't want me or maybe she was jealous of my success. Admittedly, even though she may have felt justified for wanting her own identity, I've always felt like there wasn't anything wrong with someone introducing her as "Mike Hill's wife." I actually felt like she should've been proud of that. Maybe she was, but I took it as she wasn't. Of course anything to make me feel better about my wrongdoing. *Indeed, the mind of a maniacal freak!!* Remember, she'd sacrificed a lot to follow me, putting her own dreams and aspirations on hold, so I get it. I just didn't want to get it at that time.

I noticed she was spending more and more time in Birmingham on the weekends going to see her mom. It left me in Nashville by myself, which I didn't mind. I had to work weekends, so there's that, and it also gave me the freedom to come and go anytime I wanted and do whatever I wanted to do. That meant doing no good most of the time. I didn't care what she was doing. I was too focused on what I could get away with.

I'd go home myself on occasions. It was just a 3 1/2 hour drive away. I wish I'd gone more now. I wish I'd been able to do more to save a few people who meant a lot to me. At least tried to.

Remember Durand? My friend who made the right decision by not taking me up on my "foolish" offer at his house when we were teenagers? I was hearing more stories about him and how he was going down the wrong path in Bessemer. In high school, Durand, Vincent Hudson, and I were inseparable. Vincent left to live in L.A. and is doing great as a minister today. Durand, on the other hand, stayed in Bessemer and it cost him. He was constantly getting into trouble. He started using drugs and eventually went to prison.

Durand was so caught up in drugs that he decided to rob a convenience store. Not any old convenience store, but a store that was pretty much right around the corner from his house. A store he went into all the time. A store where the employees knew his face. A store he held up with a gun, WITHOUT a mask or any kind of disguise. Not only did he do this once and went to jail for it, he actually did the same thing at the same store twice and spent time in prison for it, the second time getting a 20-year sentence. He's since gotten out and these days, he's saying and doing the right thing to stay on the right path. *Let's just hope that path doesn't lead him back to that convenience store ever again.*

The irony of Durand finding trouble *(other than him possibly saving me that time)* is that growing up, Vincent and I were envious of the things he had. He lived in a nice house in a new development. He was the one who always had brand-new clothes that we'd ask to borrow. *At least I did because Vincent is about six inches shorter than us.* Durand was the one whose family had all the new, nice cars and got to hang out late, while Vincent's and my moms were super strict and didn't allow us to do as much. Yep, Vincent and I wanted Durand's life, or at least the things he had in it. He was actually spoiled. However, Vincent and my mom gave us something more important and that was discipline, values, and the correct mindset to work for what you want. This is in no way meant to disparage Durand's mom. She would lay down the law when she had to, and she was great to me growing up. I mean, I still call her "ma" to this day.

I'm just saying having all these material things in the world growing up is not and never will be enough.

Durand wasn't the only good friend who was caught up in the wrong things during this time in my life. My friend Bice wasn't doing so great himself. I knew he was selling drugs on a low level, and we were still very close, but I saw the path he was headed down and eventually it wasn't a road I felt comfortable on.

The good thing about some of the people I grew up with is they saw something different about my mentality in that culture. It wasn't that they didn't think I couldn't handle that life; they just knew that there was something bigger for me, and they tried to protect me from it and sometimes myself. Especially Bice.

Bice was selling drugs, but when I'd come home, I'd of course still want to hang out with him. He wanted to hang too, and we did, but when he had "something" on him or he was headed into a place where, if caught, could be a game changer in my life, he ALWAYS made sure I wasn't a part of it. I ain't going to lie, sometimes I'd try to play the gangster role and tell him it was okay, but to his credit, he wasn't having it. He didn't want what he was doing wrong to have an effect on what I was building, and as you know, it certainly could have.

Because of his unselfishness, that dude meant the world to me, and I'd do anything legally in my power to help him. He didn't have much, but what he had, he'd give to you. Even though he'd make fun of the way I was talking on television, calling me "Tom & Tom," a reference to this old skit on this show "In Living Color," he was always proud of me and genuinely happy for my accomplishments. I loved that dude and always will. That's why when his sister called me at work one day to tell me he was dead, it was one of the hardest phone calls I've ever received.

He was driving in Birmingham when someone just pulled up beside him and shot him several times in the head. His car came to a rolling stop in someone's yard, and my best friend was dead. It's been over 20 years, but it's still hard to believe he's gone.

During and immediately after the funeral, I've never cried more in my life. It's like I couldn't turn off the faucet. Even though he was living that life, it was so unexpected to me. I know you may be saying, "Well, why is it unexpected if he's dealing drugs? Isn't that one of the hazards?" Yes, but if you knew Bice like I knew him, you'd ask the same question I was asking myself: "Why would anyone want to kill Darryl Bice?" A guy who had a few issues but honestly wouldn't hurt anyone who wasn't trying to hurt him or his family. RIP, my brother. You will always be missed.

Meanwhile, work was going well. I received a few Emmys for my part in Channel 2's high school football coverage. I had just signed a new two-year deal a year before, but my agent, Kris Kellam, was putting a few feelers out there. Including one to ESPN, who was showing some interest. Of course, you may know I eventually ended up there for the longest stint of any stops in my career, but believe it or not, ESPN really wasn't a place I wanted to be. I had heard so many horror stories about the workload and atmosphere, and everyone knew it was located in Bristol, Connecticut, the land of no social life. So even though many of my colleagues and friends always suggested I'd end up there, I just really didn't want to go. In fact, I was more excited about a general meeting I had in my hometown of New York than I was ESPN.

My agent set up this meeting with a guy named Mike McCarthy and MSG while I was visiting the city. MSG stands for Madison Square Garden—the TV studios were literally under the world's most famous arena. The date of my visit was May 22nd, 1998. The reason that I remember this was while I was in Mike's office, he got word that Mike Piazza, a stud catcher, had just got traded to the New York Mets. This was a major deal, and since MSG covered the New York sports scene, obviously Mike had to cut our meeting way short. I understood but was admittedly a little disappointed.

Not long after I got back to Nashville, I had another meeting that did bring some unexpected news. My boy Donnie wanted to talk to me about something. We met up, he jumped in my truck, and we went for a ride. You ever have a conversation with someone who you know wants to tell you something really bad, but they're a little nervous and don't know quite how to say it? That was Donny. Finally, he spit it out. He had reason to believe that Tamara might be having an affair.

His wife at the time, Julie, and Tamara had become super close friends, and often when Tamara was going to Birmingham to see her mom on the weekends, Julie would tag along. I never thought anything of it. I honestly just assumed they were hanging out, having fun with some of Tamara's friends. However, according to Donnie, after he confronted Julie about a matter, she came clean about some inappropriate matters, including Tamara inviting guys over to her mom's house. She also told him a name, which I won't share here, but it was the name of a person I was familiar with. Donnie didn't want to tell me but felt like he had to, which I understood and appreciated.

Ohhhh! You want to know my reaction, huh? In the car with Donnie, I played it cool. I just sort of nodded my head. Even though he didn't say what, if anything, had actually gone down, my mind went places. After I took Donnie back to his car and I was alone, I was incredulous. I remember being like, "Ah hell nawl. I just KNOW Tamara ain't cheating on ME. Me??? Shitttt!!" *You got it, another cocky as hell moment for the Mike Hill!* Soon after, I was laughing about it, like "Ain't this about a bitch? She's flipping the switch on my ass? Okay!! Game on!!" At that moment, I felt like I had my trump card. *For those not familiar with that term, it has nothing to do with an unqualified president's payment source.* I now had an excuse to continue my terrible behavior, and if I got caught, I'd have this information at my disposal to bring up at a critical time. So guess what I did when I got home and saw Tamara? Absolutely nothing.

If there was any moment I should've known that my marriage was officially over, at least in my mind, it was at that time, or when she literally got hit by a car in a parking lot and I had very little compassion for her well-being. I was emotionally detached, but I was too much of a coward to do anything about it.

I have to say, 1998 may have been one of if not the worst year of my life. There was Bice's unexpected death. There was the news that my wife might be cheating on her cheating, no-good husband. And then there was a call I got in August that I can still hear clearly to this day, as if it happened just yesterday.

It happened super early in a morning in August, and as soon as I saw the caller ID indicating it was my mom calling, I knew it wasn't good news. It wasn't. All I heard her cracking voice say while fighting back tears was, "Michael," and I knew my grandmother was gone. She had been battling health issues for awhile and was scheduled for surgery early that morning.

My mom is my rock, but my Grandma Lillian was and still is my foundation. I know I wouldn't be half the man I am today without her prayers, her many words of wisdom about staying away from the wrong crowds and drugs, and of course, her prayers. She believed in me. She knew I was destined for big things, even when I was young, and she gave me the mindset to believe that I not only could have great things in life, but I should expect to have them. I wanted to make my mom proud, but I wanted my Grandma Lillian to beam with joy. Therefore, one of the highlights of my life is her staying alive long enough to be able to see my dream of being on TV come true.

Months before her death, I had gone to New York to visit her and my mom, and during our final conversation, I told her how I was having issues in my marriage. I told her that I was being a "man," but I had checked out. My grandmother was old school New York. A jazzy chick. So her words to me were, "Don't let no broad run you," and no matter what, "Be happy." I'm choking up even writing it right now because "I love you. Be happy" was the last thing she ever said to me as I was walking out of her bedroom. When she said it, I remember looking back at her and the look on her face was so joyous. She had been pretty sick, but when I looked at her this time, I swear it was like her face had the perfect lighting and she looked healthy and good. When I saw that, something told me that would be the last time I saw her alive. It was.

I left Nashville for New York later that day, and on the way, I stopped and picked up my brother Preston, who was living in Virginia. Tamara stayed behind while we made the final arrangements but drove up with Julie and another one of her friends the day before the wake and stayed with her Aunt Kee and Michael, who were living about 20 minutes outside the city.

By this time, we were both in a bad place relationship-wise. It was like neither one of us cared at all, and my relatives could see it. My grandmother's sisters, Gladys and Arlene, really could sense it. When Tamara came over that night, she was so distant, and it really hurt Arlene's feelings, who had really grown to love her. Later, I tried to explain to my family that we were in a bad state, but Arlene was still hurt, saying, "Well, what did I do to her for her to treat me that way?" Family is everything to me, and when they're hurting, it has an adverse effect on me.

Remember how I was a teary waterfall during Bice's funeral? At my grandmother's wake, I couldn't even cry. I was emotionally drained. I can think about my grandmother now and tears will gush out, but at that moment, I was spent. I think my mom was upset at me because it appeared to her that I didn't care because I didn't cry, and that really hurt my feelings, but it's not that I wasn't sad. I was. I was just an emotional wreck.

And things just got worse for me and Tamara. The night of the wake, she went into the city with Julie, her friend, and her family to have a good time. I was hot! How could she go and have a good time immediately after her husband's grandmother's wake? When she came up with Julie and her friend, I thought they rode with her to give her support and help her drive. In this case, it appeared my grandmother's funeral was just an excuse to come to New York and party. I'm not saying it's true, but it's how I felt, and it would get worse the next day.

The day of the actual funeral, the funeral home wanted the family downstairs at 9 am so we could be loaded into the limos, line up the cars, and proceed to the cemetery. Once again, Tamara and her friends had been hanging out the night before, and she was staying with her aunt just outside of the city. I wasn't tripping hard on where she decided to spend the night, but I was adamant about her being back in the Bronx on time to ride in the limo with me. Well, my mom was the more adamant one, because despite how I was feeling at the time, she really loved Tamara and insisted she be there with the family.

It was 8:40 am and there was no sign of Tamara, and we needed to be downstairs in minutes. My mom told me to call her, so I did. Tamara was still in Bronxville, which, once again, was at least 20 minutes away from where my mom lived, and that's without traffic. She told me they were running behind because they had to eat and they were leaving then. Nine am came and my family was in the limo, but still no Tamara. I was telling my mom not to hold things up and just to leave, but my mom was holding firm when it came to waiting for Tamara. Another 15 minutes went by and still no sign. I was livid, and I almost went off on my mom because I was ready to go. She finally relented and we took off for the cemetery.

The entire ride I was seething. Remember, this was before everyone had a cell phone, so as I was riding, I still didn't know if she was coming or not. She was. Once we got to the cemetery and stopped, Tamara came to the car looking contrite and wanting to be supportive. I was so furious that I don't remember saying much to her except, "All I asked you to do is just be there on time." It was at that second I knew I was done. I was going to tell Tamara I wanted a divorce.

Chapter 10

ROTATION

AFTER THE FUNERAL, Tamara rode back with me to Nashville and we talked. I was calm, but we had to talk. I actually told her I knew about the guy in Birmingham. I didn't tell her who told me or how much I knew (because I actually didn't know myself), but I knew, and she needed to end it. To her credit, she didn't try to deny it. She just agreed to do so. Problem was she actually couldn't do it, because not long after that, I found out she was still communicating with him.

One late night, while she was sleeping, her pager was blowing up. I mean buzzing like crazy. Like I mentioned earlier, once Tamara is asleep, she sleeps hard, so she didn't hear it. Finally, I just HAD to investigate. I went into her purse and grabbed her pager. It was a 205 area code, meaning it was a Birmingham number. It was also a number I had seen pop up on her cell phone bill, which I was paying. So what did I do? What the hell do you think I did? What you probably would've done too. I called it and when the person on the other end picked up, a guy's voice said in a very cool, trying to be sexy way, "What's uppp?" I just hung up the phone. I looked at Tamara sleeping and I ain't going to lie, I actually wanted to strangle her in her sleep.

Now, I know what you're saying: "Mike, you got some damn nerves. All the shit you're doing and you're going to tell her to end a relationship and get mad because she couldn't?" "Furthermore, didn't you just say you were about to ask for a divorce?" Yep, all that is true, but once again, that was my mindset back then. I was hurt but would never admit it. Maybe it was karma. I knew it was my issues and all the pain that I brought to her that made her run into the arms of another man. I didn't care. I'm the main person that will complain about double standards, but this is one time I needed to call an audible on my own rules.

After that night, I finally got the balls to tell her that I didn't want to do this anymore and I wanted a divorce. I just kept hearing my grandmother's words to me, "Be happy," and I was far from happy. Problem was, I knew it would cost me, and I really wasn't in a financial position to do anything about it. Therefore, instead of running to a lawyer, I just went downstairs and started sleeping in the basement, while she stayed upstairs. Tamara didn't take it well. She didn't like it at all. Once again, I was the one gallivanting all over town. She was the one overhearing other women talking about me while in public bathrooms, saying the things I had done or they wanted me to do to them. *This is something she told me. I still don't know who this woman was or why she did it. Obviously she knew Tamara was my wife and probably just wanted to start some shit. She succeeded!* Tamara was the one who put her career on hold to follow me while I built mine. And now I'm telling her "I'm out" because I found out about one inappropriate relationship compared to my dozens? Yep, sounds about right.

This isn't uncommon in relationships. As men, we can hurt women many times and often do. They cry. They get mad. They forgive. They get over it, and they get back with their men because many of them are just built that way. In many situations, all it takes is for a man to be hurt once and there's no forgiving. I take that back. They may forgive, but they CAN'T forget, and it screws them up, so they have to let that woman go. It may seem unfair, and it is, but that's just facts. For the most part, women are way more emotionally forgiving than men.

You can only imagine the tension in that townhouse. Two people on the verge of divorce but still co-existing in the same home. You could cut the tension with a knife and at times, I thought I was going to get cut with one. Our families were disappointed and wanted us to work things out. We had tried counseling earlier in the marriage, after my Indianapolis tryst, but that became such a blame fest that I didn't see how it would make a difference.

Meanwhile, because of the stress at home, I felt my performance at work was suffering. My energy was way down, and I was starting to gain weight. I was keeping Z informed about what was happening, and once again, he proved to not only be the best news director I ever had, but also a great friend. He encouraged me and told me he was always there for me if I ever needed to talk, and he was. I'll always remember that about him.

Even with us staying in separate rooms, there were times that we still found "time for each other." I guess it's just human nature. The last time it happened was because my friend D.C. was in town and he was staying with us. I wasn't going to sleep downstairs with him, so I went upstairs and crawled in my old bed with Tamara, and I have to admit, it was magical and a night I'll always remember. *For several reasons!*

About a month later, around Thanksgiving of 1998, our mutual friends Winnie and her then husband Whit came to visit and stay with us for the holidays. They knew we had been having problems, but we'd known Winnie since the Philippines, so they were like family. I had just walked in from work, spoke to them both, and noticed the dining room table was full. Groceries and supplies for this Thanksgiving feast were everywhere, but there was one thing that seemed to be out of place among the items. A pregnancy test. Now, I knew Winnie and Whit had been trying to have a baby for awhile, and I got a little excited for them.

"All right, y'all going to give it a try again?" I asked Winnie. The side-eye look she gave me was like, *I know something you don't know, and when you find out, you ain't gonna like it.* Her exact words were, "Uh, this ain't for me." Not five seconds later, Tamara followed up with, "I need to talk to you for a second!" *Damn!! Oh shit. Lump in the throat. Bubble gut stomach. This can't be. Yes it is.* Tamara took me upstairs and told me she was pregnant.

I was in shock. *How could this be?? Well, duh!! Of course I know the answer to that but I thought she used her birth control! Is it mine?* These are all the thoughts that ran through my head. I know it's not a good reaction to a woman telling a man she's pregnant. In fact, it's horrible, and hindsight being what it is and the beautiful daughter I have today, I wish I could take it back. Of course, my daughter is one of the two best blessings of my life, and it's not how I feel now, but at THAT moment and at THAT time, I couldn't help but think, *This isn't the right time.* Something I remember telling Tamara over and over again. It didn't matter; we were about to have a baby together while separated.

The next few weeks were excruciating. Tamara wanted us to try and work it out for the sake of the baby, but now my mind was, *I've been set up. Oh, she wants to work it out, it must be a trap. I don't even know if the baby is mine!!* Please forgive me, world, but once again, this is how I felt at THAT TIME. I was in another dimension and couldn't or didn't want to face reality. These two forces working in different directions made an already tense living situation even more volatile. It finally came to a boiling point on New Year's Eve of 1998.

I'll always remember the date because Prince's hit song 1999 was playing on a continuous loop on MTV or VH1. I was upstairs ironing and packing because I had to leave for Arizona the next day to cover Tennessee playing in the first ever BCS title game in a few days. While I was doing this, Tamara was ON ONE. *People, a scorned woman going through a break-up while pregnant is NOT someone you want against you.* She was going in on me. As I was ironing out my wrinkled clothes, she was getting something straight with me. "You want a divorce? You can have your damn divorce, but you're going to pay for it and you're going to give me everything you ever promised me. I want that Mercedes you said you'd get me, and you are going to buy me a house."

Our friend Yoishi, who was going through her own marital issues with my friend Wisdom, was there and trying to calm Tamara down, but it wasn't working. I tried to ignore her and told her, "That's not how divorce works," but that just pissed her off even more, and she kept yelling at me.

Finally, I said, "Tamara, why are you doing this? Why are you acting like such a bitch?" *You ever seen someone go from hot to broiling? That's what Tamara did. Real quick.* Remember, this was back in the day when just about ANY black woman would lose it if they heard the word bitch in reference to them. And even though I said she was "acting" like one and not that she "was" one, it didn't matter. *Total meltdown about to commence in 3...2....1!!!!* "YOU CALLED ME A BITCH........YOUUUUUUUUU CALLED ME A BITCH!!!!" Tamara screamed in the highest pitched voice a woman could possibly have. "I'm going to show you a mother ******* bitch!!"

The next few minutes felt like a dream and still do to this day, but it was all too real. Tamara ran downstairs and Yoishi was right behind her. I was still ironing and not really thinking about anything crazy except maybe "she's lost it." All of a sudden, I heard her downstairs and in the basement. I heard banging and her opening up something metal. The next words I heard were Yoishi screaming, "Tamara!! Tamara!! Girl, what are you doing with that GUN??"

Now in my head, I'm tripping. "Gun? I didn't even know we had a GUN in the house. Where the hell did she get a gun from?"

Yoishi was begging her to put the gun down, but still I didn't move and continued ironing. Maybe I was in shock, but I wasn't going downstairs to "investigate" while she had a gun and for some reason, I didn't attempt to run out of the house as I heard her coming up from the basement. Next thing I heard was her going into the kitchen, opening and slamming shut drawers. Then there was the sound of a big knife unsheathing from a metal butcher block. Then it hit me. *Oh shit!! It's really real now. Boy, you are about to die tonight.*

At that moment, I was resigned to that. I honestly was ready to accept my fate. I stopped ironing, sat down on the bed, and just stared at the wall, stoic. Then Tamara appeared at the bedroom door, butcher's knife in hand (I guess she'd dropped the gun) with Yoishi right behind her. "Call me a bitch again," she repeated over and over again.

I sat on the bed and didn't say a word. I was scared. I was tired. I was emotionally drained and frankly, I was ready to die. Maybe I needed to. I had pushed this woman to become someone she wasn't. This was all my fault, but when she actually put the tip of that knife to my throat, that cocky, arrogant, bitter son of a bitch had to get one more petty shot off. "Go ahead and do it. I'd rather be dead than be in this marriage."

She didn't do it, obviously, but she wasn't done scaring me. She put the knife down and then picked up the iron I had been using and placed it right in my face. I could feel the heat and steam coming from it, literally making me sweat. Believe it or not, I was more afraid of her doing this than her cutting my throat because my vain ass was concerned about my precious little face being scarred and deformed. She eventually put the iron down and calmed down, but there's no way I could stay there anymore.

Before I go any further let me say, in no way was Tamara to blame for all of that. Sure, it was her actions, but hormones, mixed with my behavior, denial, and poor attitude toward her contributed heavily. I accept full responsibility, and I'm not just saying that. At the time I couldn't see it, but I wasn't a good husband or really a great person. I just had this façade of being one. No, I wasn't terrible, and maybe I had a good heart, but I was selfish and my actions nearly made another person do something foolish.

I went to my friend Tony Wyllie's house soon after and told him what happened. He said I could stay there that night and I left for Arizona the next day for a week for the BCS title game. A much-needed getaway.

Even though I had madness in my personal life back home, we killed it when it came to our coverage of the game. I got some great feedback and material for my resume reel, including an interview with Tennessee QB Tee Martin walking off the field for the last time after winning the title. I had a ball and a nice reprieve, but reality was about to creep back in.

When I got back, it was like a spouse switch took place. I went to stay with my friend Wisdom at his apartment, while his wife, Yoishi, went to stay with Tamara at my old place. *I know, it's rather bizarre.* Their relationship was just as contentious without any weapons being drawn, and Wiz was a wee bit calmer than me when it came to conflicts.

One day, I went back to my old place to grab the rest of my things, but Tamara wasn't having it, telling me since I left, I didn't have the right to any of my stuff. This caused a huge argument. Wisdom was with me, and Yoishi was going in on him too. This was becoming loud and, since both Wiz and I were on television, not a good look image wise since I'm sure neighbors could hear what was going on. In fact, I know they did because one of them called the cops. Wisdom was begging me to leave, but I was adamant I was going to leave with my stuff. When I realized that wasn't going to happen without a literal fight, I left—and just in time because I just missed the cops.

However, it got back to our job and I had to explain everything to my boss. Luckily, that was Z, and he always looked out. When I told him the back story and what had gone down on New Year's Eve, he insisted I file a restraining order against Tamara. Now even though she'd had her moment that one night, I didn't honestly think she was a serious threat to me and she was PREGNANT. However, I was made to feel like this was the only option I had if I wanted to stay out of hot water at work, so I did it. That meant I couldn't go around Tamara and she couldn't come around me and she was just two months pregnant with my child. *Damn, Mike. You suck.*

I was such an ass. I missed out on the beauty of a pregnancy. I couldn't go to check-ups, so I didn't hear my child's heartbeat for the first time. Furthermore, I left a pregnant woman by herself. It was one thing to live separately but in the same household, but now not only had I moved out, I couldn't even be around her. The one time I could was when she had a pregnancy scare and thought she was losing the baby. Unbeknownst to her, I got called to the hospital and when she saw me she freaked out, not because she was mad but because she thought she was going to go to jail because I was around. *No bueno.*

Despite all the madness, you guessed it, I was still out being a man. And since I didn't have to come home at a certain hour, have anyone to answer to, and could talk freely in my own bedroom, it was even easier.

I met this woman named Camille on a trip to Baltimore to cover a Tennessee Titans game. She was gorgeous. Former Ms. Universe contestant and carried herself with a lot of class. We met while I was still living in the house with Tamara but I, of course, lied to her (like I did many women back then) and told her I was married but was going through a divorce. Technically I was separated but to this point hadn't filed yet and made her believe it was because I had to pay all of Tamara's bills. We began talking a lot, and it developed into more than just a friendship after a short time.

Didn't take long for Tamara to find out I had moved on and it made things that much more hostile between us. Her thinking was, no matter what's happening between us or where I was living, we were still married and that meant I should've been respecting her. Maybe she was right. *And before anyone out there judges Camille for anything, remember I was making it seem like I was in the worst situation ever. And fellas, we need to stop doing this coward shit. You're lying to an unsuspecting woman, to yourself and violating your marriage. If you're unhappy, get out of the marriage first before bringing someone else INTO it. It's not fair to any of the parties involved. So stop playing little boy games and be a real man.* Regardless of my childishness, Camille had become the reason why we were breaking up in Tamara's mind. Even though in my mind, the marriage had been over long before I met Camille.

I finally had enough money to hire a divorce attorney. Scratch that. I finally found a lawyer willing to accept a payment plan to help a man with little or no money get a divorce. Attorney Robert Green agreed to help me out. He was the same attorney representing Wisdom, who was going through a divorce of his own.

Let me tell you, divorcing a woman who's pregnant and who's got her lawyer saying her husband abandoned his pregnant wife with no money or any form of support whatsoever (which was NOT true) isn't a good look for anyone. That's what I faced in that courtroom. Add to it, Tamara would show up with the rattiest, most country looking dress she could find to make it look even more terrible. Oh, did I mention the discovery judge determining my pre-alimony was the woman who actually had served as Wisdom's wife's lawyer in their divorce proceeding? So she had heard about our drama through her client and probably shouldn't have even been on our case. It didn't take long before I knew this wasn't going to turn out well.

Showing up for a few court appearances is really the only time I saw Tamara during her pregnancy. Near the end, we didn't go through the proceedings as much because she was having difficulties and was pretty much bedridden, but I have to give her props and will always thank her for something she did. Even though we were going through our drama, she decided she wanted me to be in the delivery room for the birth.

She was way past her due date, so they had to schedule a C-section. So it wasn't like there was a mad dash to the hospital because her water had broken. In fact, I remember picking her up from our old place and I was nervous as hell. How was she going to react to me? Some of her family was there, including her mom, so what kind of evil side-eyes would I get? When she opened the door, it was like I was seeing Tamara for the first time. She was big but she was absolutely beautiful. At that time, I have to admit, my mind crept into "what if" mode.

They set it out for us at Vanderbilt Hospital. I still don't know how or why we got such special treatment, but Tamara didn't just have a room, she had a suite. It was gorgeous, but it was also perfect for the perfect baby. On August 3rd, 1999, Ashlee Taylor Hill was born. At that time, it was the greatest moment of my life. Regardless of what was happening in my world with the divorce and some of the uncertainty, I was happy and proud. I was a father and for some reason, at that very moment, I felt like my life was starting to change.

Things started getting better for me and Tamara. It was far from good, but at least it wasn't as terrible as it had been. I spent time with Ashlee, even spending the night in my old place from time to time, but we were still going through with the divorce. I believe we had just gone too far to turn back.

A few months after Ashlee was born, we had our final appearance of dissolution for the marriage, and Tamara brought our newborn into the courtroom. I wasn't too happy about that, but what could I do? Seeing my newborn baby girl in that courtroom, actually looking happy, oblivious to any of the sadness or drama that was going on, will always stick with me. Maybe it's what I needed to see. In this sense, I know it's how I want it to be now. That no matter what type of strife is happening in my world, my child is shielded from it and happy.

The settlement didn't go well at all for me, but I didn't care. For everything I put Tamara through, I would've given her anything she wanted at that time. Looking back, she deserved it and more. As sad as she looked in front of the judge, I even had to chuckle when I saw her high-fiving and laughing with her friends outside of the courtroom right after.

Not long after the divorce, Tamara and Ashlee moved to Maryland while I was still in Nashville. I didn't get a chance to bond with my child like I should have. I missed out on that time and it was my fault. Tamara moved to pursue the dreams that she had put on hold and to better her life for her and our child. She did just that, and I'm super proud of her.

Look, I ain't going to lie to y'all. Around this time in my life, I was still very much an idiot. I still had many problems—or as women like to say, "Mike was a mess." I was becoming closer to Camille, and we were seeing more and more of each other, despite the distance, and work was going great, but something was seriously missing in my life. Looking back on it, I know what was missing was God. I mean, I was going to church EVERY NOW AND THEN, and I believed in God; I just wasn't walking in His path. Sometimes you need a jolt from Him in order to get there. It would happen over the next few years of my life.

Chapter 11

REMOTE BROADCAST

THE TENNESSEE TITANS had a great year in the '99-2000 season, and I got to cover Super Bowl XXXIV *(that's 34 for the ones not into Roman numerals)*. Many will remember it was a great experience and tremendous game. The Titans were playing the Rams, and it came down to the final seconds. I was in the stands most of the game, but on the final possession, when Tennessee was down seven and driving for a touchdown that could tie the game, I along with about 25 other members of the media had to watch it on a 25-inch television. We were trying to get to the field to do interviews, but security wouldn't let any media on the field until the game was over, so we were stuck in the bowels of the Georgia Dome huddled around this television (and remember, HD was out but not prominent back then) watching as the Titans came up one yard short. I, along with all those members of the media, was literally about 50 yards from the actual action and could hear the screams from the stands but was forced to watch it on the tube.

I did experience the locker room reaction in person. Damn, it felt like a funeral, and I felt terrible for those guys. I had covered the team since they moved to Nashville from Houston and watched them build the franchise into a well-respected team. I had become cool with some of the players and to see their hurt, I couldn't help but feel some of their pain too.

Because of the success of the teams I had been covering in Nashville, first the Tennessee football team the year before and now the Titans, I had one hell of a resume tape put together. Even though I thoroughly enjoyed my time in Nashville, something was telling me it was time to move on.

ESPN wanted me to fly up for an audition. Remember, I was never too keen on going to ESPN, even though many people said I was destined to be there, and the network had firmly established itself as the, well, worldwide leader in sports. However, once you hear that they want you to audition, you almost feel like you have to go. *Let me keep it all the way 100. After totally convincing myself that I didn't want to go there, I actually got super excited that they wanted me to audition. There, I said the shit.*

Before I left, Kris, my agent, gave me a heads-up about their talent guy, Al Jaffe. Anyone in the sports world knows about Al. He's legendary and brought in some of the best known sportscasters ESPN has ever hired, from Dan Patrick to Stu Scott to Kenny Mayne. People also know that Al is cross-eyed. I'm not saying this to make fun of that, but Kris' only advice to me was to not look him in his eyes, but stare at his nose. It's actually good advice but wasn't going to be enough to get me the job.

I did the audition, and knowing what I know now, I tried too hard. At the time, ESPN was full of sportscasters who were known for their "catch phrases." Stu's "cooler than the other side of the pillow." Dan Patrick's "You can't stop him, you can only hope to contain him" or his "En Fuego," etc. Even though I had become known for a few catch phrases myself *(I'll always contend that I was saying "Boo ya" before Stu, he just made it popular because of his national audience)*, I think I put a catch phrase in EVERY single highlight I did during that audition. I emptied the bag!!

Once again, knowing what I know now, I tried too hard, but at that time, I thought I had crushed that audition because my personality and ALL my catch phrases were on display for their choosing. *Such a silly little novice sportscaster.* Despite accidentally ripping my pants (embarrassing), I had a good lunch with Al at this Mexican spot and met some of the senior coordinating producers, including this guy named Mark Gross. Mark, at the time, was in charge of the network's college football coverage. He found out about my military background and we had a great conversation about how much he enjoyed his time on the road doing this show called College Game Day at WestPoint. After my great audition (I thought) and the outstanding conversations I'd had with the executives, I knew it was just a matter of time before I would be getting that offer. Well, it was a matter of time. Just not THIS time.

So I got back to Nashville and I was waiting to hear about something I just knew was happening. Long gone are those days of frustration. Seventy-four tapes for one job?? Shit!!! I'm Mike Hill. Local sportscaster but known across the nation by a few important people. I had just auditioned for a national TV gig. People in Nashville knew about this, including my peers in the press, so show me some respect, right? That's how I was thinking. Walking around with my head high and chest out. Now, there's nothing wrong with believing in yourself, but there's a fine line in quietly and modestly believing you're the shit and acting like a piece of it.

I became way more vocal. I was always outspoken, but now the cockiness was making me feel like I had to inject my opinion into every conversation. One day, I was in on a conversation at a Titans mini camp and I was giving my "hot takes" long before they were a trend. I can't remember exactly what I was harping on, but this guy Paul Kuharsky, a Titans beat reporter for a local paper, chimed in and tried his best to discredit me. *For the record, I'm not big on disrespect and even though I was cocky as shit, I've never been one to put others down or make them feel beneath me. It's something I cannot stand when someone does it, and I will not tolerate it.* Paul was also a guy I didn't really care for that much and I KNEW he didn't care for me. Our energy was just never on the same page back then. Even though we'd had disagreements before, this time I had enough of what I believed to be his elitist, entitled ways and sternly said, "Dude, why are you always in my Kool Aid and don't know the flavor?"

Of course, this wasn't an original phrase. In fact, it's a very well-known phrase in urban lexicon. Basically in my case, I was saying why are you always butting into my business, trying to dispute me when you don't know a damn thing about me? The other media guys who were around absolutely lost it. They thought it was the wildest shit ever and still, to this day, almost 20 years later, will still bring it up.

Here's what they didn't know. I was so pissed and pushed to the limit by someone I believed was just a troll that I was going to put my hands on Paul that day. However, God was looking out when I wasn't going to look out for myself. He sent me angels in the form of those other guys laughing because if they hadn't, I probably would've stepped to Paul in that violent manner. I was on edge that day, but of course, had I done that, I could've lost my job at Channel 2, which I had almost done before because of my temper, and I could've destroyed the blessings that were about to come my way.

That same day, while at that same practice, I received a phone call from Kris, my agent. She said she had good news. I had a job offer. Awesome, ESPN had finally come to its senses and they were ready to make me their next big star. Uh, not quite yet. This offer was in New York. Remember when I had a general meeting with Mike McCarthy of MSG that got cut short because of the big blockbuster Mike Piazza trade? Well, even though it was short, it paid off because Fox was starting a string of regional sports reports across the nation and one of those was in New York. MSG network would run it. Mike was in charge of it, and he wanted me to be one of the anchors. I was thrilled. Even though it wasn't a national gig, it was a top 10 city and my birthplace, so I was going home.

This opportunity would be the start of a pattern in my career. I'd be waiting for one thing to happen, but God would come along with something else out of nowhere that would lead me down a better path. *You'll see what I mean as the book continues. Keep reading, it gets better.* I didn't even know Fox was starting a string of regional networks and this happened. I didn't even care about ESPN anymore. Well, later on I found out ESPN (or at least Al Jaffe) didn't care that much about me either. It didn't matter. I didn't want to go there in the first place, right?? I was going home, and I was making over six figures (barely) for the first time in my career.

The next few weeks were pretty wild. I still had time on my contract with WKRN, but I had a top 10 or network out clause, so I was good going to New York. However, as was the case too many times in my life, I didn't want to do something alone.

Total transparency: for many years, I've been that person who never wanted to feel lonely. I love company. That's why it was rare for me to just sit in the house and a bigger reason why I was a serial dater. I always had to have some sort of companionship, especially if I didn't have my home-boys nearby to kick it with. And even though I had family in New York, at the time I didn't know a lot of single people there I could hang with that were doing the things I enjoyed doing. So I needed to change that.

Camille and I had become super close and were dating pretty solidly by then, even though she was in Baltimore and I was in Nashville. Yes, there were a few hiccups and insecurities brought on because of my questionable behavior, but I never gave her any reason or proof for her not to think I was a good dude. I was, but once again, I was far from perfect. I cared for her too. In fact, I knew I loved Camille for reasons I won't reveal here in this book. She was, and still is, smart, classy, very pretty and at the time seemed locked into me. She was my girl and with my career budding, I figured I needed this type of arm candy.

I told Camille I was moving to New York and asked her, "So are you going to move with me?"

Her reply was, "If you want me to move with you, you know what you need to do."

I, of course, knew what she meant and said, "Okay, let's just do." That's it. No getting down on one knee, horse and carriage ride through the park. No magical moment of romance. Once again, I was proposing marriage to a woman without a really strong proposal. In this case, not one at all.

Once again, here I was about to jump into something I really wasn't prepared for. First the marriage to Tamara and now this one. It's not that I didn't care for either, I just was not ready to be a married man and all that entails. However, two weeks later, I was at the altar. No big ceremony. We went to the justice of the peace in Maryland. Camille's mom and brother did come up from the Caribbean for the "event," but outside of them it was her friend Tiffany, who actually introduced us, and my boy J.R. serving as witnesses. I hadn't even gotten her a ring. In fact, Camille went and purchased two wedding bands herself. *Damn, how did I get away with some of my bullshit? Because my shit was NOT together.*

However, early on, marriage this time around was great. She and I got an overly priced but nice apartment in these twin tower like apartments in Hackensack, New Jersey. *Anyone familiar with Hackensack knows exactly the complex I'm talking about.* Camille was working at her job as a contract manager at a construction site, and for the first time in a long time, I was hardly struggling financially. In fact, we were actually kind of thriving.

Working at Fox Sports in New York, however, was not the utopia I thought it would be. I worked on a show called The New York Sports Report, and even though we were supposed to cover all the local teams, it's hard to do so when you don't have the resources. It was a lady named Sam Ryan, Bob Wischussen, Steve Cangialosi, and me working as the anchors, and while Steve and I had to also report during the week, there would be many times we actually couldn't because we didn't have a photographer to do so. The reason is we had to share resources with MSG, and since they had first priority, we got the leftovers, which usually meant less than scraps.

Our studio was as big as someone's dining room, but it was huge compared to the sports office the four of us plus three other producers had to share. They could only fit five desks inside the office, so the anchors actually had to share a desk.

The good thing about working there were the people. Not just the anchors, but the producers as well. One of them, Quentin Carter, is still a very good friend of mine, and I'm still very cordial with the other anchors, who've all gone on to do great things.

Another good thing about working there was we actually worked inside Madison Square Garden, so I got a chance to see and cover some great events. Knicks games, including Patrick Ewing's first game back after leaving the team. I was working the night Michael Jackson taped his 30th anniversary special and yes, I cringed when I saw how skinny and gaunt Whitney Houston had gotten. And I remember the Bernard Hopkins fight against Tito Trinidad. It was a lopsided fight, but what I remembered most about that night were all the Puerto Ricans who were there that looked like they wanted to whoop someone else's ass because their guy was getting his ass whooped. Since the guy whooping his ass was black, I recall not overly cheering for Hopkins. *Yeah, I was scared, but I made it out that night, so what?*

Even though I didn't get to work in New York long (tell you why in a second), besides covering my favorite football and basketball team, the Giants and Knicks, I got to fulfill a promise I made to my Grandmother Lillian a long time ago when I was a kid. As I told you earlier in the book, she literally lived right across from Yankee Stadium and I told her that one day, as I looked out her window, that I'd play inside that stadium. At the time I meant as a ball player, but since that didn't work out, working as a reporter there was the next best thing.

Covering a team I grew up rooting for and absolutely idolized was incredible. It was during some great years for the team, right at the end of their run of four titles in five years and three straight. That team had future Hall of Famers Derek Jeter and Mariano Rivera on it, along with Jorge Posada, Bernie Williams, Andy Pettite, Roger Clemens, David Justice, and Paul O'Neil.

Not in my wildest dreams that when I was losing my mind watching the Yankees win their 24th title back in '96 in a sports office in Fresno did I think that I would actually be in the stadium covering the team while it attempted to win its 27th. However, there I was, at game one watching Clemens throw a piece of a sawed-off bat at Mike Piazza, saying later he thought it was the ball. *My thing is, even if you thought it was the ball, why would you throw it at Piazza and not first base?? Bogus excuse, but I love Clemens to this day and he always shows love back.*

However, covering that World Series gave me the opportunity to meet the player I grew up putting on a pedestal.

Simply idolized. Reggie Jackson. I've had the pleasure of meeting all of my idols with the exception of Muhammad Ali in my career, but this was my first encounter with one, and it turned out to be a little strange. I was at Shea Stadium for game 3 or 4 and we were about to do our pregame show. One of the guys we were interviewing for that show? Mr. October himself. When I found out about this, I was elated. I had to talk to him beforehand, and *Please, God, don't let me sound like a bumbling idiot.*

I saw him, and of course, I was nervous, but I was still a little cocky piece of shit back then. However, anyone who knows anything about Reggie knows that he invented the word cocky. The man can't say humble. So when I walked up to him I said, in such a gleeful, innocent, childlike way, "Hey, Reggie, I'm Mike Hill, and I work at Fox Sports Net. We're going to interview you shortly, but I have to tell you, man, you were my favorite baseball player of all time growing up so it's such a great pleasure to meet you."

Reggie didn't extend his hand to shake it. He didn't say, "Aww, thank you, my man." Nope!! Reggie told me, "Hey, I know it's YOUR pleasure to meet ME," and started laughing. It wasn't said in a mean way, but it was said in a way that let you know he really did mean what he'd just said. I was a bit crushed and that Kool Aid smile I had on my face dimmed a little, but hey, I'd just had the pleasure of being semi-dissed by one of the greatest players of all time.

As for the series itself, even though it was an all New York series between the Mets and Yankees, and I was supposed to be impartial, that was pretty much impossible for me. The viewers and people at MSG/Fox knew I bled Yankee pinstripes. So when Mike Piazza flew out to Bernie Williams in game 5 to end it, it was like someone had placed me in outer space because I felt like I was literally floating. It was exhilarating and even more special getting to go down on the field while the team enjoyed it at old Shea Stadium. However, that wasn't the most breathtaking moment.

That came a few days later during the parade down the Canyon of Heroes, and since MSG was the official station of the Yankees at that time, I was one of the reporters who got to cover it. However, not just cover it from the stands or crowd. I got to ride on one of the floats WITH the team as millions of people looked on. It was the wildest experience of my life. So many people making so much noise that if someone was standing next to you and screaming in your ear, you could barely hear them. That, with paper streamers going everywhere and all the different faces, made it both exciting and frightening.

There were times when I'd get a little paranoid thinking, "The cops can't control or check all these people. What if there's a sniper or someone just starts shooting? Then what?" I know it sounds crazy, but I can't lie that it didn't cross my mind. There was one moment where I thought I had been shot.

I was on the float with the pitchers and catchers and after I did a few interviews with the guys, I decided to do my stand-up. This is where the reporter says a few words taped into the camera to either open, bridge or close his report. Remember, I could barely hear myself speak, and I was a little paranoid, so while I was in the middle of doing this standup, all of a sudden I felt something hit me really hard on my shoulder. I was startled a little, but luckily I didn't stop talking or miss a beat because it became one of the best stand-up moments of my young career. What I felt on my shoulder was Roger Clemens placing his young son on my shoulders as I was speaking, and his foot accidentally kicked me as he was putting him up there. The take was good, and it was one of the top moments people were talking about from our parade coverage. It was also good for my resume reel.

Working in New York gave me a lot of exposure, but I'll admit the working conditions at MSG brought my ego down just slightly. It had become very apparent that I wasn't one of the main priorities. In fact, Bob Wischusen, who could be a little pompous back then, basically told me I really wasn't even supposed to be there. They'd wanted to hire Curt Menefee, a local Fox anchor at the time, who of course has gone on to national prominence. For some reason they couldn't get him or work out some contract matters, so I was a last-second replacement. I was admittedly a little taken aback and hurt hearing that. First of all, why did he feel the need to share that with me? Had I been acting too cocky? Was he just being an asshole or a combo of both? I was getting a taste of feeling like I was just a number and not anyone special in this business. Unfortunately, it wouldn't be the last time I felt that way.

That feeling had nothing on the feeling I got when I got a phone call from Tamara early one morning while I was on my way to work. She was in tears and told me that Ashlee had severely burned herself. My baby was two years old. "What do you mean she burned herself? How is that possible?" Tamara told me that Ashlee had pulled a pot of boiling water down on herself in the kitchen. *Oh my God it hurts me even thinking about it now*. She suffered third degree burns on her shoulder, arms and legs, and needed skin graft surgery.

I picked up my mom and rushed down to Maryland immediately. When I walked into her hospital room, Ashlee saw me, smiled, and said, "Hi, Daddy." Despite everything that had happened between me and her mom, Ashlee always knew her daddy, even if I wasn't the best father early on. Because of that, I was overridden with guilt and second-guesses. How could I have prevented this? If I hadn't divorced Tamara, there would have been another set of eyes to help out and maybe this wouldn't have happened. Now in NO WAY is Tamara to blame for this. What happened was a freak accident. I can only imagine what it was like being a single mom of a two-year-old while holding down a job and going to school. I'm just saying had I been there for her, maybe this wouldn't have happened. Of course, that just wasn't God's will at that time, so I had to face reality. My little girl needed me to be strong for her. It was almost impossible.

The night before her surgery, I cried like a baby when she fell asleep. My mom tried to tell me to be strong, but I was really hurting knowing my daughter was in pain. To her credit, Ashlee was much stronger, and her smile and strength actually helped me through it. The only time I saw her cry was after her surgery, which was a success, when it was time for a bath. The nurse, who was just doing his job, didn't have the best bedside manner, so while he was scrubbing her and she was crying, I wanted to kill him and hug her at the same time.

She's still got the vestiges of her surgery today, but as far as I could tell, she's never lacked confidence because of them. She's a beautiful soul, strong and smart, and I'm so proud of who she's become.

Okay, now I know you've been asking yourself, what's up with the president of the creep squad? It's been a long read and we haven't heard about one single act of inappropriateness while you've been married this second time. I know you didn't just go cold turkey? Well, yes and no. I was still flirting my tail off, but not as often, and I really didn't want to follow through on anything, to be honest. I'm not saying I was cured from my "addiction," but first of all, the right opportunities never presented themselves, and Camille was VIGILANT when it came to cheating. She was a hawk, and she let you know about it.

Once, before marriage and during our long-distance relationship, she tried to call me about 4 am in the morning and she couldn't reach me. Now, we had spoken earlier that night around 11 pm and I said I was going to bed so she would think I was in for the night. This was before cell phones were prominent, so she called my house phone trying to reach me...A LOT. I wasn't home, but when I got back in, I looked down at the caller I.D and saw I had about 7-8 missed calls in a span of an hour. The light was on, indicating I had a message or in this case, MESSAGES waiting, and guess what, the phone was now ringing again. I answered with, "Hello," and immediately Camille, thinking the worst, went in, "Who's the BITCH...Who's the BITCH???"

I was like "What??" Now I was worried. Did she have a camera in here? Nope. Even if she had, I wasn't doing anything in there. What was she talking about? Regardless, I knew she was pissed, so I asked her why she was tripping. She went on about her calling so early in the morning because (a) she had to get up early for some event, and (b) her gut was telling her something was wrong from a thousand miles away. Damn, I knew she was from the islands, but I didn't know I was dating that psychic Ms. Cleo. I had to go into quick react mode. *This was critical thinking in the rule book of a player.* "Baby, I just got in from the hospital. I had an asthma attack. My inhaler wasn't working so I needed to go to Emergency for a treatment." Yup, that should take care of it. Plus she was about to feel all guilty and show some compassion for my health, right? Shiiiiiiiiit!!!

"I don't fucking believe you," she says. Now, when react mode doesn't work, you have to take it to the next level in the player handbook. False indignant mode. So I go, "You want me to f***ing prove it? I can hardly f***ing breathe still. I had to drive myself to the hospital. I just got back, and I've got to deal with THIS shit? This is unbelievable. I can't believe you're even acting like this. So what you want me to do? You want me to send you the hospital paperwork to prove to you where I've been?"

Her reply: "Yup, I want to see 'em. I have to get ready for this event, but I want to see that proof today."

At this time, I really loved Camille and didn't want to lose her, so I had to get her that proof. So, even though I was tired as hell, I actually went to the emergency room and faked an asthma attack. *They don't give a damn really. As long as you've got good insurance, they'll give you a treatment. It's pretty harmless.* I was thinking, *Okay, I've got the proof I need. Travesty avoided.* Big problem: not only was the date on that paperwork, but so was the time I checked in, and knowing the Caribbean Nancy Drew like I did, she'd certainly notice that. I was screwed.

Later that day, I talked to Camille and she still wanted that proof. I told her I would fax it (yes, this was before scanners and electronic stuff), but I also said that this was going to affect our relationship going forward. Yes, I was still pushing the lie. I continued, "We have a long-distance relationship and if you can't trust me, this will never work. So if I send this, I know you don't and won't trust me." She still wanted it. I faxed it, but I altered the time with a pen. In a fax transmission, some things come out distorted anyway, so I was hoping she would just think it was a distortion. It either worked or she may have given me props for going through all the trouble of actually going to the hospital because apparently it was enough. She didn't trip anymore. At least on that occasion.

> *I bet you want to know where I really was, huh? Maybe I'll answer this as part of a Q&A after the book comes out if someone brings it up.*

So you get the point about cheating when it came to Camille. She knew about some of my past improprieties. I've always been someone that never hid from his past. She said she didn't care about what I did in the past, but that wasn't going down with her. She even told me once that I could beat her ass and she'd get over that faster than me cheating. Now, of course, I know that was just her making a point, and I never would put my hands on a lady anyway, but she was adamant about that one rule. I knew if I ever was caught, we were done, and since I was already a one-time divorcee, I think it was a mental deterrent against any bad behavior on my part.

Not getting it anywhere else meant I wanted it all the time at home. I had a large sexual appetite and one person had to fill it. Many times I'd be left on empty. After about six months into our marriage, I began hearing, "Can I get a rain check?" when I would try to be intimate and she never initiated anything. Still, I was being good. However, I will admit, a lot of that had to do with chance and opportunity and not just Camille's one big deal-breaker.

However, when we decided to have a child, she would initiate sex. A LOT. So much that I actually used to say, "Do we have to now?" which she would turn into, "I thought you always wanted it? What's wrong now?"

I did it when it was natural. When the urge would hit. Even though making a baby is an extremely beautiful thing, for me at this time it just felt like work. As soon as I got home, "Get naked." As soon as we woke up, "Get it up." We trying to make a baby or a three-story, five-bedroom house? Because both feel about the same and require the same amount of work, it seems. It felt like a job, but fortunately what or who we created was another blessing in my life.

Chapter 12

RAMP

CAMILLE FINALLY GOT pregnant and we found out in April of 2001. Right after she got pregnant, it was like she got the juice she needed from me and I swear, we may have had sex two times during her pregnancy. The initiating was gone, and yep, I was starting to miss the days when we were trying. Hell, I need some work, Camille. Can you give a brother a job?? Nope. Okay. To be fair, some of the reason why there wasn't a lot of action was because Camille had a pregnancy scare. Since I had gone through a prior miscarriage with Tamara, I was a bit more prepared if the worst happened, but Camille was about four months at the time and her blood work came back abnormal. They had to perform an amniocentesis, which is a very dangerous procedure where they draw blood from the fetus. The procedure alone could've led to a miscarriage. Thank God it didn't, and fears of an unhealthy child were also put to rest when the results came back.

Since we were about to expand this family, it was time to get more room, so Camille and I went out to look for a house. I was excited because it was our first ever home purchase, but that excitement soon dimmed when I realized how much you had to pay for so little in return in the New York/New Jersey area. We soon settled on a nice yet modest home in Bloomfield, and since Camille was pretty much an interior decorator, we knew the inside of the home would be incredible, which it was for the most part.

However, in the process of getting the new home ready and still living in the apartment was one of the worst days in my life and of course, the history of this country.

I was still asleep when I was awakened by a phone call from my mom a little bit before 9 am. She asked me if I was home in Jersey or in the city. I was scheduled to work in the city but not 'til later that day. She then told me to turn on the news and I did. I saw smoke coming out of one of the World Trade Centers but at the time, I didn't think much of it. They were reporting that a plane had crashed into the building, but I thought maybe it was just a little prop plane that made one wrong turn somewhere. My mindset was, that sucks, but I wasn't overly concerned. Terrorism never crossed my mind at that time, so why should I be concerned? I was sorry for whoever had lost their lives, but honestly, I went back to sleep to get more rest before I had to get up for work. The TV was still on and maybe because of the sound, I woke up and as soon as I did, "boom" the second plane hit the south tower. All of sudden, that's when I realized, shit is real. America, the country I had fought for, was under attack.

I was glued to the coverage. How could this be happening? Who was behind this terrible act? I, of course, served for six years to protect this nation and this was going on? I needed answers. They weren't letting anyone in or out of the city. Luckily, Camille, who was six months pregnant, was in New Jersey working that day so she could get home, but after President Bush came on and pretty much confirmed it was terrorism, my mood went from sadness to anger. I wanted to put the uniform back on and not just wear it, I wanted to fight and even die if I had to to repay the sons of bitches who had done this.

Ironically, I lived in an apartment community known as the Twin Towers in Hackensack. I recall going to the top of my building and even though I couldn't see a lot, from where I stood, I could actually see the fire and smoke billowing as those buildings burned. Like I said, I was enraged. Then, when I went back to my apartment to continue watching the news, my anger went to complete shock and near depression as I watched those buildings actually fall to the earth. I felt my heart sink like a brick to the bottom of the ocean. I wanted to throw up and as I sat there by myself, I began to cry uncontrollably. I knew that the death toll would be astronomical.

I cried like that again when we killed that son of a bitch, Osama Bin Laden, nearly 10 years later. However, I have to say, that night and the days after 9/11 were the only times in my lifetime that I've ever felt like this country lived up to its name as the UNITED States of America. We all came together when forces came against us. Blacks, whites, Latinos, straight, gay, men, women seemed to bond together in that aftermath. Everyone was thanking law enforcement and the cops seemed to honor everyone too. It was love and most importantly, respect.

Of course, I didn't like that people ostracized and feared every Muslim after that and in a lot of ways still do. Racism and bigotry is something I can't stand and something I will always fight against as long as I have breath in my body. Maybe I'm just dense, but I don't understand why everyone doesn't feel that way and I don't understand why it takes a horrific act like 9/11 for us to realize we're all part of the human race.

The weeks after, when things had settled down a bit, everyone tried to go back to living a normal life, but I can't lie, New York changed for me after that. I had always felt like the city would always be my home, but when I looked at that skyline, especially when you see it from New Jersey as you're about to go into the Lincoln Tunnel (if you've been in that spot, you know what I mean), I just felt there was something missing. There was a huge void. The Empire State Building and Chrysler Buildings have always been great to look at, but that skyline just isn't complete without those towers. When I saw those towers, I knew I was home. I know they have the Freedom Tower in their place now, but it's not the same. Those towers could never be replaced, in my opinion.

Once again, everyone tried to go back to normal, but in a lot of ways, the terrorists had accomplished their mission. Not necessarily just the fear part, but the economic impact it would have. Something that actually would affect me too. Because just a few months after 9/11, many of the Fox regional networks had to shut down operations, including the one I worked for in New York. I heard rumors a day leading up to it. *Colleagues, other media members, and everyone knows about these things except you. In fact, you're usually the last one to find out your fate in this business.*

Mike McCarthy gathered all of us in that tiny sports office at MSG and delivered our fate. We were pretty much going out of business. Our final show was in just a few weeks. He then brought us into his office one by one and told Bob and Steve he was keeping them on at MSG in some capacity. As for me and Sam? Well, here's your separation package. We appreciate you, but we don't really have anything for you, even though we're still going to need you to work here this final month, until the last show.

Mike didn't mean any harm. He was a good guy, and I'd still do anything for him today. However, even though I was now unemployed for the first time in my broadcasting career that started in '97, I was actually excited about what my next job was going to be. I had just hired a new agent at IMG and had them call up ESPN and Al Jaffe immediately. Of course, I still didn't know at that time that Al didn't care for me or my numerous catch phrases. That wouldn't come 'til later.

So the job search was on, and I was still living life. I had savings. I had gotten a severance package of about four months. We'd moved into our new/old home in Bloomfield, New Jersey—but oh wait, I also had a wife who was now ready to deliver.

December 30th, 2001, our baby girl was past due and so we were scheduled to go and get her out with a C-section. I was ready for her. Plus, I was pretty happy she was going to be delivered before the new year, meaning I could claim her on my taxes. *I'm just keeping it real. Anyone that tells you that wouldn't matter SOME is sort of lying.* However, before her appointment, Camille woke me up in the middle of the night with a big smack across my head.

She was wearing these braces at the time because she's got carpal tunnel syndrome, so that shit hurt. Now, had I been up to no good during that time, I would've thought that I was in deep shit because she had found out something. Well, happy to say, that wasn't the case. She was just in labor.

Nineteen hours' worth of labor. That night, Kayla Noelle Hill came into the world, and as she did, I saw things in the delivery room that would make an ordinary man lose his appetite for weeks. However, I saw this precious angel with a head full of hair emerge from all that other shit...including literal shit. Childbirth ain't clean, but it's one of the two best things I've ever experienced in my life. Of course, the other happened when her sister was born.

At home I got this new bundle of joy, but now I also had this bundle of nerves. Camille's mom stayed with us for awhile after Kayla was born, so that was a huge help, but now I was done with Fox Sports New York and I was losing my mind. It was a hard pass from ESPN, who told my agent, "We already saw him and we're not interested now," and there were several openings at local stations in New York that I didn't even get an interview for. Suddenly, Mr. Hot Shit was cold as ice and it started affecting me. Why didn't anyone want to hire me? It had been months now and suddenly my savings account was dwindling. I was far from broke, but I had started collecting unemployment, and I was worried as hell. Also, because of my situation, it meant Camille had to go back to work just a month after giving birth. Every day that phone didn't ring from my agent felt like a piece of hot coal being placed in my chest. I was staying up late with Kayla, who WAS NOT a night baby, while Camille slept because she had to work mornings, and her mom would watch her during the day. I never left the house and found myself playing Playstation all the time in my TV room. I was absolutely losing my mind.

Of course, I did what a lot of people in my situation do. I really turned to God. *Oh yeah, that's what happens when things go bad, huh? "Lord, I know I ain't been the best Christian, but if you do me THIS solid, I'll be good from here on. Please God, hook a brother up."* Camille's mom was a beautiful, spiritual lady who read the Bible all the time and talked to me. She told me I just needed the faith of a mustard seed and it would all work out. I tried. I prayed a lot and tried to have faith, but I'll admit my faith was shaken pretty terribly during this time. Yes, there was a wee bit of concern when I left the military and was unemployed for two hours. This was going on three months.

Yes, I had IMG working for me, but I've always felt like no one can help you like you help yourself. So I started sending out emails to potential employers and heard absolutely nothing back, for the most part. Then I found out there was an opening for a weekend sports anchor/reporter gig at WFAA-TV Channel 8 in Dallas, Texas. This was a station I was actually pretty familiar with because Tamara's uncle Michael had once been a reporter there back in the late '80s. It was a powerhouse in the Dallas/Fort Worth area, and I felt like this would be a great opportunity for me, if I could land it. So how did I do it? Well, what I did was write one of the greatest kiss-ass emails in the history of mankind. I reached out to their legendary sports director Dale Hanson and told him how much I admired the fact that he had been so prominent in that area for so long and that I'd love the opportunity to work under and learn from someone of his caliber. Can an email like that be a blessing and a curse at the same time? In this case, it was. *More on why later.*

Dale actually responded to the email and told me to send him a tape. I had Sue Lipton, my agent, get right on it, and I waited to hear something.

Meanwhile, I had decided not to just sit around and play Playstation all day when I wasn't taking care of Kayla. One of the reasons I decided to go into TV broadcasting was because I really wanted to be an actor. I don't know what it is, but I've always felt like it's something I've just been able to do naturally. No disrespect to those who've mastered this craft, I just feel like I was born to do it. The only reason I just settled into broadcasting was because I felt like it would help me get some TV time and it was a bit more stable. However, I had just witnessed Halle Berry and Denzel Washington win the academy awards for Best Actress and Actor and got inspired to go for it. Besides, with all this free time on my hands now, it was the perfect time to try.

I called around to a few actors' workshops in New Jersey, but the one that really caught my eye was this theatre in Newark. I went out and met with the director, who encouraged me to read for a few things. Bam! I got this small part. Boom! I was working on this small project. Then POW! I was auditioning and actually getting one of the lead roles in one of their major productions called Ms. Ever's Boys.

I worked with a great cast and I enjoyed every part of it. From rehearsals to the four-week run we had at that theater. A local newspaper did a review of the play and said, "Newcomer Mike Hill was effective as Caleb." Hell, it wasn't a dazzling review, but I'd take it. Halfway through our run, the director of the theater pulled me aside and told me how proud he was of me. He knew my background. Knew I had never really acted before but told me that after just a few weeks, I had morphed into my character. I had some validation that I could actually do this.

I got more good news soon after I got my part. I got a call from Dale saying they wanted me to fly down for an interview. I was geeked. I was getting some movement. An opportunity. Getting back into the game, it appeared.

I was picked up from my hotel room by this guy named Jose Gant. Jose was a good guy. Religious. Had been there for years, starting as a photographer but now working as the pseudo sports director under Dale. He introduced me to some of the other crew there, including George Riba, one of the nicest guys you'll ever meet. Gina, who had just been hired herself as a sports reporter/fill in anchor. Arnold Payne, who without question is the best photographer I've ever worked with. Another photog named Sal and their three producers, Sean Hamilton, Carl Billick, and Jeff Collette. *Many of these names are important because of the effect they would later have on me. Stay tuned.*

Dale wasn't getting in until later, so Jose and I went to lunch downtown and I had a rare fan boy moment. As we were going into the restaurant, I saw Michael Irving, who used to be a star wide receiver for the Cowboys and future hall of famer, but he wasn't who I flipped out over. Sure, I was thrilled to see The Playmaker, but I was more excited to meet the guy he was walking with. Evangelist TD Jakes!!! His sermons had helped me through some dark times the past few months leading up to this moment, so I was super excited to meet him. I walked up to him with a huge smile and honestly, he looked a little carried aback when I did, but he spoke and shook my hand.

It felt like a sign from above when I saw him. I just knew this job was mine.

The entire sports crew, including Dale, went to the Palm for my "interview" dinner, and it was interesting. Dale didn't say or ask much, but Sean seemed to be doing most of the talking. He was telling me about this guy named Newy Scruggs, who was new to the market, and from the conversation, I could tell they were a little concerned with the dent and impact he was making. Sean mostly, but Dale would chime in about how they needed someone with personality who could "relate" to the players in the locker room. Well, I knew that wouldn't be a problem, but of course, hindsight being 20/20, I'm pretty sure I know what they meant by relate to the players since the majority of them, especially The Cowboys, were black. Oh, by the way, so is Newy!! Still, if that was really the case, that went right over my head. In fact, I was so desperate for a job, they might have been able to throw a white sheet over my head and I would've said it was cool. *I'm seriously exaggerating, but you get the point, I hope.*

I must have said and done all the right things because a few weeks later, Dale called and offered me the job. He admitted my kiss-ass email was what put me over the top. *Once again, that would come back to haunt me, but it worked at the time.* My agent worked out a decent salary, especially for Dallas. I worked out a start date a little before the 4th of July 2002 and it was now time to say goodbye to New York. Hello Big D!

> *The next two years of my life were a living nightmare.*
> *Okay, I apologize because maybe I bored you with my*
> *life the last few years, but shit is about to get interest-*
> *ing again. So hold on. I'm telling it all.*

We got to Dallas and found a beautiful, just-built four-bedroom house in Frisco, which we paid LESS for than the older house we had in Bloomfield. That house and the price it cost was the best thing I can say about my stay in Dallas. The rest wasn't so great, with a few exceptional people.

Working for Dale was the worst professional experience of my life, that would also become my biggest blessing in the end. It started off okay, but I felt there would be some issues about a month into working for him.

One of my first assignments was to go to San Antonio and cover the Cowboys' training camp for a week. It was hot as hell, but my time down there was pretty cool. It was my first time meeting some of the other media members, who I think are pretty cordial and accepting. At least, I thought so at the time. One of the guys I met was Newy, who I had heard so much about during my interview, and I think I said to him when I first met him, "It's good to actually meet you." Remember, he was the other black sportscaster at the time. I had heard so much about him during my interview process.

When I got back from training camp, I got a phone call at home from Dale. He was acting kind of odd, and he asked me if everything was all right with me. When he first asked, my naïve ass was thinking, "Ah, this is cool. He wants to make sure my transition is going well." WRONG!!! He just had to give me this critique about me being way over the top and how I was trying too hard to stand out. Here's the thing: I get it. You don't want to sock viewers in the mouth when they first see you. And I was a little different from other sportscasters in the market, but wasn't this why you hired me? Didn't you say you wanted that personality and someone the players could relate to? And I was thinking to myself as he was talking, *What's wrong with actually standing out?*

At this point, I was seven years in the business, so I'd had my share of criticism. Hell, I'd had viewers tell me I wasn't good enough to be a shoe salesman, to some even threatening my life.

True story. After Charles Woodson beat out Peyton Manning for the Heisman Trophy, Tennessee Volunteer fans called my station in Nashville and ME in particular saying the reason he lost was because of me and our affiliation with ABC/ESPN, which the fans felt had a bias against Manning that year. As soon as the announcement was over, I got about 200 phone calls from pissed fans, threatening my mom, the kids I didn't even have yet, and one told me not to crank my car that night. It was crazy.

Back to Dale's call. I've dealt with stupid shit like fan criticism for my entire career, but Dale's phone call was a bit different. It felt personal and not like he was trying to help, but hinder or hold me back. Maybe I just took it that way. Still, he was the boss and I was being receptive, but then he said something during that conversation that made me feel a little betrayed. Even hurt. I guess to get his point across, he threw this black newspaper guy way under the bus. The guy was a columnist for the Dallas Morning News at the time and according to Dale, when he spoke to him at the Cowboys' camp, he asked Dale, "Who is this Stuart Scott wannabe clown you just hired?" Okay. Like I said, I can take criticism, but not when you smile in my face and say it behind my back. When I met the paper guy at camp, he was nothing but complimentary about my style and how it was needed in the area, but when he saw Dale, the story changed. This would be a pattern during my tenure. People, for whatever reason, wanting to be in Dale's good graces, would be smiling in my face but shitting on me behind my back. It became Dale's validation.

After that, I admit, I was a little lost and unsure of myself. I had just been out of work for six months, and now after just a month on my new job, my boss wasn't too pleased. I even put up a sign near my desk that read, "Remember the Time," just to remind me of the time I spent looking for a job and to appreciate what I had now. I did appreciate it, but even when Dale found out about the sign's meaning, it was almost like he used it against me.

Work was becoming a disaster and hard to deal with, but I also had to deal with another situation. My stepdad, Richard, had been arrested for murder for hire. Some of you who've been reading this entire time may not be shocked because I told you he admitted to me about carrying out hits on people and when he shot and killed a guy in what the authorities ruled self-defense. Well, this is going to take it to the next level.

After he and my mom's divorce, he really started to spiral out of control. I talked to and saw him as often as possible, but his drinking and even drug use was getting bad. Then he met and married this sweet lady named Mary. She was much younger than him and had two young kids, but she was good for and absolutely loved her some Richard. Like he did for me, he helped raise her kids like they were his own. Mary was into the church and did her best to get him just as involved. Besides, his sister Edna's husband was the pastor of the church they attended. It didn't really work that well, but she tried.

They were together for years, but then his sickness took over his life again. I call it sickness because that's what alcoholism is, and Richard was an alcoholic who, as I've explained before, had a violent past. Mary felt this in several ways. I and others tried to talk to him about the path he was going down again. I even reminded him of him crying when my mom left and said he was f'ing this up too. It didn't work. After trying to work through it and putting up with a lot, Mary finally had enough and left him too.

Looking back, I think that may have been the day Richard's life had come to the point of no return. It got to the point where old friends were calling me, telling me how bad it was.

Admittedly, I was done with it. Now that may sound cold, me giving up on the man who raised me, but remember I had a lot of shit going on too, and besides, I had gotten to the point that I couldn't do or say anything to help him if he wasn't willing to help himself. Maybe I should've tried harder, but I didn't, and the results were fatal.

I got a phone call one day from my mom and she told me something to the effect of, "Michael, Richard had that woman killed!" *What??? Excuse me? What woman? Why?* Despite everything this man had done in the past, I was in shock. Mary had been killed and he was the main suspect.

Oh my God, what happened? *Well, I'm going to tell you, but it still makes me shake my head.*

Besides alcohol, Richard's biggest vice had always been jealousy. The mixture was devastating for whoever was in his life. So after Mary left, he became insanely jealous thinking she was fooling around with someone else. He started sending veiled threats, much like he did with my mom after she said she wasn't coming back. Mary, understandably, was scared and even told people if anything happened to her, that he should be the primary suspect. Unfortunately for her, her greatest fear or intuition did happen.

She had a job working at the church. Remember, this is the church Richard's brother-in-law, Reverend Walker, pastored. So Mary was near the parking lot of the church when a man on a bicycle approached her and shot her in the head. She died right there on the church grounds.

The man eventually got caught and confessed that it was my dad who'd hired him to do it. I'm not exactly sure how much he paid the man, but I heard it was less than $50. *Are you fucking kidding me? That woman lost her life on church grounds, due to some senseless violence that he got paid less than $50?* It wasn't long before my dad was arrested and charged with murder for hire.

In the weeks following, his lawyer reached out to me and told me he was going to try some bogus "alcoholics" excuse. I remember feeling that was bullshit. When I did talk to my dad, I was trying to be as supportive as humanly possible, but it was hard because I knew he was guilty. He was maintaining his innocence and wanted his sister and mom to bail him out, but they knew better. Everyone knew better. Jail was the best place for him. It's where he deserved to be.

I often wonder what more I could've done. I actually feel guilty at times because I asked Mary to stick with him. He'd eventually get it right. Instead he killed her and left two kids without a mom. When I think about them and what he did, I feel terrible, but I also selfishly feel relief. The reason?? That could've easily been my mom.

I didn't go back to Alabama to deal with this. I had my own crazy stuff to deal with. It wasn't getting any better at work. Dale would start having these sessions that he called "Come to Jesus" meetings with me. It was a complaint about this. A complaint about that. Anything he could find to mess with me.

Once, after I did a highlight of a Serena Williams tennis match and she was wearing a catsuit, I made a cat noise or growling sound during the highlight. Right after the show, the GM of the station saw me walking back to the sports office and told me how much she loved my highlight and the Serena Williams catsuit mention. I said, "Thanks, cousin." Just joking around since we had the same last name. I got several emails talking about how much they enjoyed it and the breath of fresh air I brought to the city. Not Dale!! He got ONE letter from a viewer. A letter in which the viewer called me "that black guy you hired," saying how much of a sexist I was for making a sound while talking about Serena's suit. He flipped out. Not about the fact the viewer mentioned my race instead of just saying "new sports guy" but because someone had a problem with my sportscast. It was almost as if I pulled my pants down on air and said, "Serena looking so good in that suit, I wish she would toss MY tennis balls." So the GM of the station could love it, but because that viewer who saw my color didn't you hated it? Got it.

The Come to Jesus meetings seemed to come the more people in the community started liking what I was doing. I'd show him ten emails praising something I did on a sportscast but he'd have one for that same sportscast that was negative and that's all that mattered. He kept telling me, "You've got to relate to Martha in Mesquite. Stop trying to be on ESPN. It's local news." Well, Dale, I've been doing local sports my entire career so far and not just for sports fans. In fact, in Nashville, a local paper called me "the best sportscaster for viewers who don't necessarily care about sports." I knew how to talk to Martha in Mesquite or Paul in Plano.

One thing I noticed about most of the email criticisms from Dale was the viewers that were sending them usually brought up my race in some sort of way. I actually brought this to his attention and he admitted some might not like me because I was black, but that didn't matter. He didn't like it and he was my boss. Which was true and his right, but he also would tell me about his past and the things he did.

He had a reputation in Dallas of actually being a bit of a racist in the black community. Early on (well, I didn't last that long so everything was early), he asked me if I wanted to be a "sportscaster or a black sportscaster"? Huh?? Uh, Dale. I don't know if you've noticed or not, but I'm black. Can I be a sportscaster who happens to be black that's not trying to sound like anyone but himself? He told me who I am wasn't what he saw on my resume reel. But bro, I been the same since Ween Dong Ho, so I know that can't be possible.

He even admitted to me that he was a bit of a bigot, but that was a long time ago. He confessed that he'd used the N-word in the past, but he was young, and besides he had changed. He told me the reason why he knew he wasn't a racist is because he had a black friend who was a judge and he played cards with him, and his daughter had a child by a black guy. Therefore, there was no way he could be racist.

Funny thing is, I don't think he really was. I was the first full-time black sportscaster he had hired in his more than 20 years at the station. I on occasion would greet some people with, "How are you, my brother?" When I say "brother," I mean it like "my sibling" or someone close to me. He took that as if I was calling him black, even though I explained what I meant by it, and got offended. So I think he was ignorant and didn't know how to deal with a black person who wasn't kissing his ass constantly. The irony is, today he's known for these viral video essays that speak up for injustices suffered by blacks, gays etc. I've reached out to him to say thanks, but there was nothing for me to be thankful for back then.

He was also a bully who got away with anything he wanted to and knew he would if he tried it. I'll admit, he was a staple in Dallas.

Meanwhile, being at home was my reprieve. Problem is, I had no social life whatsoever in Dallas. Kayla was still so young that Camille and I didn't go out much. We had good neighbors, though, especially this couple named Bob and Donna, who lived next door. They were older and became like a second mom and dad for me and Camille and would watch Kayla for us every now and then. However, everything I was going through at work could be seen on my face at home and I know that had an effect on Camille, and she was worried. Especially when this black lady named "Barbara," who worked at the station, told Camille that she should talk to me because Dale wasn't happy. And if Dale wasn't happy, I could be in trouble. *More on this lady in a second.*

I will always maintain that one of the biggest problems I had with Dale were the people that were just there to validate him. Many of them were people of color and I felt he'd go to them to justify how he treated me, even though most of them would turn around and tell me how wrong he was. To me, it always came across as his racism check. If a person of color justifies what I'm doing to this guy, then it can't possibly be racist, right? Some of them didn't really care for him, but he was a powerful man and they all wanted to kiss the ring or maybe were just afraid for their own jobs. Thing is, like the newspaper columnist when I first started, he threw a lot of them under the bus when they talked behind my back.

Like the time he told me he was talking to this black producer/photographer in our department about me "adapting," and according to Dale, the guy told him, "Mike is like my 16-year-old son. He just won't listen and is going to do what he wants." Really, bro? The same man that used to tell me, "I'm just going to pray for Dale because he ain't right. Hang in there"?? Now, when he's got you in his office, I'm a teenager? Okay. I get it. You're afraid for your job too. Self preservation kicks in for all of us when fear kicks in, I guess.

How about this photographer named "Santiago," who Dale said was killing me, talking major shit about what I was doing all the time but had nothing but smiles in my face? I could tell he was doing all he could to survive, and he was using me to stay afloat. Santiago ended up getting let go years later. I swear I hate to see anyone lose their job, but I guess that's karma.

Then there was "Barbara," the lady that told Camille that she should talk to me about Dale. She had sued the station years ago over some bullshit she had gone through, so she made it a mission to help this young black man in need. I know she might have meant well, but she actually made it worse for me. She called herself mentoring me. Monitoring and editing what I wrote. Teaching me how to adapt to what Dale wanted in my sportscast. Her mission: take every bit of personality and soul out of me.

Here's an example. I was writing a lead in for a college football game, Texas vs Tulane. In the script I wrote, "Texas hooking up with Tulane today." Very simple. Plain. Nothing clever, over the top or the least bit "urban."

Barbara freaked out. "What's that?? You can't say that, Mike." What?? Oh damn, what did I write? I was searching up and down the rest of the script and saw nothing wrong, so I asked her, "What's wrong with this?"

She said, "You can't be saying 'hooking up' on TV. That's sexual. Like a man and a woman hooking up. You got to change that." In my head I'm going, "Are you f***ing kidding me?" Right then and there, I felt defeated. I felt like if this was what I had to do or edit myself to do this, I knew I didn't want to be here at all. Dale and his followers had won. I changed what I had written, but I also knew this was a sure sign that the writing was on the wall for my ouster soon.

Chapter 13

BACK-SELL

I FELL INTO a deeper sense of not knowing who I was on air. For years, I was able to just be me, and now I was walking around like a zombie. I wasn't having fun. I've always told kids trying to figure out what they wanted to do for a living to follow their passion and not the money. Until now, I believed I had done that, and I was living a dream. I had a career doing something I absolutely loved. The best job in the world. However, at this time, I dreaded going to work.

Bruce or Kevin Frazier were always great people to call upon whenever I had an issue. One of them always had something to share with me to talk me off the ledge whenever I had a work issue. However, nothing was working now. I had been out of work for six months before getting the job at WFAA, and even though I had a job now, I was in a working hell.

What I've grown to learn is, God always has angels placed around you to help you through some of the darkest situations. My angel worked right inside the chaos of WFAA and had the whitest teeth and best smile of anyone I knew.

Nicole Block is her name, but I called her Coley Cole or Colgate because of those teeth and smile and she called me "Big Mike from The Wood" after this character in a film made in the '90s called *The Wood*. She worked as the assignment editor in the newsroom, and we just hit it off from day one. Any free time I had at work, I was at the assignment desk, hanging with her. So much so that Dale even tried to put an end to that. *I think the man just hated anything that made me happy. Now, before you go there, NO, I wasn't trying to come up and holla at Nicole. Although I wouldn't blame you if you thought that, considering my past.* I just loved absorbing her knowledge, positivity, and spirituality. We were around the same age, but her maturity stood out, and her energy just resonated with me.

One day right after he had made me sign some bogus paper basically saying I was on probation and my next infraction could be cause for termination, I saw Nicole in the newsroom. Now I was made to believe I HAD to sign this paper or the hell I was going through would be like Disneyland compared to what would come. Nicole could sense something was wrong and wanted to talk. She knew everything I was going through with Dale and had always supported me with words of encouragement or just a joke to make me laugh. However, what she said to me on THIS DAY will stick with me for the rest of my natural born life. She said, "Baby boy, you are God's child and no man, not even Dale, can stop what He has for you. Just stay strong and keep believing and NEVER LET ANYONE STEAL YOUR JOY!!!"

Those six words may have been said by a lot of people before, but it was the first time I had ever heard that statement. My eyes immediately opened, and I felt so much better. She was right. I knew there was a part of him that for WHATEVER reason didn't want me to be happy or at least stand out. That's something I couldn't understand because the more people liked me, the better it was for the sports department. However, he cared more about the handful of folks that were in his ear that didn't and wanted me to be vanilla. Once again, anytime I was starting to get some shine, he'd be right there with something he felt was terrible to try and wipe away any happiness I had. I was letting him win, and he wasn't nearly done playing. This man had so much animosity for me that he wanted to destroy me.

I tried to conform, but even though an apple and an orange are both fruits, an apple will never be mistaken for or taste like an orange, even if you cut it to its core. I was being cut to the core because he wanted me to be something I just wasn't. I remember actually filling in for him on this 30-minute sports show that was HIS BABY and I did it the way I THOUGHT he wanted it done. Just straight talk. No fluff. Excitement when needed but little or no flavor. He took it as if I was purposely mocking him, which was bullshit, and as punishment tried to demote me. Nothing I could do would be good enough for him. It just felt personal and he took everything that way. Including the final act that got me terminated.

Of all the people who played that double agent role between Dale and me while I was there, this guy named Carl Billick was the worst. At least he was the one who did me the dirtiest. Billick was my weekend producer, and I thought we were pretty damn cool. We shared a lot. He was frustrated with his role in the sports department and would vent about a number of things, including the main producer Sean Hamilton and of course, Dale. My biggest mistake was trusting him. Since he was so forthcoming about things when it came to Dale, I would vent to him about the issues I had with him too. *Yeah, I know it's dumb now, but hindsight is 20/20. However, even 20/20 vision won't see someone stabbing you in your back.*

I need to set this up for you. So one of the many things Dale demanded I stop doing was this little sign-out at the end of these sportscasts I'd tape which would run in the morning show. I'd say, "I'm Mike Hill, Keeping it Real" and I'd wink. Okay! Okay! Okay!! When I say it now, it's super corny, but at that time, people LOVED it. In fact, I had people in the streets calling me Keeping it Real Mike Hill and winking. However, like I mentioned, Dale told me to stop. So I capitulated. One night, while I was preparing to tape the sports segment, the young lady running the prompter asked me why I didn't say it anymore and my response was, "Well, I can't anymore." She said that was "too bad" because she really liked it. So before, and let me stress BEFORE, we even began taping the sportscast, I said, "I'll do it just for you off air cuz you asked." So I did it a few times. Not live. NOT on tape. It never went out over the air for any viewers to see. Just me on the set in front of the cameras and for the entertainment of a cute prompter operator. At least that's what I thought.

A few days later, Dale wanted to see me. This couldn't be good. It never was. I got to his office, and immediately I knew my intuition was right. He told me to sit down and proceeded to put a tape into the machine he had in his office. What popped up was me on the set saying my "Keeping it

Real" lines I was saying for the prompter operator. Once again, nothing that ever made air. Just the off-air recordings that someone had taped, unbeknownst to me. I didn't see the problem and frankly, I still don't see the issue, but this dude absolutely lost his top. "You have no respect for me. How dumb are you that you'd do something like this?" He was going on and on and on until after a while, his words started sounding like Charlie Brown's grandma on the cartoons. Wa-wonk-wa-wonk-wonk-wonk!!! I tried to explain to him that I didn't say this on air and what I did was for the amusement of a co-worker. That simple, innocent explanation didn't mean a damn thing to him. In his misguided opinion, I was mocking him. *Which for the record, I was NOT. Besides, that lady had no idea that it was Dale who forbade me from even using the phrase. I had told her that I just couldn't anymore.* Who cares that it wasn't seen by the viewing public; he had seen it. But how??

Once again, Carl was my sports producer, and he was in charge of taping and editing the morning sportscast. No one else had a clue what was going on that night, but he did. So for whatever fucked-up reason he had besides kissing the ass of a man he actually couldn't stand, he decided to take that raw, unedited tape to Dale and make him believe that I was, in fact, mocking him. *Once again, for the record, I wasn't.* How do I know it was Carl who did it? Dale!! As I've mentioned before, he snitched on his sources ALWAYS.

I was livid. I wanted to beat the shit out of Carl, but I didn't say anything. I got him back in a better way later. Keep reading. Karma is a cold b***h. However, I ain't going to lie, around this time, I was more worried than pissed. I knew it was just a matter of time before the inevitable but

praying that Dale would miraculously have some understanding. *I almost laughed myself at that last sentence.*

A few nights later, I got summoned to his office, and this
time when I walked in, a lady named Dee from HR was in
there too. It's a wrap. Now this man had always been an
asshole when I was in his office, but in front of this lady
from HR he was coming across all fatherly. Almost like he
was sad. He said, "Mike, we tried, but it's just not going
to work. I'm going to have to let you go. Today will be
your last day." I'll have to admit, even though I had seen it
coming, I was a little surprised it was on this day because
I had just finished a shift. My first thought was, "Mother
f***er, you couldn't have done this BEFORE I worked for
you today?" *Silly but true.* He asked me if I had any questions and I just kind of stared past him. I kept saying to
myself, *The whole time I've been here, I haven't been given
a fair chance.* Finally, it just verbally came out, and I looked
right at him and said, "You were never fair." I then looked
at Dee, whom I'd actually filed a complaint with against
Dale a few months earlier, and said, "You know he wasn't
fair, and this isn't right."

Dale actually stood up and said, "Good luck to you" and
extended his hand. I don't think I need to tell you that I left
him hanging. Dee watched me throw my belongings in a
box. She escorted me out the back door and to my car, and
I drove off the station's lot. Just eight months after joining
the station, I had been fired for the first time.

I called my agent first to tell her what happened, and then
I called Camille, which was tough because I knew she was
already super worried and overly emotional at times. She
knew what kind of person I was dealing with but still felt

like I needed to do what I could to keep my job. I honestly did. At least I thought I did. Maybe it wasn't enough. Obviously it wasn't. Dale had actually told me that I'd be fired several times in this business. He made it seem like these kinds of things are just inevitable. He said he'd been fired twice, and in a way it had turned out to be a blessing in disguise. This one turned out to be too. But damn, it took a long time and a hard road to see it that way.

The days right after that were surreal. I couldn't sleep, and when I did, I'd wake up at impossibly early times with my mind racing. I thought I was going to be out of work, but at least I was going to get paid right. I still had 16 months left on my deal and I didn't quit. You quit me. Well, that's not how WFAA saw it. They said they were firing me "for cause," meaning they were terminating my contract early AND they were going to continue to enforce my non-compete. That meant I couldn't even work in the Dallas/Ft. Worth market for the next 16 months if someone wanted to hire me. Remember that piece of paper they pretty much forced me to sign? That was the weapon they planned to use.

However, luckily, I had learned from past issues, and I had paper of my own. Remember that incident in the Air Force where the girl was trying to claim sexual harassment and the issues with Tim in Nashville? I did and I learned over a period of time to always protect your own neck. Document everything and save shit that could help you down the line. Luckily for me, Dale was so powerful, he thought he was Teflon and he could say anything he wanted to me at any time and through any forum. This included emails and instant messages on our computers. I knew things were going sideways from the start there, so guess what I did? I had all those messages saved and printed and in my files. I even had a recording of our conversations where…let's just say he'd never want anyone to hear what he said. Look, I admit, that shit is underhanded and wrong, but when you're going through crazy, unfair practices, self-preservation methods need to kick in.

Look, I was never going to really sue WFAA. In this business, if you sue a station or network, you might as well say goodbye to your career. It's rare that someone sues and finds work again. So if you do, it better be worth it, and less than a year and a half of salary wasn't. However, I had to at least make them believe I could. They wouldn't have been afraid of the small settlement that might have come about, but they were afraid of the information I had on their star sportscaster and how that would sully his and the station's brand. They caved, or at least they gave up something in a settlement. No, I didn't get my full sixteen months, but I got four months, plus they reduced the non-compete clause from sixteen to seven months. I should've gotten the non-compete even lower, but cool. I didn't have to sue. I got a nice little stack, and I could resume my career soon. In fact, immediately, because it was time to get the hell out of Dallas. Welllll, about that career resumption thing. That would take much, much, much, much, longer than I thought or would ever imagine.

The next 14 months would be the hardest, darkest and saddest days of my life. The job search was on again. Remember, I was just out of work for six months not long ago and when someone sees only an eight-month run on your last job, they want to know what happened. Well, by this time, blogs were around and the word was out about me. Even though both parties signed a non-disclosure agreement (I hope that shit has passed its legal limitations by the time this book comes out), Dale was privately telling anyone who listened what went down, and even though I didn't sue, sometimes the threat is enough to scare other stations off. Needless to say, I wasn't getting bites anywhere.

Weeks turned into months, and the panic was starting to set back in. I might be really done now. Seven years in, my career might be over. However, God has always been there for me and always shows up right when I need Him. This time, the angel he sent, ironically, was the main reason I got hired in Dallas in the first place. Newy Scruggs, who was the main sports guy at WFAA's main competitor KXAS, reached out to me one night. "Hey, dude, how you hanging in there?" I told him it was tough, but I was hanging in. He told me he knew that Dale did me wrong and just about everyone felt that way. This included his news director, Susan, and assistant news director, John Jenkins. He also said he admired my hustle and what I brought to the table and asked me when my non-compete was up.

I said, "Not 'til September."

He said when it was up if I needed something to give him a holla and he'd love to have me over there. Yes!!! At least I had that in the bag, but damn, my non-compete was still four months away.

Five months of unemployment. NO BITES. NO LEADS. NADA and I've still got two months before I was allowed to just freelance at KXAS. Camille had a job, but she was no longer in construction. She worked at Ethan Allan as a design consultant where the money was okay but our bank accounts were not. Remember, I had pretty much depleted my savings the last time I was out of work, and the nine months I was at WFAA didn't help to rebuild it. Things were starting to become scary again.

The money issues were real. That year we got a huge tax return, which was a major blessing, but pretty soon, I was scraping down to my last. I tried to keep up with my full child support payments to Tamara for Ashlee, but after awhile, I just didn't have it. I talked to Tamara about my situation. I could've easily gone back to court to request a deduction, but I wanted to pay it in full and told Tamara I would when I was back on my feet. Who knew it would take this long? Guess it's hard to get back on your feet when you've been knocked completely on your ass and someone continues to put a foot on your chest to keep you there.

However, God has always looked out for me and blessed me in an inordinate amount of ways. I just need to testify what He has done for me and how well he got me through everything. I'm not saying I didn't have troubles or worries. You'll see that as you continue to read this. Financially, though? He really got me through this time.

That July, The National Association of Black Journalists, an organization I had been a member of since my days as an intern, just so happened to be having its conference in Dallas. Every conference, there's a huge job fair, where prospects can meet news directors and potential employees to have their tapes critiqued and even possibly set up a future job. This was a huge opportunity for me to get back in front of some of these people, and thankfully it was in my city because honestly I wouldn't have been able to afford it otherwise.

These days when I go, it's like a huge reunion, full of laughs and parties. When I had to go in the summer of 2003, it was one of the most nervous times of my life. Sure, it was hot outside in Dallas, but when I walked inside the cool, air conditioned convention center, I could not stop sweating. *Not the look you want to have if you're trying to get hired, huh?* However, here's the thing: I wasn't nervous because I had to face and speak to potential employers, I was nervous because I had to face some of my peers in the industry who knew I had been fired.

I know it sounds stupid but yes, I was still dealing with a lot of pride then. It wasn't and never is healthy to do so, but it was my truth. As soon as I walked onto the floor of the job fair, I saw guys I knew. One guy named Tony Wyllie, who was the head of communications for the Houston Texans at the time. Also, my mentor I mentioned earlier, Kevin Frazier and Stuart Scott, who both worked at ESPN. Kevin and Tony were among the many who had reached out to me after I got let go, but I hadn't really seen anyone since that terrible night, so I was more ashamed than happy to see them, and I knew they could tell. Tony, who's always cracking jokes, even mentioned how much I was sweating.

I eventually pulled it together and walked around with my tape. I showed it to everyone I could. You got a TV station, I got a tape. That was my attitude. I was hustling again. Then I got to the ESPN booth. Stu was there, and although we knew of each other, I would never say I really knew him at this time. However, he's someone I respected even if I had disdain for everyone trying to compare us. He agreed to critique my tape, and when he finished watching it, he said, "I've got nothing to tell you." I was like "What?"

because I was now confused as hell. He elaborated and said, "Bruh, your tape is fine, I don't have anything to say that could make it better." I was overjoyed. Validation from the guy that is super respected in this industry.

Stu said I should show my tape to Al Jaffe. Remember him? The talent doorman who controlled the velvet ropes of ESPN? The one who had no interest after my audition there about three years back? Yep. Him. Well, guess what? He STILL had no interest. His thing was, "I've already seen what he can do, no need to watch again."

Wow! I always thought his take was interesting. It had been three years since that flawed audition and obviously people grow over a period of time. If I had to use a sports analogy, Kurt Warner's first evaluation wasn't great either coming into the NFL. Not drafted. Played in various leagues and even worked as a shelf stocker in a grocery store before the Rams gave him a try. Years later, he improves, makes the team, gets an opportunity due to an injury, wins a Super Bowl, and goes on to have a Hall of Fame career. I'm not saying I'm as great as Kurt Warner, but sometimes you deserve a second chance to make a first impression, and even though Stu had just vouched for me, Al wasn't trying to hear it.

Here's another example of God having angels in place to watch out for me and to lead me into my purpose. Standing next to Stu and Al at this time was a guy named Fred Brown. Fred was second in charge in the talent department and overheard what was happening and said he'd take a look at my tape. He did and he loved it. He asked me what my situation was, and I was upfront with him. He said he'd talk to Al more about it and be in touch if an opportunity arose. I was thankful that he'd watched but still, the wait continued.

After my seven-month non-compete ended, Newy kept his word to me and I began doing some work over at KXAS-TV. I have to give credit to Newy. He saved my career. There was nothing happening for me outside of Dallas, and had it not been for him, I might have never gotten back on the air in the city. One of the many angels that God has placed in my life to carry me through the good and tumultuous times.

However, I was only freelancing at KXAS a few days a week, if that, and the pay was hourly. I'm not going to say it was bad because when you're desperate, anything helps, but it really wasn't enough to pay all of my bills, including the child support and some of Camille's debt too. Luckily, I was able to draw some unemployment, and since I was still a member of my union, SAG/AFTRA, I and my family had insurance.

All of that helped, but I knew eventually I needed a full-time gig or I'd have to do something else soon. Camille would be at work and I'd have to take care of Kayla during the day and do whatever I needed to around the house. I was a house husband/forced to stay at home father. I didn't have a social life because I really didn't have any friends my age or with common interests to hang out with to unwind, so I had no escape. The one time I did go out around this time resulted in a huge argument between Camille and me.

I had been invited to watch basketball with Nicole and some other people from work, and for some reason, she was tripping about me going. All I knew was I NEEDED to get out of that house or I was going to lose it. I can't remember why she didn't want me to go, but she literally got in my way by standing directly in the doorway, and it's the only time I've actually put my hands on a woman. I didn't punch, slap or grab her, but since she was blocking the door, I moved her to the side to get her out of my way. Her reaction scared me because she just yelled out, "Don't you hit me!!" What?? Huh? I'm not doing anything of the sort. I got scared and I just knew I was going to be arrested when I left. I really needed to leave or escape in other ways, but reality wasn't going to allow me.

Around this time, I noticed it was becoming increasingly harder to get out of bed, and after awhile, I didn't even want to, and I damn sure didn't want to go anywhere. I was gaining weight, and while it was rare before, at this time, there was absolutely no romance happening between Camille and me. I started feeling like she wasn't attracted to me anymore, and looking back, I really couldn't blame her. I wasn't working out, so I was terribly out of shape. I had lost my drive and the little hope I had. I was starting to feel like she didn't love me or maybe she was disappointed.

At times I even felt like she resented me for getting fired, even though she knew how Dale was treating me—maybe I hadn't done enough or at least just conformed enough to keep my job. We had been married three years now, and I'd been out of work for nearly half that time. On one occasion, I overheard a conversation she had with an old roommate where she said, "This is not what I signed up for." Well, she was right. So before anyone comes down on her, she had met a guy full of confidence and ambition, and now she was married to one who was insecure, broken, and unsure. She still showed support and tried to encourage me at times. I just didn't know if she truly believed it. I really couldn't blame her. Why would you believe in someone who really didn't believe in himself?

Ten months after I got fired, I was still freelancing but still not getting any bites or really any leads for jobs. I was seriously beginning to think I'd been blackballed, and if Newy didn't KNOW what had really gone down and vouched for me, I'm sure I wouldn't have even had that freelance gig. I was seriously contemplating doing something else. Since I was in the military, I thought about becoming a government worker or working at the post office. I even went to the post office and asked for an application. However, the lady behind the counter gave me this look like, *Boy, you know you really don't want to work here.* I'm sure she didn't mean anything negative about it, but she was right. Nothing against the post office or any other government job, but I didn't want to work there. It wasn't my passion, and I probably would have been miserable. Then again, I was already past miserable. At least I'd get a paycheck. However, God had bigger plans. It didn't mean He was ready to reveal them yet, though.

I had hit the lowest point of my life. I was completely broken and didn't see any way out. I attended this great church, Shiloh Missionary Baptist Church, and everyone there, including Pastor Joshua, was incredible, but I honestly had lost faith. Where was God and why would He bring me this far to leave me? Sure, I was a bit cocky and had allowed popularity to cause me to do some unsavory things. Okay, so I hadn't gone to church as much when things were going great or given back in some other ways. But I didn't deserve this. Right? *I'm obviously being sarcastic, but then again, sometimes tone and context can't be determined when you're reading it.* The part about me struggling and losing faith though? Yeah, that's too real.

My brother Preston tried to help me. After Dale fired me, I sobbed uncontrollably as he hugged me. I was more than broken. I was shattered. *Look y'all, regardless of the type of life he's lived, no man wants to feel like he can't take care of himself or family.* Preston has always been the one person I felt I could be the most vulnerable with. *Thinking about it, I should've leaned on him more often in life. I mean, he's always been there with words of wisdom. I just don't know if I was always ready to receive them fully.*

However, my lowest point met rock bottom during Christmas time of that year. Anyone who knows me knows I love to give to others and do all I can to make them happy and smile. I was miserable, broken, and just literally financially broke. I know Christmas is more than gift giving, but I had to squeeze out a few gifts for my daughters, who, at this time, knew what Christmas was all about, and get something nice for Camille. Fortunately, I was able to scrape a few things together and did just that, but my mental progression had reached its crescendo. Anger had progressed to bitterness. Bitterness to doubt. Doubt to sadness and now sadness to full-out depression.

It's funny how your mind plays tricks on you and if you allow it, that trick could lead to your permanent disappearance. All I knew was I felt like I was just a burden, and everyone would be better off without me. At least my kids would get some insurance money. *Then again, they wouldn't get anything but the burden of burying your cowardly ass, Dad, because insurance doesn't pay for suicidal deaths.* Regardless, I started having these thoughts come into my head and they really wouldn't leave. Okay, if suicide isn't an option because of the insurance ramifications and let's face it, I was just too much of a coward to do it, how 'bout I just wish for a car accident or maybe just be in the wrong place at the wrong time around the wrong people? All I knew was I didn't want to be on this earth any longer. I felt like a failure and I wanted out.

I went to my doctor for my annual check-up. She noticed the weight gain and less than upbeat demeanor, and I told her about my job situation. She even asked me had I ever thought of hurting myself and I said it had crossed my mind. The doctor told me I should talk to someone about it and actually prescribed me some depression medication. When I got home, the meds were on my dresser and Camille's reaction was odd. She asked me why I had depression medication, and I embarrassingly told her my doctor thought I was mildly depressed. Her response was, "No you're not, Mike." I don't think she was trying to be cold, but it felt like it at the time. Maybe she thought it was all an excuse. I don't really know, but it stung when she said it, and I never did go see that therapist.

> *That decision turned out to be one of the worst decisions in my life. It wouldn't be until many years later, in fact after I had completed the first rough copy of this book, that I got the courage and admitted I needed to speak to someone. If I had only gotten a few things off my chest at THIS point in my life, it could've saved me and others so much pain. However, like a lot of black men, I decided to "man up" and power through. As you'll see, not doing so just led to more issues.*

Through my depression, I did what many of us do. Instead of being vulnerable and admitting your depression to a therapist, we turn it back over to God. Not that anything is wrong with this AT ALL. Besides, I felt I had nothing else left because at this point in my life, I wasn't as educated on mental health treatment as I am now. Back then, even though my faith had wavered, my mom and Grandmother Lillian had always taught me the power of prayer and that God would always be there for you. For some reason, I also remembered a front vanity plate that my grandmother, Richard's mom, Rose Ella, had on a station wagon that said, "Prayer changes things." I needed change, and I couldn't do it by myself anymore. I was losing, and at the time I felt that the only person who could save the day wasn't a person at all but the most high.

I've actually heard God speak to me at different times in my life. I, unfortunately, don't always listen or obey Him, but when I do it works out for my benefit. There was the night I told you about back in '96 about me moving to L.A. (keep reading, you'll see how that turned out later), and there was this one night back in 2003 that had I not listened, my career and possibly my freedom would've been over.

I had finally gotten a bite for a job interview. WFTS, the ABC affiliate in Tampa, was looking for a sportscaster to replace Jay Crawford, who had just gotten a job working on this new show called Cold Pizza on ESPN. I went in, met the news director and several of the guys in the sports department, and hit it off with each one of them. The job was mine. How do I know? Well, the news director at the time pretty much told me, "Unless we find out you're an axe murderer, the job is yours." He even sent me next door, where they had a drug testing facility, to get a piss test. *If they tell you to get a piss test, that's your gig, unless you fail the damn test.*

Unfortunately for me, I had someone putting crap in the veins and brains of the people doing the hiring at WFTS because two weeks went by and I heard absolutely NOTHING back. I asked my agent to call, but she couldn't get any answers. While I was there, I had hit it off with the sports producer, and we'd exchanged numbers. At the time, I thought I'd need it because we'd be working together. However, I was calling him now to see when or if that might happen.

When I called, I asked, "What's up, bro? When are they going to decide something?"

He very reluctantly responded with, "They're not going to do it, bro. They're not going to bring you in."

Uhhhh, excuse you?? What the hell you mean they're not hiring me? I couldn't have failed my drug test so what's the deal? Well, remember when I told you the news director said it was mine unless they found out I was an "axe murderer"? Well, Dale must have convinced them of that because the sports producer, once again, very reluctantly told me, "Your old boss in Dallas is bad-mouthing you, bro, and it scared them." I got off the phone in shock. "How could this be? Why is Dale trying to destroy me? Even if HE didn't want me around him, why is he trying to stop me from going elsewhere?" Now....I.....WAS .....PISSED!!

Next thing I knew I was in my car and headed toward WFAA, where Dale still worked, obviously. I was going to wait until he got off work, and since I probably couldn't get past security at the station to get into the employee parking lot, I was going to wait until he pulled out and when he did, I was going to pull his fat ass out of his car and I was going to hurt this man. I was either going to the hospital or jail on this night. You've fired me and now you're messing with my livelihood?? I've got money problems, and I can't fully support my kids, and now you want to affect my future income?? What he did was highly illegal but would be hard to prove. However, what I was about to do to him is also considered illegal, and I'd gladly confess to doing it.

I was rolling down the tollway and I got nearly halfway there when I began to feel super hot. Like I was about to burn up. It was around July or so in Dallas, so that's not uncommon, but it was after 9pm and the air conditioning was on full blast, yet I was still on fire. I rolled down my windows to get some fresh air and it's funny, but through the wind, I heard a voice, and I knew it was God. "What are you doing? You need to trust me. You're about to ruin it all. Just turn around." Then, all of a sudden, I felt a sense of calm. I swear. I went from infuriated to still a bit upset but totally under control. I turned around and went back home.

If I had gone down there that night, I know it would have been a disaster. If I had seen him, I was going to do everything in my power to hurt him physically like he had been mentally and emotionally hurting me. Had I done that, my career would've ended that night. Luckily, that was a time I listened to God, and even though I still had some hard times to come, as I chronicle in this book, He took care of me.

Chapter 14

GAIN

I WAS GETTING more and more work at KXAS-TV and I got refocused on that job hunt. Then, in February of 2004, my agent called because ESPN had called them. Remember Fred Brown, the guy who was second in charge to Al? He wanted to bring me in for an audition, and even though Al Jaffe objected, he said if Fred wanted to bring me in, he could.

This time I had to make it work. Fred said to just do the things he saw on that tape and I'd be fine. They had a producer named Todd Snyder helping me with my audition, and he couldn't have been more helpful. At ESPN, they have you write all of your own copy. The shot sheets they give you are typed up by the production assistants, but you can doctor them up or change anything you want to about them. I was ready. I was focused and I felt like I killed that audition. I felt good about my chances and knew it was just a matter of time before I was finally going to get another opportunity and this time at ESPN of all places.

However, a funny thing happened. Actually, it wasn't very funny at all because once again, absolutely nothing was happening. Weeks went by and I got no indication about what they were going to do at ESPN. I'll give my agent, at the time, Sue Lipton, a lot of credit because I know she pushed them, but still nothing was happening. Frustrated doesn't even begin to describe my emotions. The only good thing was I was getting plenty of work at KXAS, so at least that was keeping me busy and my mind off of me losing it.

This was one of the many times throughout my career where I've realized who was for me, who was against me, and who only came around when they thought I could provide something for them. In this particular case, I reached out to an on-air guy there who I thought would be in a great position to help me because of his standing there. This is a guy who had helped me in the past, so I knew he'd come through. I just wanted him to put in a good word with some of the senior producers on my behalf, and his response sort of threw me.

He said, "These guys aren't going to listen to me. I won't be able to help you much."

Well, I felt he could help at least "some," but it didn't appear that he even wanted to try. Then he went on to actually discourage me from wanting to get hired there because it was in Bristol. They overwork you. They underpay you, etc. I was like, "That may be YOUR position you can take, but bro, I NEED A DAMN JOB!"

He never did talk to anyone, but like I said, this has been the case for many people I thought I could rely on throughout the years and have been disappointed in the results or lack of effort. It's a reason why I will always do what I can to help anyone if I can get the positive results he or she is looking for. If they're also willing to help themselves.

I also tend to forgive those who have done me wrong in the past. Maybe it's not always the smartest thing to do, and I've definitely been burned on several occasions for doing so, but I just have a forgiving heart. I want to give you a second chance because I know we are only human. However, I ain't got to reward your ass.

Ask Carl Billick. Remember him? He's the one who secretly recorded me for Dale making an innocuous reference to the teleprompter operator? Yeah, the dude who straight-up snitched. Well, as I told you before, he really couldn't stand Dale, and he really disliked the main producer, Sean Hamilton. *Yup, I know, I'm snitching on him too, but this is Open Mike so do you really think I give... never mind.* Anyway, Billick felt like he should or could be the main producer instead of Sean. Well, he actually had an opportunity to possibly become the main producer of a sports office. At KXAS. The station where I was freelancing. Newy was looking for a new guy and just so happened to mention that Billick had asked for, applied to, and was the leading person to join the department. Shitttttttttt!!! Not today or never, if I could help it. I HAD to put an end to that. I simply told Newy what he had done to me over at WFAA and the difference in demeanor when he was in front of Dale and behind his back, and that was the end of that candidate. I then told him about a producer over there named Jeff Collette, who I thought was better anyway, and Jeff ended up getting the job.

Now some of you may think that was vindictive or bitterness. Well, hell yes it was. Some of you may ask what's the difference in what I did and what Dale did to me in Tampa? Well, first off, what Dale did was illegal because he still worked at my old shop and I never did anything to warrant what he did to me. Carl, on the other hand, was a two-faced backstabber that could not be trusted. Lastly, Jeff was a better producer anyway. A big reason why he's working for a network right now.

Look, I was really in my feelings back then. Time has healed many wounds, and I've even reached out to both Dale and Carl to wish them well. I had to learn the power of forgiveness and realize that in order to receive the blessings that were meant for me, I had to release the hate I had in my heart in order to make room for them. It's an important lesson to learn. Life should be enjoyed, and that's hard when you're allowing someone to steal your joy. As long as you're holding on to that anger, the person who's making you feel that way will always win.

God also takes us on journeys that are on rough, uncomfortable, and treacherous paths. It makes us stronger and what I've realized is that you're not stuck in something, you're going *"through"* it. Meaning eventually you'll come out if you do your part. Trust God and believe that it will happen.

What I was going through in Dallas needed to happen to me. I needed to be humbled. I needed to be chopped down in order to grow. I was being prepared for what was to come. I obviously wish I could've been taught this lesson or had it come about in a different way, but it's how God wanted me to experience it, and I'll accept it. Honestly, I didn't fully get it until a friend recently told me I needed to take responsibility for all my past issues instead of blaming others for what's happened or happening in my life. She was absolutely right. It's no one's fault if I'm not succeeding. It's my fault for allowing them to have that much power to stop me.

I'll even give credit to Dale for his special way of preparing me. He used to actually tell me that my career wouldn't really begin until I got fired. He was right. What if I hadn't gotten fired in Dallas? I'll tell you what. When I first moved there, I would've been content with just being a local sportscaster in that market. I had come to that. Between my travels in the Air Force and moving four times in seven years in my broadcasting career, I was ready to plant roots for a while and not even think about going elsewhere.

I even have to thank Dale in another way. Because he said what he said to cost me that opportunity in Tampa, that disappointment allowed me to be free to accept what God really had in store for me. I really wanted and needed a job back then, but His plans are always much bigger than ours are.

After a few months of not hearing anything from ESPN, I finally got a decision. I was a finalist, but they were going to pass. I heard they were going to hire a guy named Dari Nowkhaw. Dari turned out to be a good dude, and he's a great on-air talent, but when I first heard the news, I have to admit, I wasn't a big fan. Nothing against Dari, I was just majorly disappointed.

Here it is, the start of the many times in my career where I was up for a big role. Audition. Interview. Be a finalist but still not get the job. I was a bridesmaid for the first time but at least there was a bouquet thrown my way. ESPN was impressed enough with my audition that they wanted to fly me to New York to audition to be a part of this show they had called Cold Pizza. They needed a newsreader and wanted me to audition.

I'm thinking, *Okay, maybe this is turning out to be a blessing if I can land this.* This show was shot in New York. So I'd be going back home, in a sense, and that meant I wouldn't have to move to Bristol, Connecticut.

So here's another thing about God that you should know. Sometimes when you're in a drought, when the rain finally comes, it pours. Not only did ESPN want me to audition for First Take, but KXAS was showing me some love. This FoxSports regional network in the metroplex brought me in for an interview AND the ABC affiliate in Houston, Texas, KPRC-TV, also wanted to fly me in for an audition and interview.

In early June of 2004, I flew down to Houston for the interview. I remember thinking that people from Houston must sin on purpose just so they can cool off in hell eventually. It was hot as hell there. The interview went great, but during the audition, I remember being mesmerized by their main anchor, a lady named Dominique Sachse. She was so damn pretty, I could barely concentrate, and her beauty actually made me nervous. I've been on the set with some beautiful people before, so this was very odd for me.

The news director, a lady named Nancy Shafran, was super cool, and we seemed to hit it off. And after I left lunch with her, it didn't take long before I knew about my next move. While I was in the Houston airport waiting on my flight to go back to Dallas, I got a call from Susan, my agent. She said, "They want you." I responded, "Houston has already made an offer?" She said, "No, ESPN wants to hire you!!!" *Huh? I know I'm going to audition with them for Cold Pizza, but that's not until next week.* Sue went on to tell me that it wasn't for Cold Pizza, but for an ESPNews anchor role. They had another spot come available after one of the anchors went into radio full-time.

This was a dream. *Yeah, I know I just said a few paragraphs ago that I didn't care about going to Bristol, but kill that noise now. Let me have my moment.* I was about to do national television. More importantly, I was back in this business full-time. I was employed again. My nightmare was finally over. Thank you, Jesus!!!

I was about to get back on that plane, but I could've flown myself back to Dallas. I was floating. I didn't even call Camille to tell her the news. I decided I'd tell her when I got home in person. I will say I was actually nervous now because how my luck had been going, I would have finally gotten this opportunity of a lifetime and this plane would crash. Obviously it didn't.

I arrived back in Dallas, and I still hadn't told Camille anything yet. She asked me how things had turned out and I said great. She was in between the kitchen and living room in our home when I told her I had something to share with her. She asked, "What?" And I responded, "I'll just show you." I then turned the TV on to ESPNews. She went, "What's that mean?" I said, "That is where my next step in my career will take place. On that network. I'm going national. I got a job at ESPN." She started screaming. Ran over and hugged me, and for the first time in a very long time, I was able to put a genuine, loving smile on my wife's face. I was overjoyed. I was leaving Dallas, headed for the worldwide leader. The kingdom of all sports networks. The most recognizable four letters on cable television. I was headed for utopia. Or, at least, so I thought.

Contract negotiations were odd. ESPN had offered me a four-year contract where I'd be making below six figures for the first two years of that deal. I know it sounds like first world troubles and I'm not trying to say I wasn't grateful. However, they knew my job situation and had just hired a guy named Mike Hall who had won a reality game show they produced as an anchor and HE was making more money than me. Nothing against Mike, who's paved out a great career for himself in this business, but I had seven years of experience and been in top markets, while he was fresh out of school and won a REALITY SHOW.

Even though beggars can't possibly be choosy, I actually had a choice. Fox Sports SouthWest wanted to hire me. *Told you when it rains it pours.* The station I interviewed for in Houston ended up hiring one of the sportscasters from Fox Sports SW and they wanted to replace him with me. Now mind you, I had just found out about ESPN and was starting these negotiations. However, they really wanted me and asked me how much ESPN was offering because they would top it. Plus, I'd stay in Dallas where the cost of living was much better than Bristol. With the offers ESPN was giving, it was tempting, but I felt it was time for a change of scenery, and if I backed away from ESPN now, I might never have the opportunity to go again. So I said, "Thanks but no thanks" and I signed the four-year deal to go to ESPN.

After spending a few days in New York with my mom and stepdad, Jerry, I arrived in Bristol on July 4th, 2004. I was scheduled to start work two days later. Keith Russell, a guy I had interned with at Fox 45, was an anchor at ESPN at that time and told me about a cookout at another anchor's house named Kirk Jimenez. I went over and had a good time with them and their wives. Later, Jay Harris, who had just done the 6p SportsCenter, came over, and I was sort of thrilled to meet him because I'd always admired his work. However, it didn't appear that Jay was as thrilled. He now claims he was tired, but I just think he was being an asshole, because he didn't smile and barely spoke for like the first hour I was there. *Jay, you know you were being a prick.* Even though I was more humble, I still had a cockiness that came out every now and then. Especially if I felt like someone thought they were better than me; I'm thinking, *This dude thinks I'm trying to take his spot and I haven't even started yet.* Of course, that's how I felt at that time, but knowing Jay like I know him now, I realize he was just having one of those Bristol days that everyone who works there goes through. One of his days just happened to come during our initial meeting. Now Jay is one of my best friends in the world, and I love him like a brother.

After two days of HR training where they scare the shit out of you about sexual harassment, it was time for me to start work. And let me tell you something about ESPN: if you get a job there, YOU WILL WORK! Depending on what show you're doing, you're doing long days that turn into long nights. Starting with your show meeting and then writing about 80 percent of your own scripts. I actually enjoyed writing my own scripts because I believe no one can write the way you speak better than you.

I started off on ESPNews, which at the time, had its own programming outside of SportsCenter or the other big shows on the main network. For those not familiar, it was almost like being in the minor leagues waiting to be called up to the big leagues or sitting on the bench while the starters got all the time. In other words, if you're on ESPNews, your main goal is to get OFF of ESPNews and get a show on the main network. Some guys had been there for years and never made it. Some of them had major talent, and it still puzzles me why they never got an opportunity to move up, but when I first got there, I didn't care about the others who had been there. I was focused on making that move myself.

The most tense and even amusing time for people who had to do ESPNews shifts or anyone who vacillated between News and SportsCenter was when the schedule would be released. Every month when it was released, it would be like Christmas with all the anchors curious about what they were about to get. If you opened it and all you saw was News...News...News on your calendar, there would be major disappointment. If you opened it and happened to see a SC (SportsCenter) or NFL Live or anything else on the main network, even if it was for a date or two, you had a little smile on your face. A glimmer, if only a temporary glimmer, of hope.

After you saw what you had on your schedule, two things would follow. If all someone had was News shifts, they then went to check out the schedules of the other anchors, which anyone could access at the time, and find out what shifts "they" had. If someone who did News with you a lot started getting chances on the main network, the shadiness and hate would be real. *ESPN really should've been TNT because their motto is, "We Love Drama."* Anchors would see others getting opportunities they thought they should have, and they'd take out their frustrations on their fellow anchors and not the coordinating producers who were giving them the shifts. "How is he/she getting a SportsCenter? He just got here. The only reason why he/she is getting it is because he/she is such an ass kisser." Believe me, I heard it all. And the women there were the harshest when it came to that schedule.

I can say that, as much as I wanted to get off of ESPNews, I would never say anything about a fellow anchor getting a chance. Why shouldn't they? It wasn't their fault that someone gave them the chance. So why am I going to come down hard on them and not the people who are making the decisions if I felt like I deserved it? It never made any sense to me, but in a way, I could understand the frustration.

The second thing an anchor did after getting his/her schedule would be to look at who they had to anchor with. Especially if they had to do ESPNews. Believe me, it was a big deal. It's one thing to feel a certain way about being on News, but that feeling could turn into straight-up misery if you had to spend those long hours on set with someone you didn't quite vibe with.

The network and schedulers tried to pair anchors together they felt vibed with one another or just had chemistry. Sometimes they got it right, as was the case with Stan Verrett and Bill Pidto, JW Stewart and Keith Russell, who were pretty much the staple of the last show of the night, or the "close" show. Others weren't so successful, and I'll just leave that there.

I certainly had my favorites I worked with early on, like Steve Bunin, Anthony Amey, and Cindy Brunson. However, I also had some of those, "Oh no God! Not him/her!" moments when the schedule came out. There was this one guy who I just nicknamed "misery" because no matter how great he had it, his energy was so negative he just seemed miserable, which would bring you down. Then there was the one they paired me with early on that almost got me in some major trouble. It certainly did not give me a good early impression among the brass.

The thing is, I was warned about this person (I'm not going to say her name) before I even knew her. She got hired a little after me, and one of my old colleagues told me to be wary of her because of issues he'd had with her in the past. He told me she could be manipulative and conniving, and whatever I did, do not trust her. He disliked this person so much that he said, "I would watch her drown." *True story! That's how much he hated this person.*

Wow. That's harsh, but my thing has always been to give everyone a fair chance when it comes to me, despite what someone else thinks of them. Just because others have had a bad experience with someone doesn't mean they're a bad person. Maybe they just didn't mesh. Maybe their personalities were a bit off. Maybe they caught them at a bad time. Maybe it was really the other person's attitude that caused them to act that way. Then again, maybe the person you're being warned about could just be everything they're telling you they are.

In the beginning, everything was cool. I never even brought up my friend or let on that I even knew him. Our shows were pretty cool, and we actually got along. So much so that she started saying things to me and sending these little instant messages on the work computer that were pretty personal. How she used to date this certain actor, or the kind of men she liked and how those men she liked were usually black men. She was a pretty lady, but despite all my past creepy ways, I really wasn't interested in her like that. Besides, I had been faithful to Camille and wasn't trying to go there, and we never hung out outside of work.

While things appeared good between us, I could see a few signs of what my friend warned me about in her inter-actions with others. A bit entitled, snappy, and sometimes downright rude. In fact, our issues started because of how she treated someone else.

We were getting ready for a show, and even though we were on the set, we had some shot sheets (papers produc-tion assistants gave you to describe highlights) but didn't have our scripts, and the prompter wasn't loaded. Now, this is something that happens every so often, and while it can be irritating, there's no need to have a meltdown, espe-cially because we could've easily ad libbed the first part and gotten right into some highlights. My co-anchor was having a complete meltdown. The prompter operator was a new PA (who's actually gone on to become a huge exec-utive in the company) and she was also the one responsi-ble for sorting out and handing us our scripts. She was in the corner by the prompter doing that and the show was about to start in two minutes. She was doing her best, but since my co-anchor was in full-out "going off" mode, the PA was now a bit flustered.

I'm not going to sit up here and act like I didn't want those scripts either. It's always best to be prepared, but the military did teach me how to adapt to situations, and my nature just won't show anyone when I'm nervous. I was seeing how my co-host was treating this young PA, and I was seething on the inside because I just don't think anyone should be treated that way. Especially if they're not doing something purposely to harm you or a situation. There's nothing I could do to help this PA get those scripts together, and we were about to go on in one minute. I wanted to get off to a good start and have a good show, so I figured, "Let me just calm my co-host down."

I said to her, as she's pissed at the world and still going off, "It's going to be fine. We're pros. We'll just ad-lib this quick hello. I got the first highlight and by the time we're done with the first set up highlights in the A-block, we'll have our scripts." I was thinking to myself, "Good job, bruh. Crisis averted. We're going to have a great show."

NOPE!!!! That's when shit really got real. She turned to me and gave me a look that would make the devil scream for Jesus. Then she raised her hand and put her palm right up to my face and said, "Mike, I don't need to hear your shit right now!!!!"

Holy shit!!! What just happened? I'm trying to calm you down and now you've managed to turn on my switch. What happened next I wish I would've been able to avoid, but it was like something just took over my body because I was already low-key upset that she was treating this PA poorly.

With her hand still in my face, every bit of the Bronx and Bessemer came out of my body because I said, "Are you fucking bipolar? Putting your hand in my face?" As soon as it came out, I wished I had a rope to pull it back in, but it was too late. Now the issue was with me.

She went, "Oh great, Mike, you're calling me names?" Yep, even if he was trying to calm down a situation and she had disrespected him by putting her hand in his face and cursing him out, all anyone would see is this big black man saying something harsh to this meek, entitled woman. I knew I was fucked, just a month into my tenure at ESPN.

Our relationship changed after that. I would try to interact and there would be little to no response. It got so bad that I felt the need to address my concerns with one of the talent supervisors and let her know I thought it might be best if they didn't pair us. The supervisor told me that we were adults and we should just work it out. Not exactly the Dr. Phil advice I was looking for or needed, but okay.

It just got worse. The reason is because one of the problems I encountered at ESPN early on was it was like a high school. Cliques. People talking behind one another's backs and people who loved to stir this stupid shit up. I found out that one of those people who was doing it was someone I thought was a friend of mine. Someone I had been knowing long before I even got to ESPN. He had been there years before me and we had always been cool. However, for some reason, our relationship changed once I arrived. Maybe it was competition. Maybe something else, but it became weird somehow.

In the beginning, I felt like I could talk to him because he had been there longer and would even ask for advice on how to handle things. This includes the ongoing issue I had currently with my co-anchor. Problem is, he was also talking to her. Looking back, it was so juvenile, but he'd run back and tell her about our conversations, and he couldn't wait to tell me about theirs. It was as if he wanted us to destroy each other. Another example of me putting the blame on myself because I should not have fallen for it, but we all have those naïve moments.

Well, my issues with this co-anchor finally came to a head over those "*he said, she said*" moments. She just went in talking about how this guy couldn't wait to come and tell her that I said this and that. However, here's another issue. In this particular situation, I hadn't said ANY of the things she alleges he said I said. I tried to tell her that it was all a lie and we could talk to him together, but she wasn't having it and went off. It got worse when we walked off the set and went upstairs to where our desks were. It was about 2:30 in the morning and no one was up in that area besides us. She basically started screaming and berating me so loudly that I actually felt uncomfortable. Finally, I'd had enough. I started yelling back, "Do you really think you're just going to scream at me and I'm not going to say anything back? I got a loud voice too, so you're not the only one who can fucking yell." *Yep, I know what you're saying.* "*Why, Mike? Why did you allow her to suck you in, bro? You know how this ends.*"

All of a sudden, this woman who was coming at me with all the vitriol of hell turned into this quiet, nervous, shaking victim. I never threatened her. It's not like I picked up anything. I mean, I had to have been at least 25 feet away from her when I was screaming BACK at her. It didn't matter. All of sudden my attacker felt attacked and shut up.

You ever just have that weird situation in your body when you just feel trouble? Where you get that hot feeling in your chest? Like getting pulled over by the cops and you just don't know why? That's how I felt. It got worse a few seconds later as I was walking out to leave for the night. I had to walk past her desk in order to get to the exit and she was still in her cubicle. She had her back to me, but as I got closer she turned around and started to literally cower. No lie!! I was like what the fuck?? I wasn't even thinking about touching this girl. I just want to get the hell out of there and she's cowering?? I just kept walking, but as soon as I passed by, I heard her picking up the phone and calling someone. I knew it had to be security and as soon as I got that thought, my legs got so wobbly, I could barely make it to my car. *Remember, this was 2004. So yes, I was "Karen-ed" LONG before it was made popular in this country. A huge reason why it makes my flesh crawl to this day.*

I went home and tried to get some sleep, but as expected, my phone was ringing early the next morning. It was HR, and they wanted me to come in to meet with them. I got to the office and as expected, this woman was claiming I threatened her and she feared for her safety. She also claimed sexual harassment. *Are you kidding me? Are you freaking serious, right now?*

Yes, I was nervous, but I was also prepared. Once again, it's important to continue to learn from your past. Once again, I was armed with receipts. Documents for some "just in case" shit goes down. This was one of those times. I had all those little inner-office messages she was sending to me saved and I had printed them out before my meeting because I knew she'd be on some bullshit. I told the lady in HR, "As you can see, I'm the one who should be claiming sexual harassment." As for the threats and her fearing for her safety, I told them they should check the security footage of our interaction, since I knew they had cameras in our cubicle area, and determine who was the aggressor. At least see if I ever made any sort of threatening move toward her. Which I hadn't. I also told them, and had documentation, about the meeting I had with the person in the talent department to tell them what was brewing because I saw this coming. HR determined I had done nothing wrong, but it's a funny thing about allegations, they leave a smear. Even if you haven't done anything wrong.

It could have been a little paranoia, but I felt like some of the other anchors and producers just looked at me differently. Like, if there were rumors going around, they'd believe her over me. We had both just started, so many of the others didn't know much about either one of us, but I felt like many of my peers looked at us differently. This included the supervisors and the big boss at the time, a guy named Norby Williamson. I had a meeting with him soon after it all went down and even though HR had determined I hadn't done anything wrong, he just had to tell me how it wasn't a good impression for someone just starting. I agreed, but it seemed to affect me much more than it did her.

I just felt like I couldn't catch a break. In the last two years, I had been humbled. Depressed to the point of having suicidal thoughts. I was being a good husband. Being the best father I could be. After being out of work for 1 1/2 years, I finally had a job at a major network and now I was running into THIS drama. However, because of what I had gone through in the past, I had grown a different kind of skin and was better prepared to deal with it. So when Norby told me I hadn't made a good first impression and criticized my on-air performance, I didn't get too down. I wasn't happy, but I had gone through far worse and besides, I still had a job, right?

I was happy to have a job and to have made it to network television, but as I told you earlier, ESPN was never that high on my dream jobs list. This was for many reasons, but one of the big reasons was because Stuart Scott was already there.

Let me preface myself by saying I admired and respected the hell out of Stu. God rest his soul. He was and forever will be an icon in this business. He's a big reason why I felt comfortable being myself. I'm not about to lie and say we were close friends. We weren't at all. I knew him. He knew me and we were cordial when we saw one another, but we never had long talks, hung out, or even sat down for a meal, even though I wanted to. I'm not blaming him. He was a busy guy, and he had a life of his own. I had no big problems with Stu. However, for the longest time, I did have a bit of resentment. Not with him exactly. Just when it came to him. I'm not hating on his talents because I don't think he got ENOUGH credit for them. He was way more than just catch phrases or a gimmick; he was a solid-ass journalist who could run circles around anyone at ESPN. I even thought he didn't get enough love from the ESPN brass.

The problem I had was with all the people trying to compare me to him. I know it should be a compliment, and for those who meant it that way, like that Source magazine write-up a few years earlier, I took it that way. I'm talking about the ignorant people who said I was trying to "copy" his style or his word play. Even now it burns me the hell up because anyone that knows me off camera knows better. Those who really know me know I'm really being myself and actually holding back just a tad for television. However, because he was on national television first, and there weren't many with this style besides us, I often got called "a poor man's" version or a "biter." Funny thing is, no one ever says this about some of the "other" anchors, who sound similar to anchors who look like them. I wonder why?

Before you go, "Look at him pulling the race card!!" Slow down. This situation wasn't exclusively a white/black issue. Sure, I couldn't stand that many just couldn't believe that a black man would dare sound black on television. So of course it must be a crime that we've got two. On air. At the same network. However, I actually heard the Stu Scott comparisons more from black people than white.

For the most part, they came with good intentions. However, sometimes good intentions can come across the wrong way. Like the time I was at an NABJ convention in Vegas and two people I consider friends, who happen to be two of the biggest media personalities in the business today, decided they wanted to have a little intervention. Unsolicited, they just began to tell me how I was acting too much like Stu and how I needed to switch shit up. I know they probably meant well, but after nine years of me doing something one way, I had to change because, "Well, he was here first." I remember looking at them with amazement and saying to myself, "Get the f*** outta here with that b.s." It hurt more because these two actually knew me. Not a lot, but they had seen me behind closed doors. Away from the cameras. Then again, maybe they hadn't been exposed to enough to quite understand that "MFs, I'M JUST BEING ME!!!" It was a huge party and the brown juice was flowing heavily, so let's just blame their ignorance at the time on the alcohol.

Fans or colleagues making the comparison is one thing, but the one time it really stuck out and may have had an effect on my career came from an ESPN employee hired by management. We used to have these sessions with this talent coach named Bud Morgan, who would come in periodically to give us critiques and other feedback. Bud was a great guy, and I enjoyed meeting with him because I loved to have constructive criticism. Given and taken the right way, it only makes you better, if it's accurate. Bud was an older white guy and the reason I bring this up is because he'd tell me this just about each and every time he'd meet with me. He'd be like, "I could be wrong because I'm an older white guy but...etc. etc." I always laughed it off until this one particular session we had.

Chapter 15

SIGN OFF

I HAD BEEN at ESPN for awhile now and didn't feel like I was making any traction. I was doing a few shifts on this show called NBA Tonight, but 90 percent of the time I was still doing ESPNews and was growing increasingly frustrated. I asked coordinating producers what I needed to do better to get my chance on a few SportsCenters or other shows, and they had little or no answers. Some even told me they hadn't watched my shows to determine what I needed to do.

Now how could this be? How do you know who's ready to move up and who's not if you never watch our shows? Anyway, I asked Bud this very question, and I got the most frank, candid answer I think I'd ever been given in my entire career to that point. He started off with his usual, "Well, this is coming from an old white guy and maybe I shouldn't be telling you this, but I'm about to retire, so I don't care. You can even tell them I said it." He went on, "Mike, I like you. I think you're good, but there are some higher-ups around here that think you're too GHETTO." I...was...fucking... FLOORED!!! Ghetto?? Really?? However, he wasn't finished. He then followed that up with, "They feel like they already have someone like that." I didn't have to ask who he was talking about. I knew he was talking about Stu.

Even though I was stunned, I actually thanked Bud for being totally honest with me. He didn't have to be. Over some time, a few others would give me suggestions about my style and try to get me to avoid sounding like Stu. In other words, avoid sounding urban. I had one coordinating producer stop me in the hall and tell me to stop using the word "ain't" in my scripts because it "wasn't becoming of a SportsCenter anchor." Meanwhile, others like Scott Van Pelt used it and no one ever said anything to him. In fact, SVP, who's white by the way, used more slang than me, but no one ever accused him of sounding too ghetto. *This isn't an indictment of SVP. He's a legend and I feel a better "sportscaster," but how is it someone can be given more love who appropriates the culture than someone who actually lives it?*

I even had some suggest that I try to emulate black sportscasters at the network like the late John Saunders or Mike Tirico. *Great broadcasters but let's just say they uh never sprinkled a lot of seasoning on their food.* So, let me get this right. You don't want me sounding like this black guy over here, but it's totally cool to sound like "these" black dudes?? Okay. Got it, but not really.

Listen, let me make something very clear here. I'm not saying the reason why I never reached the levels of success I thought I should have at ESPN was strictly based on what Bud told me. I mean, it IS what HE said, but I've also swallowed enough of my ego to realize that maybe I just wasn't good enough. At least in the eyes of the people who made the decisions. The way they judge talent there is very sub-jective, and they probably just weren't digging me then, or maybe they didn't personally like me. I tried to be cool and cordial to everyone, but sometimes that just wasn't recip-rocated. I understand. It's the business.

Working at ESPN can be stressful, and the worst part about it is, there's really nothing to do locally to take your mind off of things. There was the West Hartford area that was pretty trendy, but it never was really my sort of vibe. So any chance I got, I traveled two hours south to New York City to see my mom or just to hang out. I met this dude named William Michael Reid, who introduced me to these party promoters named John and NFL Kev, who would put on Monday Night Football events at this restaurant called Justin's. There would be NFL players, other athletes, and celebrities coming through all the time and by this time, a few of them had seen me on ESPN (even if it was ESPNews) and we'd hit it off. Then something Kevin Frazier told me when I was talking to him about my frustrations with the lack of opportunities at ESPN came to mind. He said, "Yo, don't concern yourself about what they're giving you here. You should be thinking about your next move already and what you need to do to get there. So parlay this little shit they ARE giving you into something that benefits YOU." In other words, use them like they're using you.

I took that advice Kevin gave me and ran with it. When I was in New York for those Monday Night Football events, I didn't just party, I built up a network of athletes and celebrities that I could call upon, if I needed them. I also reached out to other athletes I had developed relationships with over the years. My thinking was, I had a platform on a major network, even if it was ESPNews, and I planned to use it. I'd work with the producers and tell them I could get this guy or that guy to come on and of course, I'd be the one conducting the interviews. That was good and got me some recognition, but I also needed to take it to the next level. So I started calling my interviews *Step to the Mike.* I'm sure some thought it was a little selfish and I was even told once that it's not about me but about the ESPN brand. That's true and I'm all about the brand, but I also had to give myself the boost no one else seemed willing to give me.

The downside of me going to New York was it was causing stress at home. Sure, I would have a good time. I'd party and at times get highly intoxicated, but I was also in the city taking care of business. Getting closer and securing relationships that would benefit me…take that back… US years later. *I say us because if I win, my family wins.* Camille couldn't see that, or she suspected there was much more going on than securing "professional" relationships.

It didn't help that one time I lied to her about needing her to transfer some money into an account because my truck had been towed and I had to pay all these crazy fees. In reality what had happened was I decided to buy bottles at a table one night and didn't realize HOW MUCH that cost. *Look, before then, I always had access to other people's tables because they'd invite ME to sit with them.* And yes, there were beautiful women at these events, but I can say I never cheated on Camille when I went down there. *Which, as you know, is a remarkable achievement if you've been really reading this book so far.* Nonetheless, she was not pleased, and it started putting a strain on our relationship.

Speaking of relationships. I was finally realizing that that was the key to navigating your way through ESPN. It was super important to establish them with the right people if you wanted to be noticed or survive. That place is like a country club, and if you're not a member or in good standing with the right member, you'll be on the outside looking in.

So here's how it works. *Listen up if you're currently working there and not getting the run you want.* The first thing you do is identify what show you'd like to work on. Whether it be NFL Live, First Take, a certain SportsCenter, etc. Then figure out what producers and coordinating producers run that show. Shoot the shit with them. Get to know them and let them know it's always been the show you wanted to be on. *Sure, it's a little glad handing, but play the game. Listen, there's more.* After that, spend time around that show crew. On your days off or free time, see how they run things. I did this for both NFL Live and First Take, and it worked out because they saw I was THAT dedicated to do the show. The most important step is to set up a meeting with the senior CP of that show and just ask him straight up, "How can I be a part of it?" Have a tape of some of your work in hand ready to show them just in case they're on that "I haven't seen a lot of you" tip or just why you believe you'd be a good fit. Send follow-up emails. Compliment them for good shows and even send suggestions or story ideas to make the show better. Do all of this BEFORE you get on the show and of course, watch the schedule.

I know it's a lot, and I know it doesn't guarantee you'll get that show. However, it certainly won't hurt, and you won't

hear the excuse that so many people have gotten there...
"We didn't know you were interested."

I'd say about 90 percent of the anchors at ESPN, at least
when I was there, had SportsCenter as their goal. I was part
of that other 10 percent. It's not that I didn't want to do it.
It is the flagship program and at the time, the most watched
studio program at the network. I just wanted to do more
than just highlights. I wanted to talk to people. Engage and
interview. I wanted to host.

I had my eye on *First Take*. I loved that show. Remember, I was supposed to audition for a newsreader position
when the show was called Cold Pizza before being hired at
ESPN. Well, it had moved to Bristol from New York, and I
just enjoyed the format. Oh, I forgot. For those who don't
remember, before it became a strictly debate style show, First
Take used to have more of a morning show format, with
interviews and games etc. It did have the debate segment
within it called 1st&10, but that was just a part of it. It's
what I wanted to do, and I let everyone in charge of that
show know it. I'd come in early in the morning on my days
off and observe and just hang around the crew and eventually, I started seeing opportunities pop up on my schedule.

I enjoyed working with that crew. It was a totally different environment from the SportsCenter atmosphere. It was
so much more relaxed, and the juvenile pettiness was at a
minimum. Ironically, many times I got to work with Jay
Crawford, who I would've replaced in Tampa had I not been
blocked by some powers that be in Dallas. Jay was cool and
accommodating and just fun to be around. Dana Jacobson,
on the other hand, was iffy. Some days she'd speak to me.
Some days she wouldn't even acknowledge my existence.

I really just wanted to fit in and get along. I mean, I'd go out of my way to be super nice, but on some days, she just wasn't having it. It was like she was mad at the world and taking it out on anyone in her path. We never had an argument or major fall-out, but it was like walking on eggshells sometimes when I did the show with her. It made working on the show I loved the most in the building very uncomfortable at times.

I've always just wanted everyone to get along. I know that sounds like some corny Rodney King shit, but it's true. Especially when it came to my co-workers. I've always just wanted to be accepted and liked. It can be detrimental at times, and I've been backstabbed many times because of it, but I doubt if I'll ever stop caring or change. Even when I feel like someone isn't treating me fairly or seemingly not accepting me, I'm willing to try and pick them up when they're down. This was the case with me and Dana. I'm not going to discuss exactly what she was going through, but I reached out to her while she was and let her know that I was there for her. I've always thought she was incredible on air and I told her this anytime I could, but I also needed her to know that although we didn't have the closest relationship, that I'd be praying for her. I think she really appreciated that because afterwards, our situation changed. She became way more engaging and very friendly. After that, I actually enjoyed working with her any time I could, and I'd do whatever I could for her, even to this day.

While I was figuring out how to work out my relationships at work, I wasn't doing a good job at home. It could've been my working hours. Living in Bristol. Me going to New York to network a lot, or maybe I hadn't lost the weight

I'd gained during my depression, but between Camille and me, something appeared to be off or missing. There was no affection. Barely anything happening in the bedroom and if it was, it was never initiated by her. I was really starting to think that this woman didn't love me anymore.

By this time, we had moved into another house in this nice suburb, and Kayla was doing well in school. Camille was working at Ethan Allen and doing great. In fact, her sales and bonuses were a big reason we were able to buy that house and decorate it so nicely. So the inside of our home looked great...from a furniture standpoint. Not so much when it came to our relationship. Now let me say we weren't yelling or screaming. We weren't fussing or fighting. We were just being, with little to no conversation at all.

Kayla was getting older, and I'd play with her and do whatever needed to be done to care for her. Camille would do (and still does) a hell of a job making sure Kayla was taking care of her business in school, but our relationship was more as parents instead of husband and wife, unless it came to bills, etc. At one point, I was actually jealous of Kayla because I felt like once she was born, Camille focused so much on being a great mom that she forgot to be my wife. It might not have been her intention, but it's how I felt.

I decided to approach my issues at home like I did at work when I felt like there was something I wasn't happy with or missing out on. I would have a meeting. I'd sit Camille down and I'd always start with me. I always felt the best way to let someone know you have an issue with them is to ask if you are actually the problem. So I'd say, "What can I do to be a better husband?" I just wanted to make sure I was giving her all she needed because if I wasn't, then maybe that was what was leading to me lacking in this marriage. Her response would be something like, "Play with Kayla more" or "Take her to the bus stop in the morning." The only other thing I could remember was her saying to push my chair back under the table when I got up from my seat.

I listened. I made adjustments. I tried to play with Kayla more, even though I'd be dog tired from work, and I still push my chair under a table when I get up presently. However, I'd then tell her what I felt I "needed" more of from her. Which was affection and not just sex. I'd always tell her how pretty or fine she was, unsolicited, but never heard it from her. Then again, the way I looked, I guess she probably would've just been lying to me. However, I'm a person who likes to be pushed, and if my girl tells me, "It's time to hit that gym, dude," I'm going. Especially if you hit it with me.

I also told her I'd like to have a little more support when it came to my career. I understood she wasn't a sports fan, but could she watch me every now and then just to make sure what I'm wearing was cool or tell me if my tie was straight or not. She could tell me everything Al Roker and Matt Lauer were doing on The Today Show that day, but rarely could she tell me anything I had said or done on my job. I know it sounds like I'm whining and maybe I am. I wasn't asking for her to watch the entire three hours I was on, but damn, at least you could confirm I was actually AT work that day. *I have to give y'all doses of my home life. It still drains the hell out of me. Back to work.*

Between years three and four for me at ESPN, I was actually starting to make some traction. I was doing a lot of NFL Live shifts, filling in for Trey Wingo, and I was on First

Take a lot whenever Dana or Jay was off. I also got to debut the first ESPNews show in HD with David Lloyd. Then, all of a sudden, I got called into Jay Levy's office. He was in charge of the nightly show called Baseball Tonight. He said a few people had suggested I'd be a good fit for the show and asked me if I was interested in being the secondary host behind Karl Ravech. *Full honesty here. I really didn't care much about baseball. Even though it was the first sport I fell in love with thanks to the Yankees, outside of that team, I could really give a damn about the sport.* So guess what I told him?? Hell yeah, I'm interested. Look, it wasn't that I didn't like or appreciate the game. I just wasn't passionate about it enough to watch religiously. Besides, this was too good of an opportunity for me to pass up.

The other great thing about this opportunity coming along was that my contract was coming up and being named to that post helped in negotiations. I got a good, if not great, bump in salary in my new three-year contract because of it. However, my tenure wasn't anything to write home about.

I'll admit I wasn't very good on that show. Especially early on. It was a highlight show, and since I wasn't the biggest baseball fan, some of the more foreign names felt even MORE foreign to me. The analysts I worked with on the show were great, and they helped out a lot, but it was a grind.

Like anything in my life, though, I took it as a challenge and worked hard to get better. The more reps I got, the better I got. I don't think I was ever pretty good, but at least I was decent. Karl Ravech was great to me and offered advice here and there. It's one of the reasons why I'll always have love for that dude. The producers and CPs gave me good feedback and told me I was being too hard on myself, and maybe I was, but I just felt out of my element. I wanted to add my personality and flavor and did on occasions, but it felt forced.

The reason I was offered this position in the first place was because a guy named Steve Berthiaume had left ESPN to take a job in New York at a sports station. He didn't like it there. Decided to quit and after a few months, he decided to come back. When he got rehired, I could see the writing on the wall. Just like sports, free agents leave, play elsewhere, and sometimes come back. When they come back, if they're better than the person who replaced them, they usually get the nod over that guy who filled in while they were gone. I don't have to tell you that happened to me. I will say that the powers that be did it in a nice way, telling me, "Well, you know Bert was doing this before he left and now that he's back, we just feel it's right to put him back in that role where he's familiar. This is not about you or your performance. You were good and improving. We're just making this decision based on his experience."

They could've easily said, "You suck. He's good. You're out. He's in," but they didn't, and I appreciated it. Honestly, I was a little relieved. Like I said, it was more of a grind for me than anything and well, it did benefit me in a way because I got that new contract out of it. I wasn't even looking at how some may view a demotion, no matter WHY it happened, as a stain or that it was an indication of you not being able to get the job done.

The landscape in sportscasting had changed drastically. Local stations were cutting sportscasts or getting rid of them altogether, and ESPN had no competition when it came to national networks. Fox (before FS1) and CNN had folded their sports operations years prior and so for a sportscaster, there was really nowhere else to go and the worst part about that is, the executives at ESPN knew it.

To say there was an arrogance roaming through ESPN hallways was an understatement. They knew they were the shit and couldn't be touched. They almost looked at some talent as if the talent should be paying the network to work there. While I will say it was an honor to be able to put those four letters on my resume, I do believe in treating the people who work hard for you right. At least respectfully. Let me make myself clear: I'm not saying anyone intentionally disrespected me. *I always have to preface myself when it comes to any criticism of ESPN because people think I'm still bitter. More on that later.* On occasions, I and many others just didn't feel a level of respect or appreciation for the hard work we were putting in.

I had a meeting with one of the guys in charge once, and during this meeting in his office I asked him if they listened to the fans about what they wanted to see or the anchors they liked. Like if they ever did these Q-studies. He told me, "We don't really listen to the fans. We basically just TELL THEM what they like and they'll accept it." In other words, "We're going to shove this down your throats and if you don't like it, oh well, you don't have another choice right now."

On another occasion, we had a huge talent meeting and an executive told us that all anchors and hosts aren't made alike. He said, "We will treat each and every one of you fairly, but we will not treat you equally." *Listen people. He didn't just say this to me. He said this to EVERYBODY.*

ASK A FEW OF THEM AND THEY'LL CONFIRM. It's the reason why you'll see some on-air people get slapped on the hand for an offense, while others get a 30-day suspension for a lesser crime. There are no set rules or penalties for offenses, like in a judicial system. It's all arbitrary. I felt this on several occasions during my tenure at ESPN.

I had a SportsCenter shift one day, but it wasn't just a regular show. On this day, the head of ESPN was coming to observe. I don't know why he chose our show. I think he was asked by one of our producers and he said he would. Well, needless to say, even though this particular SportsCenter wasn't on ESPN but on ESPNews, it got support from some of the senior producers like never before. In fact, it got too much attention to the point where everyone was trying to make things too perfect. This was at a time when Twitter was just becoming popular, so I tweeted out, "The big boss is observing our show today. Needless to say our show pod is tighter than a gnat's behind." I was thinking it was an innocuous tweet. Just saying that we're running a really tight ship and yes, some people may be a little tight but nothing malicious. Well, the show was going great but right before the end of it, I got an instant message from a senior CP asking me about the tweet and to see him after the show. I went into his office and explained where I was coming from and I thought the explanation was good enough. He said he didn't think it was that bad either, but a publication called Sports Business Daily picked up the tweet and used it as part of their online joke of the day. I guess they considered it that funny. Problem is, I guess ESPN wasn't laughing. A few days later, I got a call from the head of production, Mark Gross and he said some bullshit about how they needed to hold their people "accountable" and that my tweet "had brought embarrassment to the network." Are you kidding, man?? I never even said who the "big boss" was, but because another publication thought it was funny, you're mad?? Yup, that's exactly how they were thinking. I got suspended a day without pay and I was supposed to go out to L.A. to do some SportsCenters there for a few days, but they took me off the trip. The suspension hurt, but the L.A. thing really stung. Sure, I was looking forward to going out there, but it also showed me how much they valued us as workers. I wasn't going to be going out to L.A. just to enjoy the weather and scene. I was going out there to WORK for YOU and here you are treating it like you're taking a trip to Disneyland away from a child.

As I stated earlier, there was no equal treatment. It just depended on what clique you rolled with and if you had a good relationship with the person making the decision. Others had put far worse stuff on social media before me (and I know that's a huge debate there now) and nothing happened to them. However, I had to be held accountable. Right.

Anchors weren't just treated differently when it came to disciplinary issues. Bosses would come out of their side offices, walk up to a cube, and speak to some anchors and totally ignore an anchor sitting right next to him/her. No "Hi." No acknowledgement. Not even a head nod. It's a minor thing, but it's just how some in management would behave, and believe me, plenty of other anchors noticed it.

Opportunities were at their discretion too. Whether that meant inside or outside of the company. I've already told you about how they select their anchors for different shows.

A lot of politics is involved. I get that. It's how the game is played, but they also decided who's going to be doing inside promos for them too, like the *This is SportsCenter* commercials that used to be so popular there. I'm not saying I was ever treated unfairly when it came to that because I wasn't really one of their mainstay anchors on that show. However, they have killed more than one dream of mine outside of that place.

What I loved about ESPN is it was a huge platform and as you know, it was seen by plenty of people. If you were on it, more than likely you'd be seen by someone important, especially if you were on the right shows. Since I began filling in on some of the more popular programs, I was getting a little bit more exposure and recognition by athletes and A-list entertainers. As Kevin Frazier had advised me to do, I was trying to parlay this platform. If they weren't showing me major love, then get it elsewhere using their light. My agent began putting out feelers for other things, and as I said before, acting has always been a dream of mine. There was interest from a popular TV show and not just any show, one of my favorite shows on the air at the time called *The Game,* which was about a fictional football team and their homelife. I loved the creator and executive producer of this show, Mara Brock Akil. Everything this woman touch(es) turns to or has turned to gold, and this was her current baby. They wanted me to come on and play myself in not just one episode but three different episodes. I was over the roof ecstatic to do this. This would give me exposure to a totally different audience, and even if it was a small part, I was in. Problem is, when it comes to ESPN, they want to approve everything not dealing with them, even if you just want to take a shit elsewhere.

I was optimistic they'd approve this. Besides, I've seen other anchors do raunchy Adam Sandler movies and TV cameos all the time. Why would they block me? Well, here's why they say they did. In one of the opening scenes, one of the main characters was having sex with someone in the bathroom stall. This wasn't on a network like HBO, so they could only show so much, but it was enough for ESPN. At least for them to have an excuse not to let me do it. They said they were doing it for "my" benefit. They didn't think it would be a good idea for an ESPN anchor to be a part of a show with that kind of content. Wait a minute??? Just for the record, *I'm* not having sex in the bathroom. I'm not in til scene 3 at this press conference where I'm playing me. Can you take that into consideration? The producers of the show even said that they would change my name in the script, and I didn't have to mention ESPN at all. They just wanted me to be in it. I wanted it badly too. ESPN just was not having it, and so I missed out.

There was that rejection and them vetoing a second appearance of me going on a CNN news show hosted by D.L. Hughley. The only reason they allowed me to go on the first time was because D.L. is my cousin. When I made that appearance, I had done such a good job that CNN wanted me to appear again, to which ESPN flat-out said "no." Look, I get it. It's their network and my job was to be on their air, but I could never understand why some there could while others couldn't. After that, I began resenting ESPN. Problem is, I didn't have a better option, so I had to continue to play the game. Smile on the outside while having the pit of hell burning on the inside.

In my personal life, my mom had gotten married again to this guy named Jerry, who I've practically known my entire life. He treated her like the queen she is, and I respected him enough that I actually looked at him like a dad. Lord knows my other dads weren't really doing the job.

Jimmy, my biological father, was living in Tampa. I would speak to him every now and then on holidays, or he'd call me for my birthday because my sister reminded him to. Since I was on television, he'd brag to all his friends about me and he made sure to tell me how proud he was of me in his deep baritone voice. However, outside of those brief conversations, there was little or no interaction and little relationship. I'd even bet money he didn't know the name of my kids.

As for Richard, he was still in jail with little possibility of ever getting out. He knew it, but it didn't stop him from trying to pressure his sister and mom from trying. Once again, he did the crime. He'd have to do the time. I would write him every so often, but that slacked off a bit. I'd feel terrible when he'd send me a letter asking how come he hadn't heard from me. I just didn't know what to say. I had so many different emotions when it came to him. There was part pity because he was locked up, but that was overshadowed by the relief that he couldn't harm anyone else, including himself. There was anger that he could never overcome his demons that pushed him to be in his predicament in the first place. Then there was sadness because deep down I knew he had a good heart. He just took it down the wrong path.

In the nine years he spent in prison, I went to see him exactly once. One reason was my schedule. He was imprisoned in Alabama and I was living in Texas and Connecticut during the time, so it was difficult to do so. Another reason was, frankly, I just didn't want to see him locked up like that. Even though I knew he deserved his punishment, I knew it would be difficult to see him confined. However, I finally did when I went down with his mom and sister.

Going into a prison is surreal. It was my first time being in one and even though I was just a visitor, the energy was tense. You pretty much couldn't take anything inside, and honestly, it was a bit nerve-wracking. They brought us into the common room where other inmates were with their families. I was looking around, and I've got to admit, I was asking myself, "I wonder what he's in for? What if he's a stone-cold murderer? He's probably in for drugs." I threw out all kinds of stereotypes, but one thing that stood out that I could pinpoint without a doubt was, the majority of the inmates in this room were black and pretty young.

When that reality took over, I became sad and felt a bit guilty. These brothers were the same age or younger than me. Hell, this could've easily been me. Situations I was placed in or placed myself in could've ended up bringing me right HERE. How 'bout when I took that gun Richard had given me that summer and shot it carelessly or played with it around friends to scare them? What if I had been holding that gun during that drive-by in my neighborhood? What if Durand had said "yes" during that time I wrote about earlier in his house? What if I had been in the wrong place at the wrong time with Bice when he was dealing?

Only the grace of God and good family members kept me out of here. God is with these brothers too. So was it lack of family love, a corrupt system, lack of opportunities, or something else that landed them here? I'm telling you, regardless of what it is, you could see on their faces it's somewhere you do NOT want to be.

Richard was in his 60s when he went in, so he was an older guy. When he finally came into the room, it was like I was seeing him for the first time. He knew I was coming, which I thought would make him feel good, but when he saw me, he didn't look too happy. I'm not saying or thinking he should've done a jig and spun me around, but damn, the brother barely cracked a smile. I guess if I put myself in his shoes he was feeling similar to how I was. He probably didn't want me to see him this way, or maybe he had to put out a persona for the other inmates just in case they were watching. *Hell, I don't know. I ain't never been to prison and I don't ever plan on going, Lord's will.*

He also didn't look the same. He had lost a lot of weight, which was significant for him because he was already a very slim man, and his hair was cut short, which I had never seen before. The conversation started off slow but picked up and warmed up some. I apologized for not coming to see him or spend more time, and he said he understood I had a family. A family he had never seen before really. Of course, he knew Tamara, and he'd held Ashlee briefly when she was a newborn, but he had never met Camille or Kayla. He only had the pictures I had sent him.

There was a sadness in Richard's eyes that day. It was like he knew he had been locked away and would never see the outside again. Not only his body had become imprisoned but his mind too. Locked away in his own skull. Yep, I looked into the eyes of hopelessness and despair that day, and it still makes me sad now. I left that prison remembering two things. I was probably never coming back again, and I was never going to any other prison. I love my freedom too much.

Chapter 16

REACH

WORK LIFE AT ESPN was improving, slightly. A senior CP named Dave Roberts really looked out for me. He was one of only two senior CPs of color at the network, and he got me. Anytime someone would bring up that "similar to Stuart" b.s., he'd shoot it down in a staff meeting. He liked my style and wanted me to flaunt it. At one point, he was in charge of all of ESPNews and made me one of the main hosts on this show called The Hotlist, and he's the one who chose me to co-anchor the networks first show in HD. Dave was a straight-up dude who didn't take any shit from ANYONE and always seemed ready to bust someone's ass if need be. No matter who it was.

One day after one of my shows, I got called into the office of another senior CP, who I'll leave nameless. He was in charge of the day part of ESPNews under Dave, and since I worked day part, we really had developed a pretty good relationship. I actually thought the world of this dude and still do. This particular day when I went into his office and closed the door, he looked like he wanted to cry. With his voice semi trembling, he went, "Dude, you know me, right?"

I was a bit concerned now and looked at him strange, but said, "Yeah, of course, bro. What's wrong?"

His response: "Dave is insinuating that I'm a racist."

I actually sort of laughed, but not in a laughing at him type of way but laughing in a "that's crazy" way. So, of course, I had to ask him what happened. Well, from what he told me, they were in a big senior CP meeting when Dave and this guy started going back and forth, arguing about an issue. He got heated but came to a head when Dave allegedly said, "You know what your problem is? You just don't want to take orders from a nigger." From other accounts of people who know, the room was in utter shock when all of a sudden, the head of production nervously stuttered, "Uh, uh, uh...I, I don't think that's the case." Needless to say, my dude was mortified because in my opinion he was far from a racist, but it didn't mean it couldn't have been personal.

Dave eventually got promoted out of the Bristol offices and went to work in New York. That meant I really didn't have anyone in that senior CP room going to bat for me at all, and I felt it. Not long after he left, the same guy who had the incident with Dave? My friend? Took me off my day part of ESPNews, meaning I would get sent back into the regular rotation. I finally had something to call my own, and it was being taken away. Wouldn't be the last time.

My situation at home was getting worse. I can honestly say I wanted to receive love from Camille, but for whatever reason, I just didn't feel it. Maybe I had taken her through too much with all my work or non-work drama. Maybe I just wasn't attractive to her anymore because I had ballooned up to 255 pounds at one time. Even though she said she loved me every day when I left the house, I swear on everything, I really didn't feel it.

She had lost her job at Ethan Allen, so she had been out of work for awhile. That meant I had to take care of most of the bills, which I should be doing, but it was a strain, and we were barely making ends meet. She took care of the bills and accounts, so I didn't really check much. However, I did notice I was making well over six figures now but basically living paycheck to paycheck and not even putting any money to the side or investing. How could this be? I tried not to stress about it, but when you're dealing with money issues, it's hard not to.

There was still little or no intimacy, and if I tried, I'd get hit with a "Can I get a raincheck?" *For those youngsters who don't know, a raincheck is sort of a receipt they used to give out at stores when they were out of a certain supply of something on sale in the store and the receipt would guarantee that item at that same sales price when it was restocked.* I heard this a lot, and at one point I wanted to go, "But what I want is in stock NOW. You got a BOX of it right there. Looking me dead in the face." That's the kind of juvenile humor I had/have but I figured that wouldn't go over well.

She was never diagnosed, but I really think Camille suffered from a bit of postpartum depression. Thing is, she was and still is a top-flight, excellent mom. I just felt like I had lost my wife. I mentioned earlier how I was a little jealous of my own daughter early on. Now, around this time, I wasn't anymore. I had just accepted it, but it didn't stop me from longing to have the type of love, affection, and support a husband should get. I worked hard, and believe it or not, I had been faithful up to this point. *Ah, with that last sen-*

tence, *you just know some more creep shit is coming, huh?* I even washed my own clothes even though she didn't work. I actually enjoyed doing it. However, there would be nights I'd get off work after a long eight, sometimes twelve-hour day if I was doing radio too, and I'd get a text 5-10 minutes before I got home that would read, "Didn't cook. Kayla and I ate McDonald's. Fend for yourself." A few problems with this, I'm hungry as hell and you're telling me this right before I get home. Secondly, many times, it's late as hell and there really isn't anything open except a McDonald's another ten minutes out of the way. If I objected she'd sometimes say, "There are some cold cuts here. You can make YOURSELF a sandwich if you want to." I'd be incensed. I'd want to go off and say, "Your ass ain't working and you couldn't even cook me a meal or clean the house? What in the hell have you been doing at home all day?" Instead, 95 percent of the time, I just went to Mickey D's to avoid further drama. Guess that might have had something to do with that weight gain too.

One thing I've always prided myself on is being versatile. Do and learn as many different jobs as possible. Sure, you're going to be better at some than others, but versatility is one of the keys to long term success. I can honestly say without it, I wouldn't have lasted as long as I have. Especially at ESPN.

The great thing about working at ESPN was there were so many different types of jobs to do. As I said before, I never wanted to be JUST a SportsCenter anchor, reading highlights. Besides, they don't get enough facetime. *Yeah, I'm a little narcissistic, so what? Any "on-air" person who says they aren't is lying.* Seriously, it was a playground with many rides for someone like me. I ended up anchoring or hosting more than 10 different shows during my time there.

Once again, I'll admit being versatile has helped my career, but it also has hurt. I was the plug and play guy. Even utility players in baseball are rarely the stars of a team. They're an integral part, but because they don't have that one main position, their time is inconsistent, and they don't get to play every day. It was a conundrum for me. Part of me liked being on so many different shows because I got bored easily. However, I wanted to find a home and be a part of a unit on *my* show. Something I could grow.

Another negative about being the utility guy is you aren't seen as the guy IF an opportunity arose. Now I'm not saying that's the only reason. Maybe I just wasn't good enough in the eyes of those making the decisions, but I never got the chance to be the main guy on any of the shows I did or even felt like I was seriously being considered to be. Sure, there was that brief stint I had on that ESPNews day part The Hot List, which was taken away, but even that was temporary and never permanently assigned to begin with.

There was one time when reality set in like a mother-f***er. I was doing NFL Live pretty consistently. At one point, I was pretty much the #2 behind the regular host Trey Wingo. I thought I was doing a good job. The feedback I got was good and the people in charge always said they were pleased, so I had reason to believe I was solid. Well, this was around the time SportsCenter was going to expand their live shows to include early morning, and Trey was rumored to be leaving NFL Live to take over one of the shows. My thinking at the time was, "Finally, I'm going to have the chance to take over the main chair on one of the network's top shows."

What I've learned in this business is your dreams are far from other people's desires many times. While I was being "considered" for the gig, if Trey did leave, the word was the NFL Live chair would go to Josh Elliott. Nothing against Josh, but he had rarely, if EVER, hosted that show before. And this was Josh before he was even on SportsCenters consistently. Once again, nothing against him, he's a great guy, but I knew then that I would never be seriously respected by the people running that network. Sure, I was good enough to date, but they damn sure ain't gonna put a ring on it.

Trey never left the show while I was there, and eventually, they phased me off it in favor of Michael Smith. Once again, nothing against him, but at the time, he didn't have a lot of "hosting" experience. That's when Kevin's words came back to me and really sunk in this time. "Parlay this little shit they're giving you into something bigger and better for yourself." In other words, use them like they've used you. Be selfish, but be smart about it.

Look, I know some of you may think that I'm being ungrateful. "Damn, Mike, weren't you the same dude just crying to have a gig a few chapters back??" Yes, sir. That's me. The thing is I was very grateful and thankful to have a job, and to be blessed with the opportunity to grace the ESPN airwaves was remarkable. I wasn't asking to be handed something. I busted my ass to get it. I worked long hours and even stayed afterwards to make our shows better. I've even booked interviews with athletes I knew for shows I wasn't on.

> *Even though I didn't have "a" show, I'd always send*
> *ideas to the senior CPs to try and make every last show*
> *in that building better. I wanted US to win. So sure,*
> *I'm about to be a little selfish, but no one can ever say*
> *that I didn't make sure the team was going to win.*

On one of my trips to New York, I met three young ladies, Natara, Miko and Tandra, who are three of my best friends today. In fact, they're more than friends. I call them my sisters because they feel like family and they know I'd do anything for them. They've all helped me in some sort of way in my career, but it was Natara who taught me about branding myself. She was (and still is) an executive in the NFL offices and gave me a game plan on how to make "Mike Hill" stand out.

I took some of her tips and started creating more ideas for myself under the ESPN banner using some of their resources, I was able to hammer out a few things that made a difference for me. I brought back the Step to The Mike segments, within interviews, this time making it more like a hot seat for guests at the end of the interview. Then I expanded it to a web-based show using a mini recorder I bought myself. For that, I'd ask some of the guests who came through the ESPN car wash if they'd give me five minutes of their time for my own interview that wouldn't air on the network. Most said yes, including guys like Lil Wayne.

The project I'm most proud of that I created while at ESPN was another web-based show called Both Sides of the Ball. The original idea came up while I was still on ESPNews. On Fridays I used to do the Hot List with these two former football players, Ray Buchannan and Lomas

Brown. Two great but very different guys. Ray was the wild child, who could and would say just about anything, while Lomas was this giant of a guy but a lovable, country teddy bear. It was simple, but the most important element of the whole segment was that it was fun. It was sports but mostly entertainment. *Many people forget the E in ESPN stands for Entertainment.*

We'd ask sports-related questions but with a twist. Sure, we'd have them tell us their NFL game of the week (the best matchup of the weekend), but they'd also share with us their Game of the Weak (the sorriest hot garbage game and why). They'd do imitations and role play. It was like the old Chelsea Lately Show but for sports, and it worked because Lomas and Ray bought into and enjoyed it. We were even trying to make it bigger and some execs were listening, but Ray got into a little trouble and that was the end of that.

I put Both Sides of the Ball on the shelf until later when Jay Harris and I were trying to figure out something to do together. *Yeah, you remember Jay? The asshole who was mean to me my first day in Bristol. Yeah, that old dude.* Jay turned out to be one of my best friends in the world and I'd give my life for that brother. We just clicked. My best and most memorable shows were with him doing SportsCenter. We'd have so much fun we'd forget we were on television. I don't know how many times we almost cursed on air.

Before I get into our BSOTB life together, let me tell you about the most memorable show we did together, and I wish I wasn't able to because it was tragic. The date was easy to remember. July 4th, 2009, actually the anniversary of us meeting. It was a Saturday that year and we were preparing to do a 6p SportsCenter together. It was about an hour until air time and we were all sitting at our show pod when the coordinating producer that day went, "Who's Steve McNair?"

At first I was confused because I was thinking to myself, "Why would YOU, a sports producer, ask such a rhetorical question? What do you mean, who's Steve McNair?" I said to him, "He's the former QB for the Titans and Ravens. Why?"

He replied in a straightforward manner, "He's dead."

Ummm, excuse me? What did you just say? Many know the details. He was killed in a murder suicide situation in Nashville, and since I had covered him while in Nashville, I sprang into action. I actually informed his former teammate Eddie George about the matter, and we were able to get several interviews for the show. Jay came from a news background, so he was solid, and even though the situation was terrible, it showed we could handle a matter like that, even though the two of us are usually silly as hell.

Jay and I got a lot of love for that show, for the interviews I was able to secure from the guys I still knew from covering the team and for our tone. However, not long after that, I was having a session with the head of production, Mark Gross, and asked him if he'd seen it, and his reply was like, "Yeah, you guys did a good job. Maybe your tone was a little too solemn or emotional, but it was okay." I guess he was trying to give a compliment, but it came across in all the wrong ways to me. Steve McNair wasn't just a victim or a story to me, he was someone I had gotten to know and covered, so yes, the shit was solemn and emotional for me. However, this was this particular guy's m.o. No matter how many compliments I got from anyone, he'd always point out the negative and never acknowledge when things were great. At times I'd be like, "Damn, do I do anything good in your eyes?" Probably not.

Back to BSOTB. After the Ray and Lo show was a no-go, like I said, I put that on the shelf for awhile, but because Jay and I had such good chemistry, we wanted to put something together. We came up with a sketch-like, improvised comedy show that we could put on ESPN.com. It was like Curb Your Enthusiasm for Sports. Rob King was the head of dot.com and he was all on board. Digital would provide us the equipment, and they'd shoot and edit it for us as well.

It started off as Jay and me just going back and forth, ad-libbing lines about current sporting events but doing so in a comical way. What it morphed into was something I'm very proud of and I know plenty of people enjoyed. Jade Hoye, who worked in dot.com, shot and edited the pieces. A guy named Ira Fritz, who was a writer for the network, came aboard and started creating ideas and writing scripts for us. We'd still ad-lib a lot of it, but we had structure and it started to take off. Some of the episodes had Snoop Dogg, Bo Jackson, Emeril Lagassi, Rob Riggle, Steve Carrell, Donald Faison, Anthony Mackie, and others.

If we could've gotten a little promotion from the other entities, it would've been bigger, but it did get noticed by the right people. A major advertiser, Pepsi and Frito Lay, came in and offered a huge sponsorship for us and ordered four episodes that we'd put out over four weeks this particular summer.

Now, before I go any further, here's something I forgot to mention. Jay, Ira, and I were not getting paid for doing these in the first place. We were doing this in ADDITION to our jobs on SportsCenter or other shows. Our hope was for ESPN to expand it in some sort of way or for us to get this big advertiser and we'd all get paid.

Well, we GOT the advertiser, but we had a problem. Even though Pepsi was offering MAJOR money for this project, the sales team at ESPN didn't want to pay us anything. Not even a year's supply of Pepsi. Nada. Zilch. Well, I know my worth and I wasn't going to stand for that. This was a passion project, but now instead of doing this in our free time, when or IF we had time, we were now responsible to churn out four episodes by a certain date. Meaning, this is extra work that you HAVE to do, but you're not getting paid for it. I had to put my foot down, even if they wanted to chop it off.

In a move that pissed a lot of people off there, I said "no." I refused to do it. It's not fair that you're making extra money off of my extra work, that I'm not under contract to do, on a show I created. And on top of that, you don't want to give us anything? That's where Jay and I had to draw the line. Either pay us or give Pepsi its money back. Well, we knew THAT wasn't going to happen. So, after some squabbling and a pissed-off lady in sales calmed down, Rob King stepped up and took care of me and Jay out of his own budget. Considering what the network got and what WE took home, it wasn't a great amount, but it was something. More importantly than the money, for me, was the principle. *Well, I ain't gonna lie, it WAS about the money mostly.* Regardless, Rob looked out for us, and I'll always appreciate that.

Both Sides of the Ball gave me an opportunity to act a little, which I've always enjoyed doing, but creating and naming that show made me realize something else. I didn't own it. It was now the property of ESPN. Look, I get it, part of my job is to add content to the network. I enjoyed doing that, but what if I wanted to take an idea or show with me if I ever left? That's when I decided to form my own production company, which would be independent of anything I did with ESPN. I named it Thrill of Entertainment. Don't ask me why. I guess because Thrill is sort of my nickname and the... I don't know... I just did.

I've always had all these crazy ideas for show concepts. Usually talk show concepts and this would be a platform for me to write up, develop and, most importantly, own any idea I may have. It's something that's super important to me, and I encourage many others to do it too.

One of the early shows I developed was a talk show with its main premise being about relationship issues. It's a show catered toward women. Moderated by a woman but she's moderating a panel of diverse men, who will give women real opinions or advice. Not telling them what they wanted to hear, but what they needed to hear.

I came up with the idea because I've always been told by my female friends that I give really good relationship advice to them and I'm always giving it to them straight. When it comes to this, I'm like that mechanic that can fix your car, but mine is always broken down. In other words, I may be able to fix your relationship, but my shit is always a mess. Speaking of that.

I wasn't happy, but once again, I was too much of a coward to do the right thing when it came to fixing my marriage. Our little "What can we do to be a better husband/ wife" conversations turned into arguments because she felt

I was only asking how I could be better so that I could criticize her. I admit, I did say a few things that I wish I could take back. I won't say it here, but let's just say I wish I could take it back, even if it's how I felt at the time.

Honestly, during this stage in our marriage, I just didn't think my wife really loved me anymore. I heard her say it every day before I left for work but I didn't feel it. I don't know what it was. Maybe she was just worn down from all my work drama and constant moves. Maybe it was the added stress of having a child to take care of. Maybe I was just being sensitive. Maybe I couldn't feel at that time. Maybe I was disconnected because of everything that had happened on the outside of the home, but I didn't feel like we had a marriage. I felt like we had a co-existence.

No matter how bad things were going, I was not going to give up. Not this time. I'd already been divorced once, and I wasn't trying to go through another. Besides, I was already living without one of my children in my household. I wasn't trying to have two in that situation or be that stereotypical black man who's got two babies by two different women and not with either one, even if I had married both of them. I had to hold on, but then reality set in really hard on Kayla's ninth birthday. I remember saying to myself, *Only nine more years, and she'll be off to college and if I'm not happy, then I can leave. Just nine more years.* NINE!!! Damn. I ain't gonna make it that long.

When people ask me now do I think I could be in a relationship without cheating, I say "yes" because for many years of our marriage, I was faithful to Camille. I mean, sure I flirted and made little overtures here and there, but I never took it too far or followed through. *Hell yes, give me a cookie for doing what I'M SUPPOSED TO DO...* *even if I was STILL inappropriate.* However, social media was starting to take off and I was very active. That platform gave me access to something that living in Bristol couldn't. Available, attractive women.

I became a cyber cheater. Women were giving me attention and compliments I craved and something I wasn't getting from home. I was highly inappropriate, and it was fairly easy. Being on ESPN raised my exposure in many ways. Especially on social media platforms and a lot of these women that I had these "conversations" with loved sports. Or at least their boyfriends did.

Still, I was actually too afraid to do anything beyond cyber cheating. I'll be honest with you *(which I think I have been this entire book. Maybe too honest)*, I was seriously tempted several times, but I was too concerned about getting caught. Also, Camille was like a detective. I couldn't take a piss without her knowing exactly what tint of yellow it was. I blame her ex for making her such a hawk when it came to checking me, but then again, she knew my past. It was probably needed.

A person has needs. Some needs are more desirable or stronger than others and may be different for men and women in some ways, but they're still needs regardless. When those needs aren't met or satisfied in one place, you may seek that satisfaction elsewhere. For example, if a man meets a woman and tells her how beautiful she is or is extra affectionate all the time when they first meet, it's probably what that woman expects to be a constant. When that woman stops receiving that from her man, she may hunger for it, and if she's not being fed at home, she may have to eat out, so to speak. *I know what you're thinking. "Here he goes. He's about to make excuses for his terrible behavior again." And you're right, but I have to strongly emphasize where my head was at this point in my life. Cool? Not so much? Well, I'm going to tell you anyway.*

Let's just say at this time in my life, I was freaking starving. There was a lack of love, attention, and affection at home, and now I was beginning to receive it from others. Online and in person. I felt the creeping temptation coming back, but once again, I might as well have had an ankle bracelet on when it came to Camille. She was a hawk. HOWEVER, one place she couldn't track my activities was when I went on the road. Of course, I got those check-in calls in the middle of the night in my hotel rooms, but for the most part, I had a little bit more freedom to "roam."

Road trips for work and NABJ conventions made me feel "free." Let's just say I had my fun. One year, that fun took me to the next level.

By 2009, I was emotionally weakened. Sure, I was just a weak person overall, but I really didn't care much about my marriage. It sounds terrible to say, but I also felt like Camille didn't care. I remember having a talk about it with someone and told them I felt like my old dog tendencies were about to return and that person told me that they felt like Camille wouldn't even care. Even though she was such a hawk, maybe she'd just be upset by the embarrassment and not the act itself. So if I kept something on the low where no one knew about it, she'd be cool with it. *Yeah, I know. I told you my mindset was dumb as hell.*

Chapter 17

DEAD AIR

I WAS ON the road one year, and I met this lady I'll call "Kim." Kim was so pretty, with beautiful eyes and a fun, outgoing personality. There was an attraction there, but we didn't act on it. In fact, I actually had a little flirtatious relationship happening with someone she knew. Nothing went down there, but we exchanged numbers, and soon we were talking or texting almost every day. We were able to do so because she knew about my situation. In fact, she was actually going through a divorce at the time and was separated from her husband.

Here's the thing. I had flirted before. Back in the day, you know I'd done much, much more, but with this person, it was different. She was giving me something that I was starving for. Attention and validation. *Ladies, don't think you're the only people who are emotional about these things. We can be worse.* We were there for one another. I was a listening post for her and her for me. She told me all the issues she was going through, and of course my response was she deserved more and vice versa.

Then one day, she said something to me that absolutely blew my mind. She told me, "You are a king, who deserves to be treated as such." I know it sounds super simple, but that one sentence changed how I looked at her and how I viewed my marriage. NO ONE had ever called me a king before, and for a man who had felt inadequate because he wasn't receiving attention at home, it did something to me and my self-esteem. I started falling for her. It didn't have to do with desires of the flesh, but she was taking my heart. I loved this girl.

Ladies, because of what you've read so far, I may not be the best spokesperson for men who seek affection at home, but just like it's important for him to feel and understand you, you have to realize many of us men have feelings and needs too. I know some of us are greedy, but many want the things they're being offered from other women from you. Please, just take each other's feelings into consideration.

The bad thing about this situation for me was that she lived 3000 miles away. I was on the East Coast, and she was out west. Yes, I went to visit a few times under the guise of "work-related" events, but it was few and far between. She actually came to the East Coast several times, and each time I saw her, I wanted to spend more and more time with her.

All the other times I had stepped out before I was married to Camille, I felt little or nothing. This time, I was emotionally attached to "Kim." I wanted someone else but still couldn't be man enough to tell who I was with that I no longer wanted what we had. I'd become cold and really uninterested. I had even stopped asking for sex at home. I got sloppy because I just didn't care anymore. A part of me wanted to get caught. Then I did.

"Kim" had to have surgery, and since I wasn't there with her, I told her to call me and let me know once she was out and able to talk. Sure, I was at home, but I didn't care. Call me. Even if her name appeared on my phone, Camille didn't know who this person was, and besides, I already had a pretty good excuse to talk on the phone with her when she called. I'd basically make it seem like business and make it quick. Hell, Camille might not even be home when she did call.

Well, wouldn't you know it, Camille was home, and Kim called me the one instance I was "away" from my phone for a second. So when my phone rang, guess who saw it and decided to answer it for me? It wasn't Kayla. I didn't even hear my phone ring, in fact. I found out she called when Camille brought the phone to me and said, "It's your mistress." Holy freaking Law & Order shit!!! What??? I looked down at the caller ID and it was Kim's name. I was nervous as hell, but I had to play it off, right? I gave Camille a little "you're crazy" smirk, grabbed the phone, and said, "Hello, how'd it go?"

Kim knew the deal and played it off and just said, "It all went great. We'll send the invoice over later."

I said, "Thank you" and hung up. Camille was still right there in my face. She wanted answers, but obviously she already knew them after what she said, right? I didn't care. I knew Camille wasn't dumb, but I was damn sure going to test that IQ.

"That's Kim. She's in the business and she was helping me with a production thing. Why are you tripping? Why are you answering my phone?"

We went back and forth for awhile, but Camille wasn't buying it. She ended up saying, "End it" and walked off.

I retorted, "There's nothing to end." What's crazy about that moment was, I felt like I was trying to protect Kim and her reputation more than my own marriage. I was concerned she'd get harassed or Camille would find out who her husband was and say something, even though they were separated and going through a divorce. I also thought that if I continued to deny it was actually happening, she'd just believe it.

Let me put some of y'all in the mindset of how some cheaters think. If he does it and gets away with it, it almost becomes a game. Sometimes the thrill is "almost" being caught but being able to wiggle your way out of jams. I can't tell you how many times I've actually laughed after being in tight, hemmed-up situations because I looked at it like a f**king game. It's sick and it's weird, but until I got the help I needed, it's how I lived. It's also addictive, and you want to play the game more and more. Unfortunately, in these types of games, someone always ends up getting hurt. Either the person you're cheating with or cheating on. Because eventually the cheater will get caught. Especially when that cheater's feelings are involved, like mine were.

My patterns shifted. I'd go to work earlier and stay later to have more time to talk to Kim. All of a sudden, I was taking more trips and starting to hang out with "friends" (when she was in town). I was even keeping the pictures she was sending me in my phone instead of deleting them. I was in an all-out affair at this point.

I was also feeling like I was more in a relationship with Kim than Camille. We'd actually start having couples arguments and she was guilty of one of my biggest pet peeves in life. Double standards. *I fucking hate em!!* She'd get jealous about things and I wasn't even doing anything. Not even at home. However, there would be times where she'd go ghost for a while and couldn't explain where she was. Act like it wasn't a big deal or even not even answer her phone late at night. Since she was now divorced and living on her own, she'd say, "Well, it's different for me. I'm by myself." It was making me crazy. I probably deserved it. Several times I said I was going to end it but couldn't.

One day I got home from work, and Camille was there but Kayla wasn't. I asked Camille where Kayla was and she said, "I took her across the street (to our neighbors) because we need to talk." Ironically, we were at the same table where I liked to have our "what can I do to be a better husband" talks, but this time, she's calling the meeting. Her statement to me was very short. "You're a liar. You're a cheat and I want a divorce." Several things went through my head right at that moment. Shock because even though I sort of knew she was on to me, I just figured I'd never really get caught or she'd trip THIS hard. Worry because I was thinking about Kayla now and the reason why I tried to make the marriage last in the first place. And honestly, relief because she had the balls to do what I should've done and asked for a divorce and now that it was happening, I could be with Kim.

We argued and she told me she knew all about Kim. She knew about what she did. Where she lived. She knew about her ex-husband and about her two kids. Damn!!! I was so busted. There was no getting out of this, so what was my next step?? Oh, I know. Justify why I did it. I told her that

I was lacking this. I was lacking that. That she didn't pay attention to me when I was having our conversations at "this very table." That I didn't think she cared and/or even loved me anymore. I told her that I thought the only reason why she was with me was because it was out of convenience and better than starting again. I even had the gall to say it had to do with what I had, which at the time was absolutely NOTHING. *She really laughed at that one.*

Obviously, she deflected or denied any of my allegations, but then I asked her this simple question. "Name one thing that you do for ME as my wife?" She paused and it appeared like she really couldn't think of anything. I'd stumped her. Then she said, "Well, I don't cheat on you." Huh?? That's all you can think of? Hell, that's supposed to come with the standard package in relationships. Like when you buy a car, you should expect it to have brakes, but then again, I guess if I use that analogy, I just caused our relationship to have a fatal crash because I couldn't STOP my cheating.

The next few months were not pretty at all. The problem is, I was the only one working, and since we were pretty much living paycheck to paycheck, I wasn't making enough money to move out. So things were tense. We didn't talk, and if we did it was brief and hostile.

Camille was hurt, and even though we intended to move forward with this divorce, I could tell there was a part of her that didn't want it. I probably could've just said, "I'm sorry. I messed up. Let's make this work," and maybe we could have. But I was disconnected and she had just given me an out. I was also feeling like if we tried again, this time she'd be the one trying to hurt me and well, we just can't have that. Besides, would she have really learned her lesson with this affair opening her eyes to see that I have needs?? *I'm telling you, that's just the crazy stuff I used to think about.*

We actually tried to go to counseling. We said we were doing so to be good at co-parenting for Kayla, but all it turned into was a blame session and I was always the one to blame. Even in counseling, it appeared that my needs didn't matter. The reason why I became disconnected in the first place was just an afterthought to her. I'll give credit to the therapist, who tried to explain to her that a relationship is like running a business, where one person is the CEO and the other the COO. You need to work together in order to grow and maintain that business. That part went in one ear and out the other, it seemed. However, the one thing the therapist agreed with her one was that I was wrong for continuing my relationship with Kim. *Oh, did I forget to tell you? I didn't end it after I was really caught.* The therapist even asked me straight up, "Are you going to stop this relationship?" And my cocky, emboldened ass just shook my head "no." This is what I think hurt Camille the most because afterwards she cried uncontrollably.

Did I feel bad? Sort of. I feel worse today. I feel sick to my stomach today that I did that but back then, I didn't "feel" as much. It's not that I didn't want to. I just didn't. Before then, I think Camille would've taken me back. After that, I think I might as well have been dead to her.

After I met Kim, I was rejuvenated and motivated. She had a way of making me feel alive and important, and so I wanted to look that way. I actually got back into the gym heavily and started using this popular workout program at home. I dropped 25 pounds and people really started to take notice. That was like a drug too and I wanted more. *You know what I'm realizing writing this book, I really don't just want attention. I NEED attention. It's a revelation.* I always loved to play basketball, and now that I was in better shape, I played even more. I even joined a league at ESPN.

One day we were playing a game outside of the ESPN cafeteria and when I went to push off, I heard a "pop" like a small gun going off and something kicked me in my calf. Problem is, there was no one behind me and there was no gun. That pop I heard was my Achilles tendon tearing in my left foot. I actually drove myself to the hospital because I honestly didn't think Camille would come and get me. Now, I don't want anyone to think Camille is an evil person. That's never been the case. In fact, she's one of the loveliest, friendliest people you'll ever meet. However, like me, she had disconnected by now and I honestly was afraid to be around her in this vulnerable state. After it was confirmed to be torn at the hospital, I still didn't call home and ask to be picked up. I just drove back to the house myself.

After my surgery is when I saw how deep in the abyss I had pushed this beautiful, kind, loving lady, when it came to me. Let's just say, she was out of giving any F's. The kind of cast you get after an Achilles injury is tricky. They place your foot in with your toes down, making it nearly impossible to walk on it. So you really need crutches to get anywhere and if you have to carry something, you might be out of luck unless you have someone doing it for you.

Now Camille would still cook for me. Or I should say I could have whatever she made for herself and Kayla, but she wasn't going to do much else for me. And because I was so prideful, I really wasn't going to ask for much.

One day, I wanted some soup. Problem was, how was I going to get it off the stove and take a hot bowl of soup over to the area where I wanted to eat? I had to try. I took the soup from the stove. Turned around placed it on a table within arms' length in the kitchen. Slid the bowl down the table some. Hopped to the end of the table. Took the bowl off that table and placed it on a bookshelf and then hopped some more on crutches. I did this from furniture piece to furniture piece until I eventually got to the TV room and sat my soup down. Here's the kicker: the entire time I did this, Camille was right there and didn't raise a muscle or ask me if I needed help. I felt her disgust for me that day. Looking back, do I blame her? No!

It wasn't all bad. She did show support for me at a difficult time in March of 2010. The day I got the phone call from my aunt Edna that my stepfather Richard had passed away. She called me early in the morning, right before I was going on to do First Take.

When she called, I didn't even get too sad. I don't know if I just have a different way of dealing with death, but I haven't really cried at a funeral since my boy Bice was killed. Maybe I just can't process it and with Richard, I think I was emotionally numb because of his prison stint and not seeing him much. In fact, I still did the show that morning. Partly because there was little I could do. Partly because I wasn't overly sad and partly because I didn't want to put the show or ESPN in a bind at the last moment.

Anyway, Camille was very compassionate at that time. She even flew with Kayla down to Alabama to be with me for the funeral. Camille and Kayla met Richard for the first time as he lay in a coffin. Sad but true. Even though I wasn't outwardly sad, I may have been dealing with the emotions internally because I recall actually trying to have sex with Camille when she came down. This is something I hadn't even thought about in over a year, but for some reason, I needed to be held. *And I guess something more.* Luckily, Camille had her head on straight and even asked, "If we do this, what does this mean?" I knew what she meant, and I wasn't ready to get back with her. Not trying to be crass, but I just needed to release whatever emotion was pent up inside me.

Sadly, to this day, I've never fully cried over Richard's death. Doesn't mean I didn't love him. I did. He was the man who raised me, and I had a level of respect for him as my father despite his many faults. Even though I'm the man known for speaking, I didn't get up and speak during his funeral when family and friends were giving testimonies. However, what stood out to me at his funeral was who did. His stepdaughter Erica. The daughter of his wife Mary. The woman he'd had killed and spent the last nine years of his life in jail because of. When she got up and spoke, she wasn't full of vitriol, hate and condemnation. She was actually talking about how much she "loved" the "ole man" and what he meant to her and her brother Manny. Some found it to be weird. I found it to be incredibly awesome and the epitome of true forgiveness. I have so much respect for what Erica did because personally, I don't know if I could be so forgiving.

Another thing I remember about that funeral is what happened right afterwards. I had been on leave from ESPN for three days and the day after the funeral, I got a call from someone at the network asking me when I was coming back. I was livid. I thought it was crass and something they would've never done to some of the other anchors there. Remember, the morning I found out about his death, I still did the show partly because I didn't want to leave the network in a bind that day. It really made me start to absolutely hate that place. Then when I got home and saw they had sent a "single" small pear in a tiny basket as their condolences, I knew I didn't mean shit to those people. I know it's the thought that counts, but it was obvious at that point what they thought of me.

Not long after the funeral, Kim and I went our separate ways, but it didn't mean it was going to bring me and Camille together. It had gotten too far. However, here's the thing: even though she had already served me with divorce papers, we still hadn't actually gone to court to begin the proceedings. My financial situation was so dire that at the time, I didn't even have enough money to afford a lawyer. I thought about asking a few friends of mine who were athletes and had the money, but I didn't. I didn't want anyone else involved. I got myself into this. I needed to get out of it.

For the longest time, I didn't want to tell Kayla what was happening between us. She was nine and a part of me knew she could feel it, because I always felt dissension between my mom and stepdad, but I still didn't want to tell her. Camille did. At first, I thought she was bluffing because she knew how much I cared about Kayla and if she threatened to tell her, I'd be willing to work something out. However, I knew we eventually had to, and when we did, it was one of the worst feelings of my life. To hear your child scream uncontrollably is gut-wrenching and horrifying. I got mad at Camille because I felt like she insisted on doing this, but deep down, I knew it was all my fault. No matter what the reason was, I had destroyed this family and broken my little girl's heart. I will never be able to fix that, and it still hurts me today.

At work, even though I wasn't highly thought of, I was doing more and more high profile shows and my social media presence was increasing. I was one of the first to embrace Facebook and Twitter at ESPN and tried to get the network to do more. *I have to give myself a pat on the back because others won't. I've had several ideas or agendas that I brought up that fell on deaf ears, only to be resurrected by someone else and put into place. It's the business. It sucks, but it's just the way it is.*

Since I was doing more and more with social media, I was trying to find more ways to have an impact and met a young lady who said she could help. I actually met her through Twitter and we started working together, but that working relationship blossomed into something more than just work. Her name was Trang and she lived in Portland. *Yes, another long-distance relationship.* Like Kim, she was also going through a divorce when we met, and now I had finally started my proceedings with Camille. Luckily for me, I was about to become even more busy at work thanks to a pleasant surprise.

At ESPN, and I guess even now, I was very opinionated. Even when I was on SportsCenter, I'd conduct my interviews more as statements rather than questions on many occasions. This was something that didn't always go over well because SportsCenter wasn't that kind of show. After awhile people, including the head of our talent office Laurie Orlando, began asking me if I was interested in radio. I had done radio in past markets here and there as a guest on other people's shows but never anything consistent. I was interested, but I didn't want to give up TV in order to do so. *Yes, that was that vain "I need this face on TV" arrogance back then.* Despite all this talk, nothing ever came of it until I got a call one day from this guy named Scott Shapiro. He was the producer of Mike & Mike in the Morning. The was a hugely popular and top-rated show on ESPN radio, simulcast on ESPN2, and hosted by Mike Golic and Mike Greenberg. Shapiro wanted to know if I'd be interested in hosting with Golic one morning. I was caught off guard because I had NEVER done radio before at ESPN, and now I was being asked to do THE show there. Of course I said "yes," but I was curious as to why they'd asked me now. Well, Golic and I had worked together on NFL Live and he had apparently taken a liking to me. We had done the show a few times, but we had never even discussed me doing radio. Regardless, whatever our conversations were, he liked what he heard on and off camera and told the powers that be that he wanted me to do the show with him.

It's a prime example of just being cool with everyone you work with. Like I mentioned, Golic and I didn't even do a lot together, but I'm always going to try and interact with anyone I do a show with. Joke around. Get to know more about their lives away from television. Some are more interactive than others, but I will at least try. In this instance, it worked out for me.

I did that first show with Golic and crushed it. I just had fun and Golic made me feel super relaxed. I even joked that they didn't have to change the name anytime I filled in. The radio executives also thought I did a good job because all of a sudden I started getting numerous offers to fill in on different shows. It started with the overnight shift. Coming in at midnight and working from 2 to 6 in the morning. Those were tough ones and yeah, they were SOLO shifts. Meaning you had to talk BY YOURSELF for 4 hours at night in the middle of the night. Thank goodness I always have plenty to say.

Eventually, I started filling in on other shows and even had a few Mike & Mike's thrown in here and there. Then I started hearing rumblings that I might actually get part of my own. ESPN radio had an open slot coming up and they wanted Mark Schlereth to take it over. Schlereth, a former three-time Super Bowl champion, was another analyst I worked with on NFL Live, and we had a really tight relationship. The two of us would often commiserate about the way we felt we were being treated at ESPN. We both felt like we offered a lot but didn't get the respect and/or love some of the others in our position got. They weren't pity or bitch fests, per se, but we were just kindred spirits in that regard.

Word is, Mark had a huge decision in who was going to get the slot next to him, but I never heard from or even talked to him about it. I just decided that I was going to let whatever happened play out.

One night, Linda Cohn, another anchor, and I went for a game to Giants' Stadium. The three of us made an appearance for a Monday night football game for ESPN. As the car was driving us there, I received a call from my agent at the time, Ken Lindner. He said, "I've got some great news for you. ESPN is launching a new radio show and they want you to co-host it along with Mark Schlereth." I was giddy. I finally felt like I was winning. It would be a show from

7-10 Eastern and I'd still be able to do television. I couldn't say anything until contracts were done and ESPN made an announcement, but I was bursting at the seams on the inside. Even when Ken tried to tell me it was a deal he had been working "behind the scenes for quite awhile" *(which was a bold-faced lie),* I didn't stop smiling. I was going to have a show that was mine and with my name on it.

Hill & Schlereth was going to debut on January 10th, 2012, and we were even going to announce the new show on Mike & Mike. The money I got was terrible for a national radio show, but I didn't know that at the time. All I knew I was going to be making the most money I had ever made in my life, and financially things would be turning around. Slowly, word started creeping out that I was going to be getting the show, and people started asking me about it. Thing is, so did Camille and guess what, we hadn't finished negotiating a divorce settlement yet.

More money for me meant more money for her and child support. And even though my lawyer was really trying to stick it to her, deep down I knew she should get it and so she did. After 12 years of marriage, we were officially ending it. The final day we went to the judge's chambers in our collaborative proceedings was pretty hard. When the judge said, "This marriage is now officially over," Camille let out a heartfelt yelp. It was so sad and I automatically went to her to comfort her with a hug. At that moment, I was wondering if I had just made one of the biggest mistakes of my life, but it was now done.

Even in divorce, we still weren't separate. We couldn't. That's because we couldn't sell the house we were in, and even though I was making more money, I couldn't afford to pay the mortgage. All the bills. Give Camille her pre-alimony money and get my own place. I had been sleeping in the guest bedroom for months and continued to do so. The only thing really different about our conditions immediately following our divorce was that I could actually date openly now, which weirdly I still felt uncomfortable doing at first. And Camille and I actually got along better after our divorce than we had the last few years of our marriage.

> *Just for the record, let me reiterate how great of a woman Camille is. She's super sweet to everyone who meets her. She's not about drama, but she's no fool. There were many reasons why our marriage didn't work, and even though I felt some of my needs weren't met, I can't take anything away from her as a person. Like everything I've done in my life to this point in this book, I was still a lost boy, pretending to be a man. In the end, we just weren't compatible, and a lot of that was my fault. I have to take responsibility for my actions.*

Meanwhile, I was working hard. Doing a lot of double shifts. Sometimes not getting home until 2 am working at ESPN. However, the radio show was great because I was working with some phenomenal people, like our producers, Sean & Mike, and our program director, Amanda, who we called Boss Lady!! Doing radio was so different because I could just totally let loose, and they wanted me to. I mean, we took care of business but kept it light at all times. I learned a lot from everyone there and can honestly say it was the most fun I had while at ESPN.

Of course, there were moments that made me want to kick someone square in the nuts. One instance happened about three months into our run. I had a meeting with one of the higher-up bosses at ESPN radio. He said a few complimentary things, but then he asked me some asinine shit. "Is this persona who you're putting out really who you are?" I don't know verbatim how he put it, but it was obvious he was asking me if I was trying to come across as "urban." Like I said, he didn't say it word for word like that, but from talking to him more, it was very apparent to me where he was going with it. I really wanted to say, "Fuck you. I'm not trying to sound black...whatever that means... I am black, asshole." So imagine that happening in a meeting. Now imagine the person who I was talking to was ALSO a black man. Because he was.

Chapter 18

DEMO

ANOTHER MOMENT HAPPENED when Mark and I filled in one morning on Mike & Mike and there was a discussion about the BCS. The BCS at the time was the Bowl Championship System, and it was the way college football determined its national champions. Many critics of the BCS always thought there was one letter too many in the acronym because they felt like the formula was flawed. Mark and I were also huge critics, and that morning we were just hammering the system and Mark said something critical about the NCAA too. Well, of course, ESPN pays you to give your opinion on radio and all the debate shows that had sprung up, but they shudder and cower whenever one of theirs criticizes a league or organization they have a partnership with. Obviously, they had a relationship with the NCAA, and it was something the head of ESPN seriously tried to protect.

After the show, we got word that this guy was not pleased with US. Yes, us even though I didn't criticize the NCAA and Mark did. In his eyes, I was at fault because I didn't correct him. What was done was done, and we made the appropriate adjustments on our own show, but the damage had been done when it came to me. *I'll explain later.*

That was one of the big issues I had at that place while I was there. The corner offices rarely gave you a pat on the back if you did something exceptional, but they'd be the first to send word if they thought you messed up or simply forgot something. Don't get me wrong, I love feedback, but when it's all negative and never positive, you start to wonder if there's ANYTHING you're doing right.

I once got a stern email from the head of production, Mark Gross *(Damn, I'm bringing his name up a lot)* telling me I didn't announce what the next program was going to be as I was signing off a show I was doing. The thing is there was no break between shows. So as soon as I said "goodbye" on our show, the announcer on the next immediately said, "Welcome to (wherever the hell he was) and ESPN's coverage of (whatever the hell they were covering)." It wasn't like a viewer would turn the channel THAT quickly because I didn't say what was next to intrigue him to stay. It was something that simple, yet in that same show, I did an interview that the producer and everyone loved, and he didn't mention shit about it. Stuff like that happened all the time.

When I did radio, I felt like I was in a different world. Doing that as opposed to most of the studio shows, ESPE-CIALLY SportsCenter, was like being in a different environment. The best world, though, was doing the debate shows. It was like it wasn't even under ESPN's umbrella or something. Shows like First Take (which had become an all debate show), SportsNation, and Numbers Never Lie were heaven sent. When I did those shows, it didn't even feel like work, and I felt insulated from the bullshit. I would even joke with the producers on those shows about keeping me on as many as possible because I couldn't take being back in "Gen Pop." *"Gen Pop" is a term that's short for general population in prisons, where prisoners mingle with other prisoners with little or no special privileges.* I never wanted to go back because when I did the debate shows, it felt like Oz *(a popular TV show about this special prison. Then again, how special can prison actually be?).* A guy named Jamie Horowitz was in charge of these shows. He had power and he didn't come up as an ESPN guy, so he always ran and did things outside of the ESPN norm. He wasn't very popular among some of his ESPN brethren, but at the time, I loved what he was doing, and he always told me he was a big fan of mine.

I'm not a person who likes to pat himself on his back often. *I mean, I do on occasions but shit, who doesn't?* I'm about to do it now. I was a good teammate while at ESPN. Sure, I may not have agreed with some of the bosses, and I wasn't thought highly of by some of them either, but they could never say I was ever an asshole or didn't treat anyone right. If I had a disagreement, I'd try to settle it with civility. I had come a long way from that person that screamed and nearly threatened Tim Hardiman back in Nashville. I just knew how to deal with things better. It doesn't mean I didn't get pissed. I did. Several times I'd vent to a co-worker I thought I could trust, like Jay or Jack Obringer or to my guy Gerry Mattalon or Laurie Orlando. I vented to those last two because they worked in the talent department and that's what they were there for. However, no one can ever say they saw me go off on a PA for giving me a bad shot sheet or a producer for any reason. *Well, I did go off on this one producer once, but it was during a softball game and she was just a hateful, miserable person who always tried hard to get under my skin.* I played nice.

I also tried to help other anchors, even if it was to my detriment. When someone new started, I'd always make sure they had my number just in case they needed anything or just wanted to talk. A few anchors did that for me early on, and it meant the world to me. I also remember the ones who didn't and said I'd never act that way. I'd tell them the same things I explained early in this book about navigating their way on to the shows they wanted to do and once again, even if that meant they wanted to do shows "I" was hosting. My thinking was, if the higher ups believe they're better, then that's just the way it's going to be.

I never regretted helping or talking to anyone, even this one anchor who I had heard used to talk major trash about me before he was hired at ESPN. I never brought it up to him, and we got along fine. But there was one anchor that really disappointed me. I won't say his name, but he's getting a lot of run on the network even now. That wasn't always the case, and it got to him when he first got there. He, like so many others, believed he wasn't moving up fast enough through the ranks, and it made him super emotional one night. I just happened to run into him by his desk late one night, and he was nearly in tears. He was telling me about how he'd been there a year already, but he didn't seem to be making any progress. At the time, he was actually doing as many SportsCenter shows or more than me, but I STILL gave him some insight on "how to play the game" there.

He thanked me. I followed up to check on him and he said he was doing what I told him to do.

Now, I'm not saying I was responsible for his rise, because he did the work, but soon afterwards, he started getting nothing but good shows. The problem is, the more he got, the cockier and more smug he got. Far from the dude that was nearly in tears just months earlier. I wasn't the only one who noticed his change either. Don't get me wrong, I believe in confidence, and sure, you can hold your head up high and stick out your chest, but when you do that while looking down on others, I have an issue with it.

I actually started doing a lot of SportsCenters with him and he really rubbed me the wrong way one night we were doing an open and I did something out of the ordinary. Yes, it was kind of silly, but the look he gave me was like a *You are a clown and I'm embarrassed you're even next to me* look. I still see his face today and it pisses me off.

I never said anything to him because I don't care for unnecessary confrontation at work. Besides, it was an observation and nothing factual I could point to and he could just deny it. I just played it cool. Once more, I don't dislike the guy. I wish him well. In fact, there was only one anchor at ESPN I didn't care for. *Don't you wish I'd tell you, huh?? Catch me in the streets, I'll tell you for sure and even tell you why.*

My private life was doing better. Even though we were still trying to sell the house, Camille and I were actually co-existing nicely. Kayla was adjusting to our divorce and I started seriously dating Trang, who was helping take my mind off a lot. We were going on trips and really enjoying each other's company. I even felt comfortable enough for her to meet my kids on a trip I made out to L.A. Let's just say Trang tried her best, but the girls just weren't ready, and that was my fault.

That trip to L.A. was like each of the previous times I had been in the city. There was something that was drawing me there and begged me to come back. I'd had that feeling since my first trip in '96, and it was like God telling me that it's where I needed to be. That L.A. is where my ultimate is. My home. So every time I had a chance to, I was flying out to L.A.

By the end of 2012, my professional eyes were opened in a different way when I started working with Jerry Silbowitz and Evan Dick. Jerry was a manager who I'd see a lot at ESPN with his clients, and I always liked the way he did things. We'd often talk and when I was looking for an agent, he introduced me to Evan, who was a representative at CAA. Evan was a fiery, grab 'em by the balls agent, who a few in the industry felt fit his last name. I didn't care. He was doing his job for his client. Jerry was the ice to his fire. The calm, "Let's think before we jump" type of guy, and I loved that too. The two together were an awesome team, even if they didn't always see eye to eye. After a meeting between the three of us at an Italian restaurant down the street from ESPN, I loved what I heard. They even told me I was being fleeced financially for what I was doing on radio by ESPN and told me they could do better. I was sold. I was in. So were they in my life.

Even though I still had a year and a half on my ESPN contract, they started setting up general meetings with other networks and executives. Their thinking was, *It's never too early to put you on these people's radar.* One meeting was set up on one of my visits to Los Angeles. It was with Fox Sports. Of course, I knew Fox was a network that did sports, but what I didn't know at the time of the meeting was they were about to launch an all sports network to compete against ESPN called Fox Sports 1.

Jerry took me into that meeting with legendary producer Scott Ackerson, who at the time was in charge of the operation. He was pitching me on this network where they were going to bring the entertainment and fun back into sports. He was also saying how they wanted to be the opposite of ESPN and were going to dedicate the personnel and resources to this network to do so. Then he started saying he loved the things I was doing on the radio at ESPN and he thought that I would be a great fit to join what they were putting together.

All of a sudden, I realized I wasn't in just a general, get-to-know-you meeting. This was like a freaking job interview, and the more Scott talked, the more excited I got. EVERYTHING that man said in that meeting was everything I wanted to do at a sports network, and he was saying he wanted me to possibly come there and be ME. ALL ME!! It was so NOT ESPN. I felt like I was in a dream and I just knew someone (probably a boss from ESPN) was going to be waking me up soon telling me, "Sike, you know this type of shit won't happen for YOU." Luckily for me, that moment never came.

I walked out of that meeting floating. I wanted to hug Jerry. I can honestly say that I never wanted a job more in my career than the one Scott had just described. Trang and I went to a taping of the Tonight Show later, but all I could think about was Fox Sports 1. It was a great thing, but it would also cause the most excruciating anxiety of my life.

I wanted Fox Sports 1 so badly, and they wanted me to come in and audition. Here's the problem: I still had pretty much a year and a half on my contract with ESPN, and I didn't want to ask out of my deal with them unless Fox made me a firm offer first. Sure, I could've taken a chance and asked, but what if they said "no"? They'd certainly hold it against me during my next contract talks, if I was still around. And I couldn't take a chance and quit ESPN without a signed contract elsewhere. Fox Sports 1 wanted to work with me, but they legally couldn't while I was still under my ESPN deal.

This made me absolutely miserable. You ever been with someone for a long time? Your relationship has kind of run its course because even though you've had some good times, he/she has treated you like shit so much that you know it's time to leave. However, it's convenient for you. But then someone else comes along that freaking blows your mind and all you can think about is him/her? That's how I felt about my ESPN/FS1 relationship. FS1 was that new chick I had to have, but I was still married to ESPN.

When FS1 started holding auditions, Evan wanted me to do it anyway. He knew that Fox Sports 1 wanted to hire me and probably would as long as I didn't shit the bed during auditions. However, Jerry thought it was too risky and this business is too small and chatty. Someone from ESPN would've found out I was auditioning and it could've been trouble, so I agreed with Jerry and passed.

The weeks started to go by, and I was starting to hear about some of the people they were hiring. All good people, including two people I worked with a lot at ESPN, Charissa Thompson and Don Bell. They were no longer under contracts with ESPN, so they were free to walk. I have to admit, I was jealous as hell. I was dying on the inside. I just wished Fox would say, "Look, here's a 'promise' deal just in case you can get out of your ESPN contract." If that had happened I would've walked into Lauri's or Mark Gross's office and begged for my freedom. It never came, and after awhile, I honestly started feeling physically sick anytime I walked into ESPN. After feeling the energy of Fox in Los Angeles, I felt more and more of the negative energy at ESPN. It was toxic and morale was down, especially when there were rumblings of a round of lay-offs.

By May of 2013, Fox Sports 1 had pretty much hired all of its on-air staff and I wasn't one of them. I was devastated. Next to the times I had been out of work, this was one of the lowest points of my career. Sure, I still had my radio show and I was doing TV. Sure, Trang and I were great, and Camille and I had finally sold the house and I had moved into my own apartment, but like I mentioned before, I REALLY wanted this opportunity at Fox, and it wasn't happening.

By this time, it really wasn't much of a secret around ESPN that I wasn't happy. It wasn't just how I felt like I was being treated but others. It was so apparent to me and many others there was a have and have nots atmosphere going on there. It was very political, and if you were a part of the wrong political party or not in the clique of whoever was in charge at that time, you were just pretty much ass out.

I saw how they treated Robert Flores, one of the best anchors they had on SportsCenter and a guy who was funny as hell. They took him off of a morning edition of SportsCenter because he didn't "vibe" with his co-host. He got yanked off and he was better, but his co-host was a favorite of the person in charge.

I saw how they treated countless others. Never giving my guy Jay Harris his just due. Suspending Max Bretos for a big, yet honest and innocent mistake for 30 days, while others have done far worse and gotten a tenth of the punishment. How they treated countless others, who never got a shot at a SportsCenter on ESPN, although they flourished outside of Bristol. Even how radio treated Jonathan Coachman, who found out he was losing his radio show by reading a blog while he was on-air.

I was so unhappy, but I put on a happy face. I knew some could see through the façade I was putting up, and I also knew that eventually word would leak that I was secretly trying to move to L.A. and another network. I'm very sure the executives at ESPN knew. I didn't care now. I mean, I was still going to do my job and do it the best I could, but when my contract was up, I was bouncing. I was NOT going to sign another deal in Bristol. I was going to L.A. when my deal was up. It's where I knew I belonged. It's where God had been telling me I was supposed to be. I was just going to listen and take a leap of faith next year. I didn't have to wait a year, though.

Wednesday, May 15th, 2013. I got a call from this beautiful, sweet lady named Dita McKinney, who's Laurie Orlando's assistant, telling me that Laurie wanted to meet with me in Mark's office the next day at 10 am. She didn't say why, so I was super curious to know what was going on. Why would the head of talent want to meet me in the head of production's office and not her own? Did I do something wrong? No. I'd been pretty tame on social media lately and my shows had been pretty good. Maybe they were about to give me a TV show and a raise. Hmmmmmm! That's got to be it. A few days earlier, I had seen Jamie Horowitz after a debate show I did, and he called me across the newsroom and just wanted to tell me "how good" I was. He also told me I should be doing "debate" full time and he might have something for me. Yes, I'm sure that's it, right? Let me call Evan and give him a heads-up and/or maybe they've already told him. Evan had no clue why they wanted to meet with me, but he said he'd find out. About 15 minutes later, he had the answer. I was going into that meeting to be fired. Thursday would be my last day at ESPN.

My emotions were mixed. I was a bit in shock because it was so sudden and as bad as things were, I didn't think I had done anything to warrant being fired. I knew I'd flirted with another network, and they probably knew I was mentally trying to leave, but to fire me seemed extreme. It couldn't possibly be my performance because I had JUST gotten my review a month before and it was extremely positive. I was also relieved because I would be free. I can honestly say that I had no anxiety or was overly concerned about anything. It was like a weight had been lifted off my shoulders. I lost no sleep that night. Seriously, I was just more curious as to the reason they were going to give me for letting me go.

Thursday, May 16, 2013 was a surreal experience. I already had a clue what was about to go down, but it still just felt like a normal day. I was scheduled to do the 3 pm SportsCenter that day, and my production meeting was scheduled for the same time as my meeting with Laurie and Mark. No one had said I wasn't working that day, so when I got to work and everyone was acting like business as usual, I was wondering if Evan had gotten some wrong information.

I walked toward Mark's corner office on the 4th floor, and Laurie was already there. She always looked out for me and was such a sweet lady during my time there. When I saw her face, I realized that Evan's information was absolutely right. Laurie looked downright sad and said, "I'm sorry, Mike."

I actually smiled and said, "It's okay. It's part of life."

We talked for a little while inside Mark's office and then he finally walked in. He wasn't being an asshole about anything; in fact, whenever I've met with him in the past, he's always been cordial in our meetings. I didn't always agree with the things he said, how he seemed to show favoritism toward some anchors or his negative and never positive feedback, but I didn't necessarily DISLIKE him. He asked me if Laurie had already told me why I was there and I said yes. He then went into a spiel about how "this is just how the business is" and "it's not a reflection on you" and "we just feel like others are in a better position to do more shows than you." *I could only do certain shows now because of my radio schedule and I couldn't work weekends unless they forced me to work a six-day week, which luckily they didn't.* After awhile, it became like Charlie Brown's grandma talking. "Wonka..wonka... wonk...wonk wonk wonk."

After a while he asked me if I had any questions. Of course I did. I wanted to know why now? I went on to admit that had they made this decision earlier, I could've auditioned and more than likely gotten a position over at Fox Sports 1.

Laurie chimed in, "You should've said you were interested. We wouldn't have had a problem with you auditioning."

I found that very odd. "You wouldn't?" I even followed up by saying, "Well, I didn't think so since I've been telling Fox that my contract is not up 'til 2014. Had I known what I know now, I would've definitely asked you." At this point, I was a little annoyed and kicking myself because I could've been where I wanted to be by now instead of hearing this spiel about why they're letting me go NOW, which I STILL couldn't understand.

Something didn't feel right. I was just thinking to myself, *They're just going to let me walk and eat almost 15 months of my contract. I can just sit at home. I can get paid and chill until I find a new gig. Maybe it's not too late for me to go over to Fox Sports.* So one more time, I expressed to them, "I could've been gone before today. I've been telling everyone I'm not up 'til 2014."

I said this at least four times and then finally Laurie said, "Mike, you keep mentioning 2014. What's happening in 2014?" *Let me just hold this moment here for a second because it was one of the most satisfying moments of my entire career.* It was at that moment that I realized that they DIDN'T realize something very important. And so with a little, I'll admit, smugness, I looked at Laurie before turning to Mark, smiling and saying, "Well, 2014 is when my current deal is up." *Mic drop!!* The look on Mark's face was priceless. The lump in his throat was better. All of a sudden I heard Laurie racing through some papers before she said, "They told me it was July of 2013." Nope, I'd signed a three-year, NO CUT contract back in 2011.

Mark then put on a strong face and said, "I guess it's too late to go back now." At that point, they could've asked me to come back with a raise and I would've turned it down. I was SO DONE. I was emotionally, mentally, and even physically over that place, and I was relieved it was happening. Mark said, "Well, I guess you can just hang out at home doing nothing and get paid if you want to." And with that, I said, "Thank you for the opportunity," shook his hand, packed some of my stuff in a box, and with Laurie beside me, walked out of ESPN for the very last time.

> *Side note! Here's my final word about how I feel about ESPN. For the longest time, I was bitter. Not about how things ended but because of how things were many of the years I was there. I knew just how great that place could actually be if not for all the politics and biases I FELT. I felt like there was a reason why most of the people who leave there rarely say they miss it or long to come back, unless they're out of other good options. It took me a while to get that bitterness out of my heart.*
>
> *However, I will say NOW that I appreciate the time I had there. It was a major, magnificent platform, and it opened so many doors for me. I did nine years there and have ESPN on my resume. That means something to a lot of people, and it's a reason why I STILL get recognized by so many today. It's also the reason why I am where I am today. That's how big and powerful that place was and still is. I honestly want to thank*

> *everyone who I encountered. Some I saw eye to eye
> with. Some I became great friends with. Some I worked
> well with and learned from. Some I didn't necessarily
> care much for, but every one of them had an impact on
> me in some way, and that's why I have to be grateful
> for them helping shape my life and pave my path. The
> feelings I wrote about earlier don't express my feelings
> for the place or any of the people now. Because of my
> maturity and walk with Christ, I know it was all part
> of God's plan. And He continues to walk with me.*

It was all God's plan for me to be let go at that time.
The reason why is it opened up the door to the happiest
time in my life both professionally and personally. At least
it would be the façade I'd present *because I was still dying
inside. More on this later.* Because of ESPN's error, I knew
I'd at least have a full paycheck coming to me for more than
a year, but I wasn't going to just sit around collecting it. I
wanted to work, and I knew exactly where I wanted to go.

Like I said before, even had I stayed at ESPN through my
contract in 2014, I likely would not have re-signed unless
there was an opportunity for me in L.A. God's schedule is
always better for you, and the contract snafu allowed me
to make that move earlier than expected. Jerry and Evan
reached out to Scott and the folks at Fox Sports, and the
very next day after I left ESPN, I was on a plane to the
West Coast.

I made a stop in Portland to visit Trang, but a few days
later, I was off to Los Angeles for my audition. I'll admit, I
was nervous as hell. One reason was because the network
had already signed all of its on-air talent, so I was wonder-

ing if they even had a spot for me. However, at that point, I didn't even care. I just wanted to be on the team in some capacity. Another reason I was nervous was because I really wanted and needed this. Sure, I had the money coming in from ESPN to fall back on, but I needed to be back on the air as soon as possible. The longer you're off the air, the harder it is for you to get back on.

When I went in to audition, I hosted a panel segment with Donovan McNabb, Gary Payton, and a few others. The good thing about doing it with them is I had already met them before. So they were already familiar with me and I with them. Even so, I was about to hyperventilate beforehand, but I don't think it came across on camera. I got through it. I wouldn't say it was my best, though. I was really doubting myself until Donovan actually came over and just out of the blue said, "You were superb." It's funny in this business, how you can sometimes think you've had a horrible audition and everyone thinks it was great, but the ones you think you crushed, sometimes nothing ever comes out of it. With this one, I just didn't know.

Before I left, Scott said they'd "be in touch." His body language and smile made me think positively, but I'd been in this business too long to get overly excited. I've been extremely disappointed thinking I had something in the bag before. *Remember Tampa? Once again, that turned out to be a blessing, but at the time, I couldn't see it.* This time, I just prayed about it and asked God that if it was His will, then let it be done. Regardless, I had already made up my mind that I was going to move to L.A. because it was where I felt I needed to be.

Leaving Connecticut wasn't hard, but leaving Kayla was. Even though I hadn't been living with her for the past few months, I would never go more than a few days without being able to see her. Now, I was going to be 3000 miles away from her AND Ashlee, but again, it's what I had to do. The great thing about it was they were both excited because I'd be in Los Angeles and they loved L.A.

I have to address something about my kids here. They're my world. They're who I go hard for every day and my first priority. If you accept me, you have to accept them. I get a lot of credit from a lot of people for being a great dad. I will say out of any accomplishments or titles I've ever garnered, it's the one I'm most proud of. I love them unconditionally and always have, but I haven't always been such a good father. At times, I just didn't know how to.

Kayla and I were super tight early in her life. She was my buddy and we played like best friends. However, the divorce between me and her mom and the things she overheard leading up to that divorce had a big impact on damaging that relationship for a while. Luckily, we've gotten back on track. As for my relationship with Ashlee, it was almost the opposite. Early on, we didn't have much of a relationship. A lot of that had to do with me not seeing her a lot. Issues her mom and I had that got filtered into her and honestly, I just didn't know her. As she's gotten older, our relationship has gotten tighter, and now I feel like I can just about talk about anything with both of them, and they feel comfortable doing the same with me.

Look, as you've gathered in this book, I never had a great father in my life, so what I was doing or learning was always on the fly, and I've made plenty of mistakes. I'm not trying to make excuses. Anything I've done wrong has been because of me and me only. I've always been able to learn from the mistakes of my fathers when it comes to certain things. It's why I'll never hit a woman. However, the life lessons they failed to teach me should have also inspired me to be a better father. It did in some ways, but I failed too many times. Luckily, I've been able to grow in life as a person and as a father.

I've had to learn how to really think and analyze something through before making a major life decision. My two marriages were jerk reactions to something I didn't fully expect, and now I was about to do it again. *Guess my silly ass still hadn't learned too much, huh?* Trang and I had been dating for a little over a year, and it had always been long distance. Now I was moving to the West Coast. And even though it would be closer, she was still in Portland while I'd be in Los Angeles. She wanted to move to Los Angeles. I was all for that, but she wanted us to move in together. Now, admittedly, I was a bit hesitant to do that. I just felt like we should both be in the same city and date exclusively but live separately. She wasn't having that. She said if we were going to be together, we were going to be TOGETHER, and besides, rent was expensive in L.A., and she was going to be splitting all the costs with me. When she put it like that and also made it seem like it was that or we were done, I capitulated. I'm not going to say it's not what I wanted. I did. Once again, I just wasn't ready for it. *I've said that a lot, haven't I?*

I was now in Los Angeles kind of knowing that I'd be on with Fox Sports 1 in some capacity but not fully sure what that would be. I just knew I'd be working there. It wasn't cockiness or anything anyone said. I just trusted God and felt like this was supposed to be happening.

That faith paid off. Finally, Fox Sports 1 made an offer. Since they had already made their hires for their flagship show Fox Sports Live and their other dailies, they were going to bring me in as the "utility guy." Once again, this is where being versatile in this career field really paid off for me. I was going to be a fill-in on Fox Sports Live and a show called Fox Football Daily. I would do news updates and host some of their college basketball and college football studio shows. I was just going to be that guy they could go to when someone needed a day off and I was THRILLED to have that role.

The way my reps and Fox worked my initial deal, I was also supposed to eventually have my own radio show on Fox Sports radio. Even though there wasn't a slot open yet, there was talk of that changing in the near future, and I'd slide right in. Contract already signed and delivered. The problem with the radio deal was I wasn't going to get paid for that until the radio show actually came to fruition. It was exactly half of my compensation for the entire contract, so early on, I wasn't getting paid for that.

Chapter 19

LOG

LIVING IN LOS Angeles, making far less than I was being paid in Bristol could've been a disaster, but God has always provided. Before signing with Fox, Evan and CAA worked a buyout of the remainder of my ESPN deal. With that lump payment, that was a huge chunk in the bank and with Trang paying for half of everything, my financial situation was actually flourishing. Life was good and was about to get better. At least professionally.

I still hadn't learned how to be a good man in relationships, and Trang was a good woman. She was super helpful to my mom when her husband passed away, so my mom loved and appreciated her. I appreciated her too, but as many of my friends have said to me, I just wasn't ready.

> *I know. I know. You're saying, "Mike, you're just a mess." I've heard it plenty of times. Always that guy that most women will describe as "Nice but he's a mess." I never knew exactly what that meant until recently. As much as I've "talked" about having my life in order, I never did anything to truly fix it. And it had an effect on my and Trang's situation.*

We had a long-distance relationship for over a year and a half and NEVER had much of an argument about cheating at all. In fact, I might have been way more concerned about what she could've been up to than her. Not that she ever gave me any reason to be. However, because of all my creep shit, I was actually starting to think karma would catch up to me eventually. Once we started living together, things flipped.

I first noticed she was searching for something when we went to visit her family in Washington. We were in a hotel and I jumped in the shower. Now, you ever get in the shower and immediately realize you forgot something and have to jump out? So that's what happened to me. I jumped right out and without even grabbing a towel, I opened the bathroom door and saw her holding my phone, which was on the charger. My sudden appearance startled her, and she straight-up dropped my phone and said, "Uh, uh, uh, I need your cord to charge my iPad." Now, I'm a fool but not a new one. I smelled something fishy. I walked over and looked at my phone and when I did, I could see that my lock screen ain't locked no more. Obviously she'd figured out my code. Typed it in and unlocked the phone, which you don't need to do IF you're just getting the cord. She was adamant that she wasn't looking in my phone, but once again, I ain't that big of a fool.

The next incident nearly broke us up for sure. She was ignoring me all day while I was at work and when I got home, she wasn't there. When she came in she was pissed and going off about me sending flowers to a female friend of mine. Obviously not a good look and I can understand with my history why you wouldn't think I was innocent, but I was in THIS situation.

This particular friend and her mom lived in Atlanta and had been extra helpful to my mom when her husband was going through his treatments. So I sent flowers and on the card it said *I Love You*, which I meant, but not in the way in which Trang took it.

Now, I'm not blaming Trang for seeing this and being upset with me telling another woman, who wasn't family and she didn't know, that I loved her, but it was more out of appreciation than anything. I tried to tell her that, but it didn't matter. She saw what she saw and she was livid and was seriously questioning me and even her judgment about moving in with me. She kept saying how much of a fool she was thinking I had changed.

Here's a crazy nugget about me. I have gotten super emotionally defensive in relationships when I've been accused of doing something wrong and I wasn't. I guess in my warped mind there are so many faults I have or bad shit that I've done that are actually true that you don't need to *find* the other stuff. Or maybe I'm just happy when I'm innocent for real. I've done this several times in MANY relationships and I'm still that way today. Well, I have to be honest, when I thought my situation with Trang was going to end over this, I admittedly got emotional and pleaded with her to stay. It worked because she stuck around, but at the same time, the situation did damage to our relationship. The reason why? Well, now I couldn't trust her.

I know it sounds crazy and maybe it was, but now I had to flip this on her. It's another thing I've done in multiple relationships, and it's another nugget about me. If I think you're lying about how you've gotten information, I then become leery about trusting you. *There you go again, being all sane and judging me. It may be sad, but it's very true.*

The reason Trang knew I had sent flowers to someone else is because she was going through my emails. Now, in some relationships, that may be cool and I actually wouldn't have a problem with it too much myself, but if I ask you how you got your info and I just KNOW you're not telling the truth, I'll start to wonder about your integrity. *Stop it!! Don't judge me. I told you, I'm insane when it comes to these things.* Anyway, here's my argument. If you are searching, whether it's secretly digging through my DMs/text or emails, and I ask you how you got that information you're bringing to my attention, just be honest. Be honest and tell me how you got it and most importantly WHY you were even searching in the first place. If I'm wrong, then I have to pay the price and who cares how you got the info?

In this instance, Trang told me she was in my emails because she needed to use my laptop and when she opened it, the email was right in her face. Not believing that. That couldn't have been the case because the email was so old that she would have actually had to do a search to retrieve it. That, added to her "I needed your charger" story when I caught her red-handed with my unlocked phone in her hands, made me question her integrity.

Let me explain. This is NOT an indictment on Trang. She did what most women would've done had they been in a relationship with me back then. Hell, maybe even today. Hell, there were probably numerous things that she observed that she never brought to my attention that caused her to search for more. So I'm not blaming her at all. She's a great woman. However, here's where it became dangerous in my warped mind. I started thinking, *Hmmmm, if she's so worried about what I'm doing wrong (and as of this point, the answer was nothing), what is SHE doing?*

Therein lies another one of my biggest issues. I have had a hard time trusting people. Mainly because they're human and they're bound to let you down but partly because I HAVE been let down a lot. On the real, I think that trust isn't something that should just be handed out anyway. Trust has to be earned. With Trang I certainly trusted her, but my mind just started playing tricks on me because subconsciously now I was thinking her conscience was bothering her. I mean, why else would she suspect ME of anything? *Don't answer that damn question. It's obviously rhetorical, but since I've changed my ways... Not buying it, huh?*

My past. I just have to shake my head thinking about it because it's what I believe has had an ill effect on relationships. Me being honest and coming clean about my past has really hurt. *Imagine what people will think once they read this book, huh?* I have come clean about the things I've done. Mainly in my marriages because, well, when you've been married twice, people are curious as to what happened. I've always felt the best way to go was to be honest. Most times it's been a detriment because once you admit that you're a convict, you're going to be looked at as a convict. Not to say it's totally wrong because if someone looks suspiciously at a convicted burglar when something valuable goes missing, who can totally blame them? It happens. It happened to me when it came to infidelity in relationships, and it had a lot to do with me and Trang starting to struggle.

Meanwhile, work at FS1 was cool. I was having a blast, even though in the beginning I was mainly doing update shifts, where I'd do little 15-second hits they called "Three Things You Should Know." I made those 15 seconds different and entertaining, especially the teases beforehand. A lot of stuff I did was corny or way over the top, but I was just going for it and the great thing about it was the people at Fox, from top to bottom, encouraged and loved it.

I kept my head down, and even though I was just filling in for someone here and there and the ratings for the network weren't that great, I was extremely happy. It wasn't just because I was working in L.A. (although that was a huge reason why), but I have to say the atmosphere inside the network at the time was extremely positive. Ninety-nine percent of the people I worked with had super good energy. If someone had a bad attitude about something, it was an aberration and certainly not the norm. It was so good inside that place that I actually looked forward to going to work. Sure, I wanted to be more consistent on the other shows I was doing and not just updates, but I treated the update producer like I'd treat a producer on SportsCenter. It didn't matter. We had a good group and I finally felt like I had a superb work family.

Speaking of family, I loved Trang's family and still do, but it was becoming obvious that we wouldn't be having one of our own together. We had always said that we weren't going to have any children and that we would never get married again. In fact, when someone would ask us if we ever thought we'd get married, our standard reply would be as if someone asked us if we'd ever swim with piranhas: "Ah helllll nawl." It wasn't a diss toward either one of us.

It was how we felt about marriage. We were cool just living together. So I thought.

One day Trang and I were having a normal conversation when out of the blue she just went, "I'd consider getting married again. I just wouldn't marry you." Okay. Where in the hell did that come from and why?? She continued, "Nothing against you, I just know how you feel about marriage." Well, I thought we BOTH felt that way. Something had changed, and I didn't know what it was or why, but my feelings about marriage hadn't. I didn't stress it, but it was at that point that I knew for sure that we weren't going to make it. She was thinking about something that I couldn't give her or I wasn't willing to even consider at this time. It was still too soon for me. I loved her, but now I felt like I'd never be able to give her her ultimate happiness or her day. She deserved that. I just wasn't the one for her.

In the past before therapy, this has always been the danger for me in relationships. Not having a reason but finding one to slide out of the backdoor. This isn't necessarily the reason why things rapidly began to deteriorate for us, but it was certainly a contributor. My mind has not always been the strongest, and I've often been too much of a child to admit I've had a change of heart or I've just been afraid of really hurting the other person, even if I felt like I was lacking something. With my mind heading in that direction, our relationship had no chance, but I still stuck around.

I kind of had to stick around or should I say, Trang was there for me because I seriously needed her to be. Can you believe I tore the Achilles tendon in my OTHER foot. Four years after the first injury, I suffered the same injury again, doing exactly the same thing, playing basketball. As soon as I went down, I knew it was torn and my emotions took over. I just kept screaming, "Not again. Not again," but that wasn't going to change a thing. Sitting on that gym floor, I thought about two things. The long-ass rehab I had to go through again and oh DAMN, I'm going to have to go through this shit again while living in a place with a woman I'm having relationship issues with. We all remember the soup story from Camille earlier in this book, the first time around.

I didn't even know who was going to take me to the hospital. I couldn't drive this time because this injury was to my right foot. The crazy thing was, the gym I was playing in was right around the corner from where Trang worked. So I called her and without delay, this lady was right there for me, taking me to the hospital.

All of a sudden, our issues seemed over. Trang stepped up. She was there for my surgery. She even spent the night with me the night of my surgery after I had some minor complications. And even when my mom came to help out, she didn't slack off at all.

I was simply amazed and sort of embarrassed because of the way I had acted, but she didn't seem to hold any grudges. Maybe I was doing this all wrong. Maybe I was overreacting to her actions and I should've just been more patient. This woman truly loved me. Right? So let's try to stay together and make this work. For now.

Meanwhile, things couldn't have been better at work. Fox sent me to do a few shows in New York during Super Bowl XLVIII, and while I was there, Scott Ackerson pulled me to the side. He said that I had done everything they had asked me to do and told me that because of my positive attitude and skill set, they wanted to talk about a new contract with me. Also, he hinted at the possibility of a new show being developed.

I thought I was dreaming. I'm sure I orgasmed because this was sounding too good to be true. I had just signed a contract five months earlier, and even though the radio thing hadn't come to fruition yet, word was it was going to be happening in a few weeks. That may have been the reason why talks of a new contract were brought up because one of the things Scott asked me is if I'd consider just doing TV and forgoing the radio part. My answer was quick and simple. HELL, YES.

Soon Jerry and Evan were negotiating a new three-year deal with Fox, and all of a sudden I was making more money than I could have ever dreamed of making just a few years earlier. This is how God has always worked it out for me. Giving me more than I could ever imagine for myself. Under this deal, I was now making way more money doing this one job than I would've made doing both TV AND radio.

Whose life is this and how did I get to be a part of it? Wow. And why is it about to get better? Soon after, there were talks of a new show replacing Fox Sports 1's daily NFL SHOW, and I was going to be one of the candidates to host it. I couldn't wait. I was finally going to get my opportunity.

The initial concept for the show was to be a daily show that would get you ready for that night's action. We'd utilize all the regional assets Fox Sports had to take you to different arenas and ballparks before the games started for an in-depth preview of the big events for that night. It was called America's Pregame and it was supposed to be hosted by two people. In fact, that's how they had us audition: with a co-host. However, soon after they decided that there would only be one host and a newsreader.

I felt like my audition went well, although I couldn't do all the walking the show was designed to have because I was still recovering from my Achilles surgery. And when I thought it was a show with two hosts, I'll admit I was sort of confident that I'd be one of those hosts. Especially since they had just given me a huge contract. I doubt they would've done that and been cool with me just filling in, like I had been. However, when I heard the whispers that it was going to be just one host, I was a bit concerned.

I can't remember how long it took them to decide. I know it was within a day or two, but I do remember not being able to sleep well until they did. Even though I had been given a strong indication from an inside source that I'd be named the host, if you've been reading this book, you'll know it wouldn't be smart for me to get my hopes up too high until it was official.

I got it!! Scott gave me the news and said that I was the choice and a young lady who also started when I did named Molly McGrath would do the updates. I was so grateful. I got on my knees and just said, "Thank you, Jesus!!!"

All the things I had gone through in my career, some of my own doing and some brought on by others, was all worth it because it had led to this point. I was going to be THE HOST of my own show on a major cable network. Not the back-up. I was the true #1 starter for the first time. Outside of my kids being born and me giving my life to Christ, this was the proudest moment of my life.

Trang was happy for me. And even though issues started creeping up again between us, she fully supported me by giving the show a strong social media push and even baking pastries for my crew. *Damn this girl was super sweet. She didn't deserve the shit I put her through. Then again, not many of the women in my life actually did.*

Getting that show was also one of the first times I remember my kids telling me they were proud of me. Ashlee was a teenager now and Kayla has always been a little more mature than her age or just more "grown" than I'd like her to be at times. Hearing my pride and joy tell me they were happy for me was everything.

I loved America's Pregame, or APG, as it became known. It was mine and I did my best to nurture, love, and protect it. That means everyone who was a part of it was a family member to me and I hope they felt that from me. I always said that if I ever had the opportunity to have a show, that's how I would treat the crew. I wanted everyone on that show to know they were appreciated. I've always felt like if you give these professionals the respect they deserve and treat them fair AND equally, they'll run through walls for you, and that's exactly how they reacted. I've never been a yeller or a screamer, and even though some told me I needed to be a little tougher, I didn't feel like it was warranted, as long as they TRIED their very best. *Besides, Scott was already the one they feared. I'm just joking...well, some did fear him...but I love Scott and would do anything for him. He did more for my career than any other TV executive I've worked with, and I will always appreciate him for that.*

Once again, even though I hosted the show and yes, I felt like it was mine, I publicly shared it with anyone who was a part of it. I even started saying Molly was my "co-host" and not just the update person. This was something that Evan would get super pissed about. I understood where he was coming from, and I know 95 percent of the hosts in my position would never do that, but I wanted every-one to feel great and empowered on that show, so that we could make it the greatest possible. I was also super proud of Molly, who was like a sister and made major strides in a short amount of time at the network.

It's funny how broadcasting or just entertainment period works at times. When it rains it pours, and that's not always a bad thing. I've given you several times in my career when my droughts have turned into flash floods, and it was about to happen again with this new show. This platform was giving me exposure, and with that came opportunities that I'd simply dreamed about before.

Not long after APG launched, Jerry gave me a call and said the daily syndicated entertainment show Entertain-ment Tonight was looking for a new host and wanted me to audition. I think my initial reaction was, "Get the ***k out of here. You bullshitting." He wasn't.

I had never met with them, and when I asked him if he had sent them a tape or something, he said "no." He said there was an executive over there who liked me and wanted me to come in if I was interested.

I was super interested. There were only two problems. I had just signed this new deal with Fox and gotten this new show AND Charissa Thompson, who got hired for the launch of the network, had just informed them that she was breaking out for another job with the entertain-ment show *Extra* herself. So I was excited about the possibility but I was also in a conundrum, if things went great. After all Scott had done for me, I didn't want to make it seem like I was being disloyal by rolling out on him, and if he found out I was even auditioning, I was sure he'd be pissed. Especially since the Charissa situation had JUST happened weeks before.

Well, a few days before they wanted me to come in, Scott did find out and right before I was about to go on the air for APG, he walked up to me with a smiling smirk on his face and coldly said, "So you're auditioning for another show, huh?" And then added an "Okay," as if to say, *I see how your unappreciative ass is going to act.* Right then and there, I was shook. I got nervous as hell. I was like, "Ah damn, I'm going to HAVE to audition because I'm about to lose this shit." However, after talking to him and letting him know where my head and heart was, he was cool.

I auditioned. Wouldn't hurt to audition, right? Jerry and I talked about it and we concluded that it would be good to just be in front of TV people outside of sports. Something I wanted to transition into anyway and maybe there might be a crazy way I could do both. So let's go for it.

I went in for the audition and the staff couldn't have been any nicer. I would be on set with the longtime host of the show, Nancy O'Dell, and while I was sitting next to her, I just remember thinking how pretty she was. Nothing disrespectful or creepworthy, but her beauty was distracting, and I had to focus.

During the audition, she was the greatest and made me feel so at ease. The audition was pretty much just an ad-libbed conversation between us, and usually these things take about 5-7 minutes. Ours went about 25. I was AWESOME. One of the best auditions I've had. I could tell I was killing it because I could hear the executive producer, Brad Bessey, through Nancy's earpiece laughing loudly and saying, "Oh my gosh, we love him. Keep this going. Keep this going."

Afterward, Brad came to the set and basically said the same thing to me. He knew my situation and asked, "How can we make this work?" I didn't have the answer to that, but now I was hooked on THIS drug. I wanted to figure out HOW to make it work. I had to.

E.T. wanted to, too. The audition went well enough that they wanted me to actually host an episode alongside Nancy. Oh my gosh!! Pinch me. This isn't happening, is it? We worked out a date and as long as I was done by a certain time, I was good to go because I still had to host APG that day.

Everyone was on board. Even Scott. Although I'm sure there was still a little hesitation, he wasn't tripping on it. The one person who didn't know I was about to do this show or even had auditioned was my agent, Evan. Jerry and I had decided not to say anything to him because he hadn't even brought it to my attention that E.T. was looking for a host in the first place. He knew that I wanted to transition out of sports and into other avenues of hosting, and although he had other clients who auditioned, he never even told me there was an opening. Needless to say, I wasn't happy about that.

He eventually found out and I'll say his reasoning made sense but wasn't completely satisfying. His thinking was that I had just signed with Fox and gotten a new show and so it wouldn't be a good look to quit if E.T. was seriously interested. I agree. I wrote about it earlier in this chapter, but my thinking was, as his client, he should always at least provide me with the options and allow ME to decide. I mean, I'm all for his opinion or choreography, but when it comes to my career give ME the choice. He understood.

I later got the opportunity to host E.T., and it was incredible. Ironically, one of the main stories we did had to do with sports. It was an interview with Vi Stiviano, the lady who secretly recorded and eventually took down former Clippers owner Donald Sterling for his dumb racially-charged comments.

Everyone was so accommodating, and the show went great. Afterwards, I was in a rush to get back across the hill to shoot my own show, but Brad Bessey kept asking me, "How can we make this work?" He was asking if it was possible for me to do both of these shows. I don't know how serious he really was, but I know I wanted to so badly. I was hoping to make it work, but deep down inside, I knew it was damn near impossible with how the schedule of the shows coincided.

I was still happy, though. I had my own show, APG, but now had the bug. I wanted to host other shows outside of sports. The euphoria I had at this time felt like the first night I was ever in Los Angeles and KNEW it would be my future home. I was here for this reason. I just had to find the right path.

My foot was healed, but my relationship with Trang was torn. We had reached a point of no return. I won't go into too many details, but I became paranoid. I started thinking she was up to no good. I started going through her phone and not trusting her. *Ain't that a bitch??* Meanwhile, I once again disconnected, and as we know, that's always spelled doom for my relationships.

This time, though, I was a little bit more mature. I told her I wasn't happy anymore, and I felt we should end it. We decided that I would keep the apartment but there would be some time before her new place would be ready, so she continued to live with me. This became especially uncomfortable when my mom and children came to visit for a few weeks during the summer. It got worse.

I started fooling around with someone we both knew, and she found out about it. It wasn't pretty and it shouldn't have been, but it made Trang become someone way outside of her character. She was snarky, and the things that she would just do for me because it's her nature weren't happening anymore. That's understandable, but she wasn't even her normal cheery self around anyone I knew. I had made this sweet, beautiful lady into someone ice cold.

Our situation really came to a head one day when my kids wanted to go to the movies and me, my mom and Trang were going to join. Yeah, I know, it wasn't the greatest idea in the world, but my mom loved Trang and wanted her to go. She had really endeared herself to her when she was instrumental in helping my mom with her husband Jerry's funeral arrangements. My mom also thought Trang was really good for me and took care of me. Which she did very well. However, once again, Trang was not herself at this time.

With Trang in the front passenger seat and my mom and kids in the back, we took off for the movies. Not even a mile from the house, there was a topic brought up. I don't remember what it was, but it was something that sparked a very smart, sarcastic comment from Trang. Now, one thing I DO NOT like to do is have arguments in front of people, especially my kids. At the time, they were fourteen and twelve, and even though they knew Trang and I were breaking up, they didn't need to be a part of this drama. So I told Trang, "We're not going to do this right now." Trang said something else, and I repeated myself. "We're not going to do this right now."

All of a sudden, from the backseat, my mom went, "Why do you always start stuff?" And she was talking to ME. What? I'm starting stuff? First of all, when do I ever start stuff? Secondly, what did I say to make you think I started THIS, and lastly, why are you jumping in my business anyway? Now, I may or may not have verbally said that last part to my mom in a certain way. I'm lying, I straight up told her exactly that. Needless to say, this didn't go over well. All of a sudden, words out of her mouth weren't the only things flying from the backseat, her hands were flying too, and they were landing on ME!!! "You ain't gonna disrespect me!!"

I'm having words yelled at me and fists hitting me WHILE I'm driving. I was trying to cover up and NOT crash, and the next thing I heard her say was, "Let me out!!" "Let me out!!" At this moment, I heard my youngest daughter screaming and bawling her eyes out. There's something about hearing your child cry or in any kind of pain that makes another instinct kick in. It's a feeling that could give you superhuman strength or make you even snap. So with my mom hitting and yelling at me and my daughter basically traumatized, I did what any son/father would do in that situation. I pulled over and told my mom to "Get the fuck out of my car!!" *I know. Looking back this is unforgivable. No one should ever speak or disrespect his/her mother like that. Remember, this was before therapy and me even realizing I had so much trauma and pain inside me.* And then I looked at Trang and said, "You need to join her."

I pulled over and my mom got out of the car, mumbling curse words as she walked away. Trang kept telling me that I was wrong and that she couldn't believe I had just done that and I retorted by saying that she was the cause of this even happening and "Why are YOU still in my car?" She wasn't getting out, though, and as for my mom, she was swiftly walking away.

Yes, the Son of the Year recipient for 2014 continued to drive away as Ashlee was comforting Kayla, who was still nearly inconsolable. After about three minutes, I circled back trying to find my mom. By the time I did, she was in this residential area and both Trang and I were asking her to get back into the car, but she was stubborn and not having it. I don't know if it was something we finally said, if her feet started to hurt, or if she just didn't know exactly how to get back the apartment, but she finally relented and got back into the car.

Needless to say, we never went to the movies that night, but the tension continued over the next few days. I was done with my own mom at that point. I may have been wrong to actually put my own mother out, but the father in me FELT like she was bringing harm to my child and I reacted. Also, when it came to my relationships, I felt like she always took the side of the woman I was having issues with. Yes, I was at fault in many ways, but there may have been other issues that I would never discuss with her because it wasn't her business and I would never try to disparage someone I'm with to my mother. She could never understand that back then, and I always felt like she thought I was just a bad guy.

I was numb and had nothing to say to her. I even told my brother that after she left, I would be freeing myself from her. I was just tired of drama. Even if I was partly responsible for it. I just didn't want it anymore. She could feel my numbness and after a few days, she pulled me to the side, told me she loved me, and apologized. What's ironic is that situation actually helped my relationship with my mom because our issue made us bounce back stronger and with more understanding. It did NOTHING to improve my relationship with Trang. Soon after, she moved out.

America's Pregame was my baby and I treated it as such. My only regret is I wish it had gotten the promotion it deserved. Don't get me wrong, I'm not blaming anyone at Fox for this, but outside of a small ad on Fox Sports 1, the show really got no publicity. Once again, I'm not saying this was the only reason for the poor ratings. There were poor ratings across the board on the network in the beginning. I just believe we could've made more of a dent had it gotten the love I see some of the shows on the network today get.

Many people who watched me on ESPN didn't even have an idea I was at Fox. *That's kind of still the case today because I'll have someone trolling me on social media about what ESPN is and isn't doing every now and then.* I don't know how many times I've gotten, "Damn, bruh, when did you leave ESPN?" At the time it had been more than a year, but obviously no one knew that, and I just honestly believe the network hadn't done a good enough job of letting anyone know.

We had some really good times on the show and some memorable moments. Many of them, for some reason, involved the UFC. Like the time Chael Sonnen and I got into a heated conversation after he was busted for a tainted drug sample. The time Rhonda Rousey and I had one of the most awkward moments of the year when I brought up the issues she had with Floyd Mayweather and she acted like it never happened. However, I have never been in a more intense moment in my broadcasting career than the time when I conducted an interview with Conner McGregor, who was fighting José Aldo. I could feel the hate and disgust for those two guys in the air and I had to sit between the two of them while they hurled insults back and forth. Most of them coming from McGregor's not-made-for-family-TV mouth.

The biggest thing APG did for me was give me a platform and when you've got YOUR platform in this business, other people will be more inclined to do business with you. It's the "you're more attractive when someone else has got ya" situation.

Chapter 20

ON-AIR SHIFT

IN ADDITION TO the opportunity I got on Entertainment Tonight, I got to do several shows on a popular local show in L.A. called Good Day L.A. and was a guest panelist on the Jim Rome show on Showtime. I even had a super strong audition to host the long-time show Inside the NFL. *Catch me in the streets and I'll tell you an interesting story about who called me and why on that day I auditioned in New York.*

So although I wasn't getting much promotion or not generating the ratings I had hoped on APG, it did pay off in other ways.

However, about a year and a half after the show launched, my "Oprah," Scott Ackerson, was set to retire and I knew there would be some major changes. I was worried. No, let me be straight-up honest: I was terrified. Change can be good, but in this business, if you don't have that advocate in the right place, you can be totally screwed. I just felt like it was a matter of time before it was time for me to bend over.

I was a bit relieved and partly excited when I found out the company was about to hire Jamie Horowitz, though.

Jamie was the guy who was in charge of so many of the debate shows I hosted at ESPN, like First Take, Numbers Never Lie, and SportsNation. He had always said he was a fan and actually was the one who wanted me to expand my duties outside of being just a host and being more of a pundit. You'll remember he's the one who called me from across the newsroom at ESPN just to tell me how good he thought I was and said he might have something for me. Of course, a week later, I wasn't with ESPN anymore. However, I just knew that if he was hired, my future at FS1 would be fine. *Once again, you should never get overconfident or fully trust anyone in this business. Maybe I'm jaded, but hell, you may not be able to blame me.*

With Jamie in the mix, programming became more debate oriented. Even APG had more of a debate structure, which was fine with me. I had already been doing my own rants called "Open Mike," and I created a segment on the show called "America's Talking," which was a segment with me and a guest panel, delving out strong opinions about major issues in the sports world.

Many thought the show was getting stronger and expanding, including myself, but the only person who mattered was Jamie. He wasn't impressed. It just wasn't his KIND of show because it wasn't the embrace debate shows he was known for. I'll give him credit for one thing: he actually told me this not long after he had gotten there. I thought maybe he'd revamp it. Tweak it. Make a few adjustments here and there, and we'd be stronger. ESPECIALLY if he could convince them to finally start promoting the damn show on Big Fox and billboards. Uhhhhh, that didn't happen. What's the opposite of promotion?

September 28th, 2015, we were getting ready for the show, but honestly, I could sense something was off. A few of the coordinating producers, Azzie McKenzie and Bill Dallman, just didn't seem like themselves. Our executive assistant, Dana Fisher, was a little subdued too. In fact, she had been for a few weeks, and I recall her sad reaction when I saw this nice America's Pregame jacket on her desk and told her I wanted one. *Her reaction was almost like, you better hope THIS ONE fits because it's the only one that's ever going to be ordered.*

One of the things I enjoyed about FS1 is that if someone was having a bad or off day, it was an aberration and not the norm. Everyone's demeanor was usually spot on, unless a producer wasn't "paying attention to detail" and Scott Ackerson had to correct them. *I just made a few of my former producers tighten up a bit with that one.* So to have a weird vibe by so many on this day just seemed odd, but the show went on, and we got through it without a hitch. Afterwards, I realized they already knew what I was about to find out.

After the show, Molly and I got called to Jamie's office, while the rest of the staff was called into a group meeting. I changed clothes first and when I walked up to the 5th floor and Jamie's office, Molly was already inside. Now, I wasn't completely lost. I had a feeling what was taking place and I was keeping cool. I actually hopped up and sat on some filing cabinets, swinging my legs back and forth outside of Jamie's office while he and Molly met inside.

When the door opened, Molly looked as if he had just told her a family member had died. She was in shock and as soon as she saw me, she burst into tears. She was crying uncontrollably and at that moment, I knew for sure America's Pregame had been canceled. As much as it hurt, I was more concerned about Molly's well-being. Remember, I was much older, with way more experiences, good and bad, in this business. In fact, I had been in this business (20 years) almost as long as Molly had been alive (25 years) at this point. I kept trying to calm her down and promised her she and everyone else would be all right. Of course, at that point, I didn't know for sure, but that's what I felt at that time.

With Molly's situation more under control, I walked into Jamie's office, where he had this look of concern but at the same time, trying to make me feel secure. He, of course, told me he was canceling the show. Explained that it just wasn't HIS show and the ratings weren't high enough for him to keep it around. Then he assured me that I would be fine. He reiterated how much of a "fan" he was and that he'd have something for me down the line. His words were, "Just be patient. I don't know what it is yet, but I'm going to find something for you here. I know you may get a little antsy but once again, just be patient." He told me he'd had this same conversation with ESPN host Michael Smith back when they both were at ESPN.

I wasn't worried too much because, at this point, I still had nearly a year and a half left on a nice sized contract. So I figured he not only would find something for me to do, he'd probably have to do it to justify my salary. Therefore, I just knew when he started developing shows, I'd be right in the mix. Well, that day never came under Jamie Horowitz. I got to audition ONCE, on ONE segment of a show they were developing and never again. I have my suspicions as to why, but I can't prove it, so I'll leave it alone.

This is another reason why it's hard to trust anyone in this business. I'm not going to come down on Jamie. He's no longer with the company because of a huge scandal, so who knows if he would have EVENTUALLY found something with my name on it. All I know is he was still there when it was time to renegotiate my deal, and by this time, he had created some programming, bringing in some high-priced talent from ESPN and elsewhere. Although I was the person he said he was a "fan" of, his side of the FS1 company had nothing for me. Not even a guest appearance on any of the shows he created. It's something that befuddled me because I was on all his high-rated shows at ESPN because he wanted me to be, but I couldn't even get a sniff on these new shows, which were struggling in the ratings. I could never understand that. I probably never will.

Thank God for John Entz. Another man I'll call my Oprah. I first met Entz when he was an executive at the MLB Network while I was still at ESPN. Before I signed my final contract with them, he brought me down to New Jersey for an interview with him and the head of the company, Tony Petiti. We met in this Italian restaurant that was straight out of Goodfellas or The Sopranos. I swear the whole time I was there, I just knew I was going to get "whacked." I felt set up. Even though nothing ever came out of that meeting, Entz and I really hit it off, and now he is a senior executive at Fox.

Entz was and still is in charge of the live events and studio shows that support events. He's never said he was a "fan" or given me that type of treatment, but I could always tell that he trusted me to do a good job on his shows, and he's ALWAYS been cool with me each time I saw him. Even though Jamie didn't have any work for me, Entz did, and so when it came time to renew my contract, he and a few others directly under him, like Kent Camera and Bardi Shah-Rais, stepped up and showed me some love.

Once again, the lesson in all this is to be versatile. If I didn't already possess the hosting experience I had, I probably would've been ass out at Fox. However, as I write this book, I'm still very much employed there. In fact, of all the on-air people who came to launch the network, only Charissa Thompson and I are still doing things there on a regular basis. The others have left, and I'm happy to say, they're all doing quite nicely for themselves in other places. They're good people, and they deserve it.

HEY Y'ALL, I'M writing this book like I speak in life. Sometimes that may be all over the place and disorganized. **I think my Pulitzer Prize went out the door with my first sentence.** However, as you can tell, my life has been dysfunctional and unorganized at times too.

Let me tell you a little secret. It's March of 2020 as I'm writing this very passage. I actually finished the first draft and have been talking about Open Mike on social media for the last year and a half. It's gotten to the point that some may think it will never see the light of day. Well, obviously if you're reading this, it has. It's just been a long, drawn-out process. Part of that reason is because some people warned me against putting it out. I'm giving away too much of my personal life, and that would have an effect on me and my career. However, God is pushing me in this direction.

Even if this book doesn't do well sales wise, it's already served a big purpose. It saved my life. What I've realized at this point is that writing this book was needed. Even if I was putting on the mask of a happy man, I was really a crying little boy who was afraid to admit he was hurting. Like many black men, I would never seek therapy because I was made to believe you kept your business to yourself. Besides, if I did, I was admitting I was weak. Writing this book became that help I needed. At least the start. I uncovered trauma that I didn't even know existed because I had suppressed it for so long. Believe me, since I let it go, I feel so much better. I understand what I did and a big reason why I did it.

I can't change the past, but I can do my part to help the future. That includes continuing to help myself. I have to in order to walk into my God-given purpose and to finally become the MAN my daughters, friends, family, and God want me to be.

It's not just about me, it's about hopefully helping someone else that may have the same issues and need to get help. Another reason is because there's been a lot that's happened in the last 18 months. Someone has come into my life and absolutely changed it for the better. Someone I was finally ready for because I had become whole. Her name is Cynthia Bailey.

I WAS CO-HOSTING a radio show for Fox Sports Radio with Ephraim Salaam. **Now let me tell y'all something. Even though this was supposed to be a "sports" show, there would be many times where E and I would talk about just about anything but sports.** Mainly we would talk about my dating life and how I was running these L.A. streets. I was having fun. A lot of fun. I was single so I could, and I'll just leave it at that. However, I always admired Ephraim and the love and respect he had for his wife of 13 years, Reiniece.

Honestly, and I'm not trying to throw anyone else under the bus *(so ladies, if I've ever hung with your husbands a lot over the years, don't try and overanalyze my words here),* but at this time, I had never been around another man who loved, respected and was as SUPER FAITHFUL to his wife outside of my brother, Preston. I mean, this man worships his wife, and she puts him on a pedestal that is equally as high. They have two boys, and I know every family has its issues, but they are the quintessential perfect family to me. I wanted that and would tell E that numerous times, but his response would always be, "You ain't ready."

I knew what he meant. I could say it, but if my actions didn't show it, I shouldn't do it. You should never go into major situations in your life without truly knowing deep down that you're ready for it. At this time, I wasn't ready, but since I had finally opened my heart to the possibility, I knew that if I met the "right" person, I could certainly get there.

One day during a break on our show, E asked me if I'd be willing to be a guest on the talk show that comedian Steve Harvey had at the time. He told me some producers he knew had reached out to him asking if he knew of any eligible bachelors that might want to come on to participate in this dating game Steve played called The Dating Pool. E told me that, if I was interested, I'd be one of the bachelors trying to woo one of The Housewives of Atlanta. Immediately, my first response was, "Which one??" No disrespect to any of the ladies on the show, but that part DID matter. He asked me if I was familiar with Cynthia Bailey, and I was. In fact, years before, I used to watch RHOA with Camille, and ironically, one of our favorites on the show was Cynthia. Of course I didn't know her at that time, but on television she appeared super classy and carried herself with grace for many years, which is a rarity in the reality world. Still, I was a bit hesitant. Am I really going to find the woman of my dreams on a dating show? Am I even looking for the woman of my dreams right now? The answer to that question was no. Remember, I was open to discovering, but I wasn't exactly looking. Also, why was she going on there? She's gorgeous. I had seen her once before in person, so I knew it wasn't just a television thing. I had a lot to think about.

Here's why I went on that show **and this is Open Mike, so it's all the way real now.** For years, I had wanted to cross over into the entertainment space. I had made strides in the sports world, but I've always wanted to expand. It's one of the reasons why I was so excited to be in L.A. Steve Harvey's show was a completely different audience for me and honestly, going on it would allow me to be seen in another way. Remember, at this time, I was thinking the only reason Cynthia was on there was for some sort of publicity. Not to find true love. So if she was doing it, why shouldn't I?

Now before anyone goes off, and I know someone already has, it wasn't the ONLY reason I went on there. Remember, I wouldn't have gone on there if it was a housewife I didn't really get good vibes from. Don't ask, I'm not telling you which of the ladies that might be. At least not today. I was curious to meet Cynthia and see if she was who she appeared to be on that show. If she was, I also felt like we could at the very least be friends. So I decided to go through with it.

God wanted me to meet Cynthia Bailey. It didn't take long before I knew she was supposed to be in my life. I didn't know what the capacity would be, but I just knew she was supposed to be a part of it. My first indication was because of how everything played out the day we taped The Steve Harvey Show. I almost didn't do it.

We had a call time of 1 pm and we'd tape the show at 3ish. Done no later than 4:30-5. At least that's what I was told. Shit didn't work out like that. Steve's birthday was that day and production got pushed back at least an hour and a half. Usually this wouldn't be a problem, but I had to be at work later that day and I didn't have a lot of time to spare. During the delay, the producers kept coming in to assure us things would be starting soon, but they also knew I had a hard out (meaning the time I HAD to go) at five, so that I could make it to work. Next thing I know, it was four something and I was looking at my watch thinking, "I got to get the hell up out of here." I mean, meeting Ms. Bailey and being on the show would be good and everything, but my job was so much better, and I ain't risking losing that. Not for the "possibility" of winning a date. Hell, not for the date itself. I actually remember telling the producer, "Thanks for the opportunity, but I gotta go." I don't know who told who what, but next thing I know, they did whatever they needed to do to get things started.

Even when the show began, it was shot in order, so our segment didn't come on right away. About 15 minutes in, they escorted us "bachelors" from the green room to the studio and it was about to go down. During a break, I saw her across the way. Damn she looked good in that white pant suit. I honestly was thinking, "This lady is fine as hell. I gotta win this shit!"

When they brought us onto the stage to start the segment, she didn't really look at any of us. I was thinking, "Well damn, she ain't feeling none of us." Now that I know her better, I realized she was a bit nervous and shy. Now her ass ain't always shy, as you know, but Cynt isn't overly gregarious when she really doesn't know someone. However, once the cameras came on and Steve began talking, I saw that spark in her eyes that I have come to know and love. She's an angel and an absolutely joyful person with a pure heart. I felt that energy, even in that moment. That's when it went from "I gotta win this" to "I am gonna win this." It wasn't being cocky. I just felt it. I had a small feeling that this wasn't just some publicity stunt for her. She wouldn't do that. I still didn't think she needed this to find LOVE, but I love good, positive, genuine people, and I could tell, just from being on that set with her, that she was one of those people. I at least had to meet her. Therefore, I had to win.

The producers had given us some of the questions she might ask us ahead of time and before the show had gone over each of them with us. I remember the segment producer reading them to me and wanted to know how I was going to answer each question. She was a cool sister, but I remember telling her, "I've been doing TV for years. I just like to let answers come off the top of my head." Like I said, I can feel energy and I remember her energy was like, "F the top of your head, I need to know the words that will be coming out of your mouth, right now." I picked that up and told her how I planned to answer each of them. However, when we actually got on the show and Cynthia started her questioning, something else just kicked in. It wasn't scripted. It wasn't acting. It was just genuine. I just took over. I was on another level. Some may call it extra, but I was going to win my prize. I was answering the questions posed to the other bachelors and of course, making the most of the ones directed toward me. Now here's the thing: I'm a spiritual person. I wouldn't say I'm highly religious, but I know God is good and where my strength comes from. However, if you had heard me answer most of those questions, you would've thought I had just graduated from divinity school. I think I mentioned God or Jesus at least 5-6 times during that segment. I think I mentioned God so much, Steve sent around a tray for the tithes afterwards. Here's the thing. Every...single...answer that came out of my mouth during that show was exactly how I felt. One hundred percent genuine. Well, the crowd loved it. Steve loved it, and God answers prayers because Cynt loved it too. So much that she chose me.

Now, the producers never told us what to do if you were chosen. However, if you've ever seen a clip of that show, you know once she said, "I think I'm going to go with Mike," I get up out of my chair, stroll right over to Ms. Bailey, give her a hug and a kiss on her cheek and then say, "You're very beautiful." She often asks me what made me get up. Well, watch the clip again and you'll see me briefly look to my right before getting up. I don't know who it was or where it came from…maybe it was God Himself…but I heard a voice that said, "Mike, go over there." So I did.

Many of y'all think that we've been inseparable since. WRONG!!! In fact, right after I hugged her for the first time and Steve wrapped up the segment, I said, "It was nice meeting you, but I gotta go!" I mean, just like that. We were supposed to actually go on a date RIGHT AFTER the show, but I was running late for my own show, and I had to roll. She would later tell me that her reaction was like, "Damn, well, nice to meet you too."

I honestly thought that would be it for us. God's honest truth. I mean, I knew I'd probably run into her again and if I did, I could be like, "Hey, remember me from the Steve Harvey show?" and then maybe hold it over her head that she owed me a date. However, the producers of the Steve Harvey Show had other plans, and it's actually the reason we're even together now. **Once again, God's plan!**

About a week after we taped the show, I got an email from one of the producers saying something like, *Hey Mike, Cynthia just can't stop thinking about you and is BEGGING US to give you her number. We know you're busy and have your choice in L.A. women, but would you please just give her a call and just make her feel good? And if you decide to do so, maybe you could take her out on a small date. We'd greatly appreciate it and we know she would.* Oh, y'all ain't buying that, huh? Well, maybe it was more like, *Cynthia is actually interested in your busted ass and we would like to have footage of your date for content. The* ACTUAL *correspondence may have been something* in between those two scenarios, but the bottom line is, the producers reached out to me trying to hook us up, making it seem like she was interested. Unbeknownst to me at the time, they were playing out the SAME scenario, just flipping the rhetoric by reaching out to Cynt and saying I really wanted her number. Regardless, it worked, and I am so thankful to God and those producers that it did.

Our first date still didn't happen until about a month after we met. Of course, she's based in Atlanta and I'm in L.A., so even though we would text and talk back and forth every so often, we had to wait until one of us was in the other's city. She just happened to make it back to L.A. first.

She was in town for some press and to see some dude. Oh, did I forget to mention Ms. Bailey was sort of seeing somebody when she came on Steve's show? I mean, it wasn't an exclusive relationship, and I was kind of in these streets too, but that's not the point. She had an option. However, we decided while she was in town. As some of you know, she's also cool with Claudia Jordan, who was on the RHOA with her. CJ and I both work for Fox Soul now, but back then, we were co-hosts of a podcast. In fact, it was Claudia who encouraged me to do Steve's show when I was sort of on the fence once Ephraim told me about it. Anyway, Claudia booked Cynthia to be on our podcast and so CB and I decided we'd just go and get some lunch afterwards. Our first official date. She loves sushi so we ended up going to this spot on Sunset.

Chapter 21

CANS

THE FIRST TIME I was SURE Cynthia was someone special and someone I at least wanted to be friends with for a long time was during that walk from the parking garage to the restaurant. I'll never forget it. We were walking past Roscoe's Chicken and Waffles when all of a sudden this young lady, who was about 19 or 20 years old, literally came RUNNING up to Cynt. At first, I wanted to jump in front of her and make sure she wasn't going to harm Cynthia, but I could tell she wasn't shook, and the lady looked friendly. So I just took it all in. She came right up to CB and they embraced as if they were relatives who hadn't seen each other in years. The young lady said something like, "You're my favorite," and just like that, she walked off. Now I've been around my share of celebrities, so I know the reactions they sometimes get in public. This was different. I mean, once again, this encounter was as if Cynthia had known this lady for years. When she walked off, I even asked her, "Y'all related?" and her response was, "Nope. Never seen her in my life."

She wasn't fazed by it. She didn't complain about a random woman coming and hugging her. She didn't act bothered AT ALL. Once again, I've been around a lot of celebrities and a lot of times that's not the case when it comes to fan interaction. Cynthia seemed just as happy to meet that young lady as she was to meet Cynthia. I don't know why that stuck with me, but right then and there I just knew that that class, grace and genuine energy that I had witnessed before on television and had felt on that stage with her on the Steve Harvey show was absolutely real. This is one person I would love to have in my life forever.

I even still felt that way after our first date. A date in which she spent pretty much the entire time on the phone talking to the producer of a TV show she was going to be on. However, that actually did more to help than harm our budding "situation-ship." You see, I'm about taking care of business too, and I need to be with someone who understands that sometimes you HAVE to put business first so that you can enjoy all the personal luxuries that come with it. Even though she profusely apologized throughout the phone conversation, I got it. I understood. Once again, it was a plus for her in my eyes.

In fact, because of that, I realized then that Cynthia actually exemplified every quality I've ever wanted in a woman. Someone I was mentally and physically attracted to. Check! Someone who matched my hunger and drive when it came to career. Check! And someone who cared about others as much as she cared about herself. Not just people who could do things for her but for all good people.

With that said, some may think we jumped right into things, fell in love, and wanted to spend the rest of our lives together almost immediately after meeting. Not at all. Our relationship in the beginning was a slow burn. In fact, it was more like the eye of the stove was on, but the flames were so low they were flickering and you could probably smell gas. Obviously, you still have to get to know a person. Make sure they're not sending a representative to the table. And remember, she was dealing with a "distraction." And since I'm throwing her under the bus, I need to join her. I was actually dealing with someone too who had some of my attention, but I WAS NOT IN A RELATIONSHIP.

I've said several times that, since the first time I met her, I knew Cynthia was supposed to be in my life in some capacity. However, there was one time, early on in our "friendship," I doubted that.

After our initial date, we saw each other in New York for a quick drink, but when she came back to L.A. for some work, we decided to hook up again. The day she arrived, we agreed to go to lunch. So I picked her up from her hotel. We went to lunch in Beverly Hills and had a great time. It was so good we decided that we'd hook up later that night after I got off work around nine. Once again, this is Open Mike, and it's time for another Open Moment. When we decided to get together later that night, I was coming strapped. Not that she gave me any indication that anything was going down, but I still had a little cocky side to me. We had kissed before. Nothing passionate, but once again, I was on some "just in case shit." So, in other words, I was gonna at least TRY and get it. So I got off and admittedly, I was kind of excited to see her. I hit her with the text. "Hey. Just got off. Are you still at the hotel?" Now usually, Cynthia is a quick draw texter. When she receives a text, she's hitting you right back unless she's working. This time, I didn't even get crickets. No text bubbles. Absolutely nothing. 10 minutes later, I called her. I mean, even if the previous text said "delivered," you never know. Her carrier MUST BE TRIPPING. I got voicemail. Well, I didn't even get that because the little white woman's voice told me that Cynthia had "a phone that has yet to set up voice mail service...... GOODBYE." I'm not the thirsty kind. I'm not desperate. I try not to sweat anybody, BUT I waited about 30 minutes and texted AND CALLED her again. No dice. I had officially been "curved." Yup, that's urban slang for "her ass done stood me the hell up."

Needless to say, I wasn't happy about it. Look, I know she didn't "owe me" anything, but here's why. I'm a huge stickler about time and more importantly, valuing someone else's time. Once again, we weren't in a relationship. She didn't owe me anything. Even if she changed her mind or something came up, she could've just let me know. Even though I had turned down some other options that night to spend more time with her, I would've totally understood if she had just informed me that she "couldn't make it...sorry." Would I have been a little disappointed? Sure. However, would I have understood? Absolutely. Once again, even though there was a mutual attraction, we were free to do whatever we wanted. However, as I said before, just tell me and not waste my time and not have me worried that something may have happened to you. Which briefly, I was.

She eventually texted me back a few days later, explaining "something came up." I knew what that meant. I act a fool, but I'm not one. It's cool, but I admit, I was somewhat in my feelings. It's not the act, it's the principle that mattered to me. And when you don't really know someone that well, it's a red flag that's hard to overcome. I almost didn't. In fact, I barely spoke to or texted her after that. Was I being petty? You're damn right I was, but for some reason... FOOL, YOU KNOW IT WAS GOD...I still truly felt like this woman was supposed to be in my life. I just knew it.

Maybe we would just be good friends. Hell, at one time, I thought maybe I'd introduce her to her next serious relationship. That's the thing about me. I don't believe God brings anyone into your life without a reason. For some reason, I was super curious to figure out what part Cynthia Bailey would play in my life or me in hers. So I stayed in touch here and there. Sent her a care package and some fruit (which she hates) when she had a health scare and encouraged or congratulated her when necessary. You know, things an extended friend would do. I was cool with that. I was happy with my life, and so was she.

Around May, four months after we met, was when I saw the shift. I admit, a thirst trap picture she put on Instagram is what flipped the switch. She was in Mexico with her daughter Noelle, living her best life and taking selfies on the beach. There was one she took in a black bikini and so, of course, I HAD to let her know that she was raising the temperature in Mexico and yes, she got a rise out of me too. I don't know exactly what I texted her, but she responded with "Hey, you wanna FaceTime?" Here's the thing, we had NEVER FaceTimed before. So I was a little caught off guard, but if you're telling me that you're on the beach right now and you want to allow me to see what you're working with? The answer is a resounding "YES." Of course, I was probably all suave and shit with my text response and said something like "Sure, that's cool!"

I hit her up and we talked for maybe a half hour or even more. That's amazing to me because I actually hate talking for long periods of time on the phone. With her it was different. It helps that she talks about 80 percent of the time in our conversations, but that's not the main point. What I liked and what I still love about our conversations is that I'm actually intrigued and interested in what she has to say. We clicked that day, and it had nothing to do with the way she was looking. Okay, maybe for the first five minutes, it was 50 percent visual and 50 percent verbal, but after that, I wasn't into her looks. I was into her mind. Her soul. Her spirit. I was into her. Since that day, there has not been a day that we have not AT LEAST spoken on the phone at least three times when we've been apart. That day, our connection was stronger than any 5G signal or anything else I had ever felt in my life.

Everything in my life is God's will and it was God's will and time that are the main reasons why we're still together. Timing is everything, and the way things played out made it a perfect time for us to be together. I actually saw her two years prior to that dating show at a birthday party. I didn't meet her. I wanted to, but the timing wasn't right. She was already divorced at the time, but she didn't seem too available. I'll just leave it at that. And it's a good thing I didn't meet her then because even though I was very available, I wasn't ready to be in any kind of committed relationship with someone like Cynthia. In fact, if I'd met her and we'd started dating at that time, I truly believe it would not have ended well. Like Ephraim used to tell me, I wasn't ready.

Time and therapy, including writing this very book, prepared me. Made me look back at all the issues I had and
gave me the opportunity to address them. That help from
God and his earthly angels called therapists have helped
shape me into the man I am presently. Now I know I'm
ready. Thank God she is too.

So where am I now? Well, my contract at Fox isn't nearly
as good financially as it was before, but now it allows me
the opportunity to do other things, which is just as important. I always wanted to expand my horizons, and over the
last few years, I've been able to do just that. I've become a
TV talk show host on this streaming platform called Fox
Soul, and I've done a series for Netflix. I've even gotten a
little involved with more acting.

This is still Open Mike, so I have to be completely open
with you. I've had some days, weeks, and months over the
last few years that have been extremely tough. Fortunately,
it wasn't from a financial standpoint, but at times frustration mounted because I felt like my career was at a standstill.
It hurt, and while I didn't reach the depths of depression, I
was emotionally frustrated and excruciatingly disappointed
because I hadn't been able to take that NEXT big step professionally.

Here's the thing, though: what has happened for me since
APG went off the air has been exactly what I needed. Sometimes you need to take a step back or just sit still until the
right blessing comes. I've gotten promoted and taken the
next step in my life *spiritually,* and that's helped me become
a better person all around. The things I used to complain
about or the jobs that I don't get don't bother me as much.

Sure, I still get a little frustrated, but I know that what God has in store for me is for me.

I told you, I get these feelings. These inclinations and visions for what's in store for me. I know something incredible is about to happen in my life. Maybe even by the time this book is out and published, it will have come to fruition. If not, it's coming. That's because I feel it in my purpose, and I believe and trust in God.

Honestly, with God and continued mental therapy, I'm already doing fine. Despite some of the disappointments, the last few years have been the best years of my life, and it's actually genuine now. No more mask. I'm actually happy professionally and personally and not just pretending to be.

First and foremost, my relationships with my daughters have been good, but I'm still learning HOW to be a good father. I make a lot of mistakes and I'm thankful they're forgiving young ladies. We're not friends, but we sure act friendly. I'm like a big brother/cool daddy who they can talk to about anything, and I feel like I can talk to them about my issues too. Of all the accomplishments I've ever been able to achieve, the title of "dad" is my biggest one.

As they have gotten older, my concerns have grown because they're now at that age where boys are in their lives. Karma is something I'm deathly afraid of. You would think it would be me being hurt by Cynthia because of the things I've done in the past to women. I'm actually way more concerned about some dude acting just like me in the past and breaking their hearts. I don't want them to have to pay for the sins of the past of their nasty-ass father. It's why I've been honest with them about my past. Including the shit I did to their mothers, so that they could have their antennas up when it comes to dealing with guys. Don't get me wrong, I'm not trying to discourage them from dating guys with flaws. I just want them to protect their hearts and make sure that a guy deserves to have it. Make him earn it and even after he does, he needs to do what's necessary to protect and keep it. If not, take that shit back. Ultimately, ladies, it's YOUR heart.

I've realized some things through writing this book and continued therapy. One is that a reason I wasn't able to fully open up, in addition to that time Jackie broke my heart in high school, was I was afraid that if I did, someone was going to hurt me. It's why I wouldn't just "fall." *Sorry, ladies, I know you can get hurt three times a year and want to jump back out there to give the right guy a shot. For many of us guys, if we're hurt once, it affects many of us for LIFE. Pray for me.*

Even though I have for the first time with Cynthia (FALLING IN LOVE and loving someone are totally different in my book), I still have some trust and insecurity issues. Don't get me wrong, I'm not a jealous dude. I mean, I ain't no fool either. However, before therapy, my insecurities were strong enough that I always felt like I needed to have an "in case of emergency" back-up plan. Meaning, even if I was with you, I had to have someone on standby for that soft landing. Through my therapy, I've learned other ways to get past that and using other women as an escape to get past the times when I feel inadequate or insufficient. Believe me, learning that my insecurities and stress were a trigger for me to do inappropriate things was a huge blessing. It's not an excuse, but learning that part in therapy has changed my world.

A big reason why I even wanted to publish this is to tell other men that they can get past their "hoe demons" too. Being with a multitude of women while you've got a loving, loyal, faithful partner doesn't make you more of a man. It actually makes you less of one. I allowed the way I was raised, what I saw growing up, and just my plain dumbness dictate and destroy past relationships. I wasn't ready. I truly believe I am now. With continued counseling and prayer, I know I'm ready to be the man that not only Cynthia needs me to be but the man God intends for me to be. I know if I can do it, so can every other man that's "ready" to put away childish things.

With Cynthia now being my fiancée, I've obviously made huge strides, but let's just say, God ain't done with me yet. I mean, don't get me wrong, I'm nowhere near the boy I used to be. I know I'm a man, but that's just it... I'm just a man. A man who learns from but isn't immune to mistakes.

Let me clarify this for the masses. I ain't out here messing around on Cynthia. I just now have a sense of awareness of who I am. They say "once a cheater, always a cheater!" And guess what? I agree. When it's said, it sounds scandalous on the surface. And for many people it is. However, let me peel back the layers of what I mean by that phrase. Yes, I've been a cheater. I had a problem. I admit that. I've gotten and continue to get help for that. Not just from God but from therapy. No, I'm not a sex addict. I just did dumb shit because of a multitude of reasons I've already discussed in this book. So yes, in a sense, I'm a cheater. I always will be. It's a label that will be stuck on me for life. Just like a person who goes to jail will forever be a convict. Alcoholics will always be alcoholics and addicts will forever be addicts. It's the label, but it doesn't have to define you if you don't sub-scribe to the characteristics that make those labels what they are. I wholeheartedly believe people can change, but only if they want to and put in the work necessary to change. I continue to do that. And I vow I always will.

I've been doing a lot of praying. I want to get it right, and I've apologized to all the women I've hurt in the past. I never want to hurt anyone. I couldn't love them the right way because I didn't fully love myself. Also, I just didn't know how to do it and I have always just loved WOMEN.

I've made many mistakes and I've tried to learn from them. I know a few of the women I've dated are reading that saying, "that motherf***er is a slow learner," but I really am trying.

As much as many of my close friends, like Wisdom, Steve, D.C., Chuck, Vanessa, Nat, and Nickol are laughing at that last statement, I know my friends like J.R., Hud, Jay, Natara, Miko, and Tandra are happy I've made strides to address and fix it. At least they're all praying for me.

Prayer works. After saying I'd never marry again, I've opened up my heart and will do so again with Miss Bailey soon. As much as I'd like to have another kid, I'm too old to raise one. Sure, I'd love to have a boy, but I'd be in my 60s when he became a teenager and that's just not going to be a good look. If I raise this man, I want to be able to show him everything he needs to be to be one. A MAN. Mentally, I'd be capable. Physically, I'm not sure. Although I have been focused on getting my body in order recently. That's helpful.

I'm not going to end this book by preaching to you, but everything I've gone through in my life and the people I've gone through it with have been for my ultimate purpose. It's made me who I am, and I have no regrets because of that. Don't get me wrong, I'm sorry for the other people affected in a negative way, but I pray for their forgiveness and hope they understand that everything we've gone through has just been God's will.

In fact, I'll leave you with this from T.D. Jakes in a sermon:

You can't win without a struggle

You can't gain wisdom without mistakes

Mistakes give you wisdom

It's not always what I did right that informed me...it's what I did wrong that informed me

But if I can never ADMIT that I did things wrong

I can never grow to the freedom that makes you free...

INDEED.

This has been my "Open Mike." I'll keep it open as my journey continues. God's will, my next chapters are going to be my best yet!!!!!

LETTERS FROM MY HEART

TO MY MOM

First and foremost, thank you. I know you've lived a very hard life. You made a lot of sacrifices for me and my brother, and I want to show you how much I appreciate you and how much gratitude I have toward you for doing that. You've lived a very tumultuous life where you did everything to make everybody else happy. One of the biggest things I wanted to do in my life is to make sure I'm doing things to put a smile on your face. Hopefully, I've done those things. I've made you proud. Thank you for still continuing to be that disciplinarian. For straightening my ass out when I know I'm going wrong even though I'm almost 50 years old. I appreciate you even though sometimes I don't always show it. I know I'm wrong for that, but at the same time, always know the love and admiration, the respect, and the ability to be a good father is because you were such a great mom. Thank you so very much. I just want to continue to do the things and instill those life lessons you have given to me to make me better and the world a better place to live in.

TO MY DAUGHTERS

First and foremost, I'm sorry I wasn't the right example of a man that I would want you to have in your lives early on. Secondly, I apologize for breaking up our families. I wasn't there. Growing up, I always wanted to be a father who did the things that my father would never do or was never able to do for whatever reason, but because of my transgressions I failed.

Not being able to have the family that I dreamed of and not being in your homes consistently to help and watch you grow up pained me. I want you to know that I'm trying. I'm still flawed, and I've made mistakes. There are still things I'm learning on the fly. Fathering is on-the-job training for me somewhat.

I want you to know that no matter what, I am here for you. I want you to know that because of my mistakes I can actually be a better guide to help you to avoid the pitfalls that your moms had to go through with me. There are red flags and signs that you must be aware of in men who are not ready or deserving of your hearts.

Admittedly, I've always been afraid of the things that I've done in my past when it came to how I mistreated women. I wondered how karma was going to treat me. Would I eventually fall in love with someone and then they would turn the tables on me and hurt me the way I hurt others? Today I recognize that the karma that plagues me is the pain in your eyes. The disappointment that lives in your heart and reflects on your face is something that I have to live with. For this, I apologize.

Instead of allowing the pain to take up residence inside of you, know that I am here to recover anything that has been lost and to heal anything that has been broken. I am here to give you my all as you navigate the relationships of your lives. Eventually you will discover the love that you deserve, and if it is God's will, I will be there with you every step of the way.

My prayer is that you honor the spirit of compassion that you so gracefully carry. Remember to do what feels right and good for your soul. It is in this space that true happiness thrives. Remember to trust God in all things. When you let God into your life, you can't fail. You have the opportunity and potential to be the best, but only if you put in the effort. No one can do this for you. And even though you have an abundance of support, never take for granted your independence. You owe it to yourselves to stand firmly on your own two feet.

Never stop learning. Never stop loving each other. Never stop loving yourselves. Continue to love society and be genuine when it comes to helping people. Push the envelope for every goal that your ambition directs you to chase. Believing in yourself is half the battle. Construct a game plan, and never fail to execute. There will be obstacles, but the will to win is in your DNA.

Remember to get rid of the things that weigh you down. Cut the anchors when you need to and swim toward destiny. The torch of light and of love has been passed to you; take it and run as fast as you can toward your dreams. I'm so proud of you. Your divine destiny awaits.

TO MY EX-WIVES

I want to sincerely apologize for the hurt that I caused. For the pain I inflicted. I always tried to be a good man, but unfortunately, the two of you had to feel the things I was going through. I think you two, besides my kids, were the ones that felt it the most. I'm sorry I wasn't the man that I should've been or could've been when I was married to you. I decided to make you a queen, but I didn't do a good job being a king with the transgressions I made. I wasn't a terrible human being, but I was far from perfect, and for that I apologize. We had some good times. Some great times. I know the ratio of wonderful, beautiful times was much better than the horrible times. The good times don't justify the bad, but thank you for providing me with two precious human beings by giving life to my two daughters. They are the biggest blessings of my life. Thank you for being such exceptional mothers. Even though our marriages didn't work, I cannot thank you enough for the job you have done in raising our children. They have grown into beautiful girls and beautiful young ladies, and for that I have to give you credit. Yes, I was there on occasions and did my part, but I had to learn how to be a good father, and I'm still getting there. So thank you for your patience. Thank you for forgiving me for the things that I have done. Just know had I been a more mature person and not gone through the things that I went through when I was younger and realized the hurt I was going through, perhaps if I was mature enough to go and get the help that I needed, maybe the outcome would have been different. But at the same time, we all know that God doesn't make mistakes, and we go through things for a reason. We're great friends now and I'm grateful for the respect we now have for each other. Just know that I will always love you no matter what. No matter what anybody says, I will always love you, and I am very thankful for the great times, and the love that you gave to me. I appreciate that and I am always here for you.

TO CYNTHIA

First, thank you. God has really blessed me by bringing you into my life. Thank you for coming into my life and for adding to the wholeness that I already have. I'm thankful to God that He brought you into my life at the right time and we found one another. You are everything that I have ever desired to have in a woman and a soul mate. You are somebody that provides for me in a mental, emotional, and physical aspect, but you're also so kind and beautiful to others. That's one of the reasons that I love you so much. Thank God you came into my life at the right time because it was at a point where I finally had the ability to fall in love with someone. The help I finally got allowed me to open up to the kind of love you give to a man. Thank you, and I can't wait to see where the rest of our lives takes us because we will be spending the rest of our lives together. You are an amazing person. You are an amazing mother and I am blessed with a bonus daughter in Noelle. Thank you for accepting me for my past. Thank you for walking with me in my present, and I can't wait to spend my forever with you.

TO MIKE

From a professional standpoint, I've always wanted to build an empire to pass down to my kids. I'm always thinking about generational wealth. As a people, we must all consider how to even the playing field by creating wealth for generations to come. My work to produce TV shows as well as a dating show that has been developed and acquired with Cynthia is a part of my pursuit to take my work to the next level.

It's gonna be great for me and for Cynthia with the things we have in store to do together. Producing projects for ourselves and other people that will be groundbreaking, earth-shattering, monumental, and of course money making, which will always be something that happens for the Hill-Bailey household.

Personally, I want to keep God first and build my family structure on solid ground. I will work relentlessly to help my daughters with what they need to do in building their careers and to fulfill their dreams. I am well aware that I will always be a flawed man, but I will continue to do what I need to do to correct the mistakes that I have been making so I can be a better person, a better human being, a better follower of God, a better husband, a better father, better coworker, better friend.

Even though I recognize that God isn't done with me yet, I am proud of where I am now. I'm blessed that I had the strength to realize that I needed help, and that I took the steps to seek it.

That's one of the messages I want to get out in this book. No matter what you've accomplished or how good people think you have it, if you realize you're hurting on the inside, you need to ask for help. To me, asking for help is a bold step. When a man can admit that he is weak, he becomes strong.

Had I continued down the path of self-destruction I am certain that I would have lost my life because of the stress and unacknowledged trauma. I lost so many other things because I couldn't or wouldn't deal with my demons sooner. But after fooling so many, including myself honestly, I finally admitted *I need to change to make myself better.* I will still make mistakes, but I know I can forgive myself and ask God for forgiveness and move on. I'm still learning, but I'm getting better. All I want to do every day is to continue to improve and let God guide me. My steps are already ordered. I just want to carry out His will. I promise to put in the work in all aspects of my life. I will be somebody that people will be proud of. I will make this world a better place to live in, and I will leave a legacy that will have a tremendously positive impact on the world to come. I promise.

Not having anyone else in the home besides my mom and my stepdad meant I had to endure and deal with the nightmares of their volatile relationship all alone. Remember how I told you my first memory of my life is my mom getting her ass beaten by a man? That first memory was by my biological father. As for my stepfather, I could write a book entitled Richard Hill's Greatest Hits. Richard Hill was my stepfather. I took his name when he adopted me when I was fifteen years old, but thank God I didn't take his penchant for domestic violence. If you know me or you've seen or heard me on television/radio, you know how I feel about a man putting his hands on a woman. He's not a man. Well, this outrage should be self-explanatory for most but comes from firsthand accounts of seeing and mainly hearing it up close and personal in my own home.

I would never call Richard a terrible human being. He was actually a good-hearted man. He was kind most of the time. He had a sense of humor and honestly, y'all, I can genuinely say he had love for me. Even though I wasn't his blood, I was his son, and he treated me like his DNA ran through my body. And I have to admit I loved him too. I called him Daddy. He was the only one I truly had that was there for me. The problem was, he was flawed. Misguided. Ignorant at times, and he had a sickness. Alcoholism. He also had a temper and a jealous streak. The combination of those three, as you know, can be deadly. As a matter of fact, it turned out to be. We'll get to that later in the book.

Richard and my mom were married, I believe, 18 years. I don't think I can count 18 total days where they seemed absolutely thrilled to be together. I don't remember them being overly affectionate in front of me. Of course, there would be the occasional kiss goodbye before he went to work or something, but from how I remember it, it was never lovey dovey and I NEVER saw them hold hands while walking together. Not once!! They were married but not together. And when I say "not together," I mean on just about anything.

About

MIKE HILL

WITH THE EXTRAORDINARY gift of engaging people, born James Michael Hill in Bronx, New York, Mike Hill is a proven veteran in the world of broadcasting as an Emmy award-winning sports journalist with more than 20 years of experience under his belt. With the climate of today's media being full of sensationalized platforms Hill is a polished, versatile, credible, talent that refers to himself as an "infotainer," an on-air personality that delivers important news with an effortless ability to cross over from sports to pop culture. Hill has demonstrated his aptitude across a variety of platforms and prior to his broadcast career, he was enlisted in the Air Force from 1988-95 and also spent time working for the government as an analyst providing classified reports to the National Security Agency, FBI and CIA.

Currently, Hill is wearing many important hats as an accomplished sports journalist, TV host, book author, reality TV Personality, father and future husband. Hill started his sports career in Hagerstown, MD, then went on to Fresno, CA followed by a short stint in Nashville. Hill made the biggest move of his career by joining ESPN in 2004, appearing as a host on Sports Center, NFL Live, Baseball Tonight, and NBA Tonight among others. Hill joined FOX Sports in August of 2013 as part of the networks launch. Currently he is hosting the networks college football and basketball studio shows, as well as host of America's Pregame and MLB Whip-around, during baseball season. Additionally he created the FOXsports.com web series 'Keeping It Real with Mike Hill.'

Connect with Author

MIKE HILL ON SOCIAL MEDIA

INSTAGRAM:

@ITSMIKEHILL

TWITTER:

@ITSMIKEHILL

EMAIL:

MHILL@THRILLOFENTERTAINMENT.COM